Mikhail Minakov, Gwendolyn Sasse,
Daria Isachenko (Eds.)

POST-SOVIET SECESSIONISM

Nation-Building and State-Failure after Communism

Bibliografische Information der Deutschen Nationalbibliothek

Die Deutsche Nationalbibliothek verzeichnet diese Publikation in der Deutschen Nationalbibliografie; detaillierte bibliografische Daten sind im Internet über http://dnb.d-nb.de abrufbar.

Bibliographic information published by the Deutsche Nationalbibliothek

Die Deutsche Nationalbibliothek lists this publication in the Deutsche Nationalbibliografie; detailed bibliographic data are available in the Internet at http://dnb.d-nb.de.

Cover picture: © copyright 2020 by Mikhail Minakov. Printed with kind permission

ISBN-13: 978-3-8382-1538-9
© *ibidem*-Verlag, Stuttgart 2021
Alle Rechte vorbehalten

Das Werk einschließlich aller seiner Teile ist urheberrechtlich geschützt. Jede Verwertung außerhalb der engen Grenzen des Urheberrechtsgesetzes ist ohne Zustimmung des Verlages unzulässig und strafbar. Dies gilt insbesondere für Vervielfältigungen, Übersetzungen, Mikroverfilmungen und elektronische Speicherformen sowie die Einspeicherung und Verarbeitung in elektronischen Systemen.

All rights reserved. No part of this publication may be reproduced, stored in or introduced into a retrieval system, or transmitted, in any form, or by any means (electronic, mechanical, photocopying, recording or otherwise) without the prior written permission of the publisher. Any person who does any unauthorized act in relation to this publication may be liable to criminal prosecution and civil claims for damages.

Printed in the EU

Soviet and Post-Soviet Politics and Society (SPPS)   Vol. 226
ISSN 1614-3515

General Editor: Andreas Umland,
Institute for Euro-Atlantic Cooperation, Kyiv, umland@stanfordalumni.org

Commissioning Editor: Max Jakob Horstmann,
London, mjh@ibidem.eu

EDITORIAL COMMITTEE*

DOMESTIC & COMPARATIVE POLITICS
Prof. **Ellen Bos**, *Andrássy University of Budapest*
Dr. **Gergana Dimova**, *University of Winchester*
Dr. **Andrey Kazantsev**, *MGIMO (U) MID RF, Moscow*
Prof. **Heiko Pleines**, *University of Bremen*
Prof. **Richard Sakwa**, *University of Kent at Canterbury*
Dr. **Sarah Whitmore**, *Oxford Brookes University*
Dr. **Harald Wydra**, *University of Cambridge*

SOCIETY, CLASS & ETHNICITY
Col. **David Glantz**, *"Journal of Slavic Military Studies"*
Dr. **Marlène Laruelle**, *George Washington University*
Dr. **Stephen Shulman**, *Southern Illinois University*
Prof. **Stefan Troebst**, *University of Leipzig*

POLITICAL ECONOMY & PUBLIC POLICY
Dr. **Andreas Goldthau**, *Central European University*
Dr. **Robert Kravchuk**, *University of North Carolina*
Dr. **David Lane**, *University of Cambridge*
Dr. **Carol Leonard**, *Higher School of Economics, Moscow*
Dr. **Maria Popova**, *McGill University, Montreal*

FOREIGN POLICY & INTERNATIONAL AFFAIRS
Dr. **Peter Duncan**, *University College London*
Prof. **Andreas Heinemann-Grüder**, *University of Bonn*
Prof. **Gerhard Mangott**, *University of Innsbruck*
Dr. **Diana Schmidt-Pfister**, *University of Konstanz*
Dr. **Lisbeth Tarlow**, *Harvard University, Cambridge*
Dr. **Christian Wipperfürth**, *N-Ost Network, Berlin*
Dr. **William Zimmerman**, *University of Michigan*

HISTORY, CULTURE & THOUGHT
Dr. **Catherine Andreyev**, *University of Oxford*
Prof. **Mark Bassin**, *Södertörn University*
Prof. **Karsten Brüggemann**, *Tallinn University*
Dr. **Alexander Etkind**, *University of Cambridge*
Dr. **Gasan Gusejnov**, *Moscow State University*
Prof. **Leonid Luks**, *Catholic University of Eichstaett*
Dr. **Olga Malinova**, *Russian Academy of Sciences*
Dr. **Richard Mole**, *University College London*
Prof. **Andrei Rogatchevski**, *University of Tromsø*
Dr. **Mark Tauger**, *West Virginia University*

ADVISORY BOARD*

Prof. **Dominique Arel**, *University of Ottawa*
Prof. **Jörg Baberowski**, *Humboldt University of Berlin*
Prof. **Margarita Balmaceda**, *Seton Hall University*
Dr. **John Barber**, *University of Cambridge*
Prof. **Timm Beichelt**, *European University Viadrina*
Dr. **Katrin Boeckh**, *University of Munich*
Prof. em. **Archie Brown**, *University of Oxford*
Dr. **Vyacheslav Bryukhovetsky**, *Kyiv-Mohyla Academy*
Prof. **Timothy Colton**, *Harvard University, Cambridge*
Prof. **Paul D'Anieri**, *University of Florida*
Dr. **Heike Dörrenbächer**, *Friedrich Naumann Foundation*
Dr. **John Dunlop**, *Hoover Institution, Stanford, California*
Dr. **Sabine Fischer**, *SWP, Berlin*
Dr. **Geir Flikke**, *NUPI, Oslo*
Prof. **David Galbreath**, *University of Aberdeen*
Prof. **Alexander Galkin**, *Russian Academy of Sciences*
Prof. **Frank Golczewski**, *University of Hamburg*
Dr. **Nikolas Gvosdev**, *Naval War College, Newport, RI*
Prof. **Mark von Hagen**, *Arizona State University*
Dr. **Guido Hausmann**, *University of Munich*
Prof. **Dale Herspring**, *Kansas State University*
Dr. **Stefani Hoffman**, *Hebrew University of Jerusalem*
Prof. **Mikhail Ilyin**, *MGIMO (U) MID RF, Moscow*
Prof. **Vladimir Kantor**, *Higher School of Economics*
Dr. **Ivan Katchanovski**, *University of Ottawa*
Prof. em. **Andrzej Korbonski**, *University of California*
Dr. **Iris Kempe**, *"Caucasus Analytical Digest"*
Prof. **Herbert Küpper**, *Institut für Ostrecht Regensburg*
Dr. **Rainer Lindner**, *CEEER, Berlin*
Dr. **Vladimir Malakhov**, *Russian Academy of Sciences*

Dr. **Luke March**, *University of Edinburgh*
Prof. **Michael McFaul**, *Stanford University, Palo Alto*
Prof. **Birgit Menzel**, *University of Mainz-Germersheim*
Prof. **Valery Mikhailenko**, *The Urals State University*
Prof. **Emil Pain**, *Higher School of Economics, Moscow*
Dr. **Oleg Podvintsev**, *Russian Academy of Sciences*
Prof. **Olga Popova**, *St. Petersburg State University*
Dr. **Alex Pravda**, *University of Oxford*
Dr. **Erik van Ree**, *University of Amsterdam*
Dr. **Joachim Rogall**, *Robert Bosch Foundation Stuttgart*
Prof. **Peter Rutland**, *Wesleyan University, Middletown*
Prof. **Marat Salikov**, *The Urals State Law Academy*
Dr. **Gwendolyn Sasse**, *University of Oxford*
Prof. **Jutta Scherrer**, *EHESS, Paris*
Prof. **Robert Service**, *University of Oxford*
Mr. **James Sherr**, *RIIA Chatham House London*
Dr. **Oxana Shevel**, *Tufts University, Medford*
Prof. **Eberhard Schneider**, *University of Siegen*
Prof. **Olexander Shnyrkov**, *Shevchenko University, Kyiv*
Prof. **Hans-Henning Schröder**, *SWP, Berlin*
Prof. **Yuri Shapoval**, *Ukrainian Academy of Sciences*
Prof. **Viktor Shnirelman**, *Russian Academy of Sciences*
Dr. **Lisa Sundstrom**, *University of British Columbia*
Dr. **Philip Walters**, *"Religion, State and Society"*, Oxford
Prof. **Zenon Wasyliw**, *Ithaca College, New York State*
Dr. **Lucan Way**, *University of Toronto*
Dr. **Markus Wehner**, *"Frankfurter Allgemeine Zeitung"*
Dr. **Andrew Wilson**, *University College London*
Prof. **Jan Zielonka**, *University of Oxford*
Prof. **Andrei Zorin**, *University of Oxford*

* While the Editorial Committee and Advisory Board support the General Editor in the choice and improvement of manuscripts for publication, responsibility for remaining errors and misinterpretations in the series' volumes lies with the books' authors.

Soviet and Post-Soviet Politics and Society (SPPS)
ISSN 1614-3515

Founded in 2004 and refereed since 2007, SPPS makes available affordable English-, German-, and Russian-language studies on the history of the countries of the former Soviet bloc from the late Tsarist period to today. It publishes between 5 and 20 volumes per year and focuses on issues in transitions to and from democracy such as economic crisis, identity formation, civil society development, and constitutional reform in CEE and the NIS. SPPS also aims to highlight so far understudied themes in East European studies such as right-wing radicalism, religious life, higher education, or human rights protection. The authors and titles of all previously published volumes are listed at the end of this book. For a full description of the series and reviews of its books, see www.ibidem-verlag.de/red/spps.

Editorial correspondence & manuscripts should be sent to: Dr. Andreas Umland, Institute for Euro-Atlantic Cooperation, vul. Volodymyrska 42, off. 21, UA-01030 Kyiv, Ukraine

Business correspondence & review copy requests should be sent to: *ibidem* Press, Leuschnerstr. 40, 30457 Hannover, Germany; tel.: +49 511 2622200; fax: +49 511 2622201; spps@ibidem.eu.

Authors, reviewers, referees, and editors for (as well as all other persons sympathetic to) SPPS are invited to join its networks at www.facebook.com/group.php?gid=52638198614
www.linkedin.com/groups?about=&gid=103012
www.xing.com/net/spps-ibidem-verlag/

Recent Volumes

217 Jakob Mischke, Oleksandr Zabirko (Hgg.)
Protestbewegungen im langen Schatten des Kreml
Aufbruch und Resignation in Russland und der Ukraine
ISBN 978-3-8382-0926-5

218 Oksana Huss
How Corruption and Anti-Corruption Policies Sustain Hybrid Regimes
Strategies of Political Domination under Ukraine's Presidents in 1994-2014
With a foreword by Tobias Debiel and Andrea Gawrich
ISBN 978-3-8382-1430-6

219 Dmitry Travin, Vladimir Gel'man, Otar Marganiya
The Russian Path
Ideas, Interests, Institutions, Illusions
With a foreword by Vladimir Ryzhkov
ISBN 978-3-8382-1421-4

220 Gergana Dimova
Political Uncertainty
A Comparative Exploration
With a foreword by Todor Yalamov and Rumena Filipova
ISBN 978-3-8382-1385-9

221 Torben Waschke
Russland in Transition
Geopolitik zwischen Raum, Identität und Machtinteressen
Mit einem Vorwort von Andreas Dittmann
ISBN 978-3-8382-1480-1

222 Steven Jobbitt, Zsolt Bottlik, Marton Berki (Eds.)
Power and Identity in the Post-Soviet Realm
Geographies of Ethnicity and Nationality after 1991
ISBN 978-3-8382-1399-6

223 Daria Buteiko
Erinnerungsort: Ort des Gedenkens, der Erholung oder der Einkehr?
Kommunismus-Erinnerung an einem historischen Ort am Beispiel der Gedenkstätte Berliner Mauer sowie des Soloveckij-Klosters und -Museumsparks
Mit einem Vorwort von Sigrit Jacobeit
ISBN 978-3-8382-1367-5

224 Olga Bertelsen (Ed.)
Russian Active Measures
Yesterday, Today, Tomorrow
With a foreword by Jan Goldman
ISBN 978-3-8382-1529-7

225 David Mandel
"Optimizing" Higher Education in Russia
University Teachers and Their Union "Universitetskaya solidarnost'"
ISBN 978-3-8382-1519-8

Contents

Mikhail Minakov, Gwendolyn Sasse and Daria Isachenko
Post-Soviet Secessionism: Introductory Remarks 7

Bruno Coppieters
Abkhazia, Transnistria and North Cyprus: Recognition and
Non-Recognition in Ceasefire and Trade Agreements 15

Mikhail Minakov
The World-System and Post-Soviet *De Facto* States 59

Petra Colmorgen
Small State or Big Bargainer? Azerbaijan's and Georgia's
Agency in Russia's and Turkey's Near Abroad 113

Gwendolyn Sasse and Alice Lackner
War and State-Making in Ukraine: Forging a Civic Identity
from Below? 161

Nataliia Kasianenko
Internal Legitimacy and Governance in the Absence of
Recognition: The Cases of the Donetsk and Luhansk
"People's Republics" 191

Jan Claas Behrends
Post-Soviet Separatism in Historical Perspective 213

Our Authors 243

Index 247

Post-Soviet Secessionism
Introductory Remarks

Mikhail Minakov, Gwendolyn Sasse and Daria Isachenko

In spite of development of international and global institutions, the modern state remains a powerful construct as the legitimate means of political organization and the exclusive location of political authority. Contemporary states went through a long process of institutionalization marked by the milestones like the Westphalian peace, age of the world imperial system, The Montevideo Convention on the Rights and Duties of States, decolonization, Helsinki treaty, and globalization. Despite this long history, the modern state system does not fully deliver on its promise of order and security, and often leads to contestation of territorial integrity and alternative claims to sovereignty. Such claims occur within existing recognized states from groups which feel themselves excluded and prefer to aspire to their own statehood and international status. By implication, competing claims to statehood can turn into seemingly 'frozen conflicts', as local authorities embark upon their state-building projects in the absence of international recognition, while still participating in peace talks.

Contemporary Europe has evolved into a complex and contradictory set of states within an international order at risk. In the last three decades, the political geography of the European continent has been shaped by two simultaneous, yet contradictory processes. On the one hand, West European countries have undergone a deep, peaceful and comprehensive integration, which has resulted in the creation of a political centre in the form of the European Union (EU) and a more balanced redistribution of power between the Union and national and local governments. (As Brexit, Scotland's referendum attempts, and Catalonian separatism show, EU did not solve all center-periphery issues, however it created legal and political frameworks for peaceful resolution of any secession attempt). On the other hand, Eastern European countries have witnessed the disintegration of complex state and regional unions, such as Yugoslavia, Czechoslovakia and the USSR. In the former Eastern Bloc, the collapse of the old political institutions has stimulated an upsurge of nationalism and conservatism, resulting in the creation of newly independent, recognised states. Moreover, it has ignited irredentist and secessionist movements, which in some cases have led to the creation of de facto states.

The USSR is a good case in point here. Its dissolution resulted in the creation of fifteen new recognised states and four non-recognized statelets (Nagorno-Karabakh, South Ossetia, Abkhazia and Transnistria). These polities comprise a stable network with state-like elements that have been contesting the territorial integrity of the parental states (Azerbaijan, Georgia, and Moldova) since the early 1990ies. Each of these state-like entities has its peculiar forms of legitimacy and political economy and demonstrates systemic dependence on their sponsor states (Russia and Armenia).

Even though the post-Soviet state-like entities were long regarded as a security threat limited to Caucasus and Eastern Europe, they have developed into a source of secessionist practices and ideologies that have proliferated across parts of the continent, eventually becoming a factor of attraction for secessionist movements in Ukraine and other European countries. For example, before 2008, the population of Nagorni Karabakh, South Ossetia, Abkhazia and Transnistria was approximately one million while their governments were under international sanctions and were not recognised by other states. After the Russian-Georgian War in 2008, South Ossetia and Abkhazia enlarged their territories while obtaining partial recognition from states such as Russia, Nicaragua and Syria. In 2014, the outburst of Russian-backed secessionist movements in Donbas led to the creation of two more parastates, the Donetsk People Republic (DNR) and Luhansk People Republic (LNR), whose leadership used the state- and nation-building experience of the 'older' de facto states to institutionalise their own secessionist endeavours. As of today, this growing network of de facto states counts a population of over 4 million people. Furthermore, horizontal ties between the six de facto post-Soviet nations are growing at the level of government, trade unions and local communities while Western European secessionist movements and their activists are ardently involved in the political and military processes in Donbas.

How can we explain the evolution of post-Soviet secessionism from a phenomenon of regional importance to one that may have a bigger impact on EU member-states and their stability?

So far, studies of post-Soviet and post-communist secessionism have adopted either a macro- or micro-political approach. A group of scholars considered post-Soviet secessionism to be a part of the bigger process of transition from the Soviet Union to post-Soviet states, suggesting that smaller ethnic groups managed to secede from their mother states by using the contradictions between bigger national players. Moving from a traditional nation-state perspective, V. Tishkov (1997), N. Bougai (1996), R. Sunny and T. Martin (2001), and R. Brubaker (2011) posited that contemporary interethnic conflicts and secessionism in the region have their roots in Soviet nationality policies. However, others, such as T. De Waal (2003), D. Aphraidze & D. Siroky (2011), C. Ciobanu (2008), Ch. Zürcher (2007) and J. Hughes and G. Sasse (2011), paid more attention to the mistakes made by the elites of the new independent states, which led to interethnic clashes, secessions and frozen conflicts.

Another group of scholars focused on the internal dynamics among the populations living in the de facto states, seeking to understand how individuals, communities and economies manage to survive under the combined pressure of external sanctions and internal autocratic or warlordist regimes. V. Kolossov & J. O'Loughlin (2011), P. Kolstø (2006) and S. Fischer (2016) suggest that after almost thirty years of existence, the Eastern European de facto states evolved into a specific political reality that has its own shared political culture, model of development and peculiar role in the pan-European political environment.

There is also a tendency in secessionism studies to endorse a narrative that characterises post-Soviet secessionism as a uniquely Eastern European phenomenon. Similarly, scholars of Western European secessionist movements, such as L. Hooghe (1995), A. Bourne (2014), D. Muro and M. Vlaskamp (2016) underestimate the growing linkages between Eastern and Western European separatists.

To address this issue and to draw attention to different dimensions of secessionism in Eastern European—as well as larger Europe's—contexts, the Ideology and Politics Journal published a special multilingual issue in 2019 (Minakov, Sasse and Isachenko 2019). The issue focused on the analysis of the complex relationships between parental states and sponsor states with unrecognized statelets in the East and West of Europe as well as the internal state-building challenges in the paternal states.

After the publication of the issue, the academic discussion continued and evolved into this volume. This book consists of papers from the published IPJ issue, some of them updated, as well as new contributions that jointly address a number of important questions. How do post-Soviet de facto states survive and continue to grow? Is there anything specific about the political ecology of Eastern Europe that provides secessionism with the possibility to launch state-making processes in spite of international sanctions and counteractions of their parental states? How are these secessionist movements embedded in a wider network of separatism in Eastern and Western Europe? And what is the impact of secessionism and war on the parental states?

This book starts with the article written by Bruno Coppieters. The author argues that seceded authorities and parental states countering secession may enter into negotiations with regard to a ceasefire or some trade agreements without implying the recognition of statehood. Coppieters shows how such processes of communication regarding the non-use of force and trade lead to the de-escalation of conflicts, but do not suspend political contestation. Which means that policies of recognition and non-recognition provide the conflicting parties with tools to defend their statuses and identities, as well as to preserve or to strengthen international security. In his article, Coppieters refers to the cases of recognition- and non-recognition-policies regarding Abkhazia, North Cyprus and Transdniestria.

In the second chapter, Mikhail Minakov applies a world-system analysis to define the status of post-Soviet non-recognised states. The author argues that these non-recognised states constitute an 'extreme periphery' in relation to 'the global centre.' In the decades after the dissolution of the USSR, these breakaway territories or communities turned into a fairly stable network of polities that oppose international law and the global order. This opposition creates a state model that has proved to be sustainable in spite of conflicts and sanctions, and that proliferates across Europe. Minakov also shows how the establishment of the two non-recognised statelets of the so-called 'Donetsk People's Republic' and 'Lugansk People's Republic' was affected not only by the political, military and economic sponsorship of Russia, but also benefitted from cooperation with the 'governments' and societies of Transnistria and Abkhazia. This leads the author to the conclusion that the states on the 'extreme periphery' tend to cooperate and proliferate regardless of international law and order.

In the third chapter, Petra Colmorgen analyses the parental states facing challenges to their sovereignty. The chapters focuses on Azerbaijan and Georgia in their entangled relations to the de facto statelets and communities living in the non-controlled territories of Nagorno-Karabakh, Abkhazia and South Ossetia, and in neighbouring Russia and Turkey. Both parental states share fundamental similarities as peripheral states whose sovereignty has been compromised. But, at the same time, their foreign policy objectives in their relations with Russia and Turkey differ significantly. Emphasizing the ability to exert influence instead of focusing solely on the weakness of smaller states, Colmorgen demonstrates Azerbaijan's and Georgia's agency in dealing with their powerful neighbours.

In the fourth chapter, Gwendolyn Sasse and Alice Lackner revisit the famous dictum of Charles Tilly about the link between war-making and state-making. Based on original survey data from 2017 and 2018, Sasse and Lackner analyse Ukrainian society amidst the ongoing war in eastern Ukraine, a case of secessionism encouraged and supported by neighbouring Russia. The authors identify a significant shift towards a civic identity centered on the Ukrainian polity, which contradicts the official Ukrainian state rhetoric at the time which focused on a narrower ethno-linguistic definition of the Ukrainian nation and its state. Thus, war does not necessarily increase polarization but can instead encourage a civic sense of belonging.

In the fifth chapter of this book, Nataliia Kasianenko contributes to an examination of the strategies used by the self-proclaimed governments of the 'Donetsk People's Republic' and the 'Luhansk People's Republic' for achieving internal legitimacy. The author reviews how the two regimes use direct democracy for their purposes in the eastern Ukraine. Kasianenko argues that it is possible to attain legitimacy in the absence of external recognition and sovereignty. She shows that the two de facto authorities managed to gain some level of internal legitimacy due to the provision of basic public goods and services for the residents of the non-government-controlled territories of Ukraine.

In a concluding essay Jan Claas Behrends argues that the key to understanding post-Soviet separatism lies in the 20th century history of international and civil conflicts that shaped the unstable geopolitical order in Eastern Europe. The long-term driving force of this underlying instability is the dialectical relationship between nationalist and imperial politics. This dialectic helps to contrast post-Soviet secessionism with examples from Europe and other post-colonial settings.

We hope that our book with its discussion of secessionism challenges will encourage a wider research community to develop more nuanced perspectives on state-dissolving and -building processes in Eastern Europe and to see Europe as one region where macro- and meso-political processes are interconnected rather than being clearly separated into "east" and "west".

Bibliography

Aphrasidze, D., & Siroky, D. (2011). Frozen Transitions and Unfrozen Conflicts, or What went Wrong in Georgia. *Yale Journal of International Affairs* 5: 120–129.

Bougai, N. (1996). *The Deportation of Peoples in the Soviet Union*. NY: Nova Publishers.

Bourne, A. K. (2014). Europeanization and secession: The cases of Catalonia and Scotland. *JEMIE* 13: 94–120.

Brubaker, R. (2011). Nationalizing states revisited: projects and processes of nationalization in post-Soviet states. *Ethnic and Racial Studies* 34(11): 1785–1814.

Ciobanu, C. (2008). *Frozen and Forgotten Conflicts in the Post-Soviet States: Genesis, Political Economy and Prospects for Solution*. Richmond: United States Institute of Peace.

De Waal, Th. (2003). *Black garden: Armenia and Azerbaijan through peace and war*. NY: NY University Press.

Fischer, S. (ed.). (2016). *Not Frozen! The Unresolved Conflicts over Transnistria, Abkhazia, South Ossetia and Nagorno-Karabakh in Light of the Crisis over Ukraine*. Berlin: Stiftung Wissenschaft und Politik.

Hooghe, L. (1995). Subnational mobilisation in the European Union. *West European Politics* 18(3): 175–198.

Hughes, J., Sasse, G. (2001). *Ethnicity and Territory in the Former Soviet Union: Regions in Conflict*. London: Frank Cass.

Jessop, B. (2004). Multilevel governance and multilevel metagovernance. Changes in the EU as integral moments in the transformation and reorientation of contemporary statehood. *Multi-level governance* 2: 49–74.

Kolossov, V., O'Loughlin, J. (2011). After the Wars in the South Caucasus State of Georgia: Economic Insecurities and Migration in the "De Facto" States of Abkhazia and South Ossetia. *Eurasian Geography and Economics* 52: 631–654.

Kolstø, P. (2006). The sustainability and future of unrecognized quasi-states. *Journal of peace research* 43(6): 723–740.

Minakov, M., Sasse, G., Isachenko, D. (eds.) (2019). Secessionisms in Europe: Societies, Political Systems and International Order under Stress. *Ideology and Politics Journal* 12(1).

Minakov, M. (2016). Novorossiya and the Transnationalism of Unrecognized Post-Soviet Nations. In *Transnational Ukraine?: Networks and Ties that Influence (d) Contemporary Ukraine*, Beichelt, T., Worschech, S. (eds.). NY: Columbia University Press, 216–230.

Molle, W. (2017). *The economics of European integration: theory, practice, policy*. London: Routledge.

Muro, D. & Vlaskamp, M. (2016). How do prospects of EU membership influence support for secession? A survey experiment in Catalonia and Scotland. *West European Politics* 39(6): 1115–1138.

New Eastern Europe. (2018). Para-States. Life Beyond Geopolitcs. *New Eastern Europe* 3-4, http://neweasterneurope.eu/2018/04/26/issue-3-4-2018-para-states-life-beyond-geopolitics/ (accessed 1 October 2019).

Pelczynska-Nalecz, K., Strachota, K. & Falkowski, M. (2008). Para-States in the Post-Soviet Area from 1991 to 2007. *International Studies Review* 10: 370–387.

Pollack, M.A. (2015). *Policy-making in the European Union.* Oxford: Oxford University Press.

Stanislawski, B.H. (2008). Para-States, Quasi-States, and Black Spots: Perhaps Not States, But Not "Ungoverned Territories," Either. *International Studies Review* 10: 366–70.

Suny R. G. & Martin T. (2001). *A State of Nations. Empire and Nation-Making in the Age of Lenin and Stalin.* New York and Oxford: OUP.

Tilly, Ch. (1990). *Coercion, Capital, and European States, AD 990–1990.* New York: Blackwell.

Tishkov, V. (1997). *Ethnicity, Nationalism and Conflict in and after the Soviet Union: The Mind Aflame.* Oslo: Sage Publications.

von Benda-Beckmann, F., von Benda-Beckmann, K. (2016). Rules of law and laws of ruling: law and governance between past and future. *Rules of Law and Laws of Ruling.* Routledge 1: 17–46.

Willis, G. B. (2015). *Analysis of the cognitive interview in questionnaire design.* Oxford: Oxford University Press.

Zürcher, Ch. (2007). *The post-Soviet wars: rebellion, ethnic conflict, and nationhood in the Caucasus.* NY: NY University Press.

Abkhazia, Transnistria and North Cyprus
Recognition and Non-Recognition in Ceasefire and Trade Agreements[1]

Bruno Coppieters

1. Introduction

Secessionist conflicts over territories under the control of contested states involve antagonistic positions regarding the recognition and non-recognition of status and identity. Each of the parties defends a specific position regarding the status and identity they desire for themselves or that they are willing to attribute to the other. Such activities are referred to in the present analysis as "policies of recognition." In addition, conflicting parties also have specific political positions on the status and identity they do not want to be associated with or that they do not want to be attributed to the other, which are referred to in this chapter as "policies of non-recognition."

Conflicting parties may have to acknowledge, or even be forced to accept, a particular status or identity for themselves, or for the other party, that is not to their liking, due to the fact that such a status or identity contradicts their policies of recognition or non-recognition. These kinds of acknowledgements should also be considered as forms of recognition, and the parties may then try to redress such a situation in the long term through new policies of recognition and non-recognition.

It is also possible that the objectives of the policies of recognition and non-recognition of a conflicting party do not coincide, which creates tension between the policies. For instance, the conflicting party may wish to reach an agreement with the other party, as this would allow them to have their rights recognized and

---

[1] I wish to thank Pasha L. Hsieh, Daria Isachenko, Vjosa Musliu, Gëzim Visoka, Linda Hamid and Catherine Woollard for their comments on this chapter and to Susan Sellars and Christy Monet for copyediting.

also impose some duties on the other party, but such an agreement may require them to accept that the other party has a certain status in the negotiations, or in the agreement itself, that is not in line with their policy of non-recognition. Such a compromise implies that the first objective prevails over the second, or, in other words, that the policy of recognition takes precedence over the policy of non-recognition.

The present chapter aims to explore the policies of recognition and non-recognition of status and identity in secessionist conflicts involving contested states, where status and identity do not exclusively refer to statehood. In certain situations, contested states may be recognized as non-state actors by the government confronting breakaway, particularly in relation to negotiations on ceasefire and trade agreements, including trade regulations. Such agreements can give non-recognized entities a political and legal status in respect to their armed forces or as a trade entity, and thus a certain form of equality with the other signatories. The party that is recognized in this way may consider this to be an achievement, as this legal status grants them rights and obligations, even if it does not correspond to the status of sovereign equal that they are seeking. This chapter examines the reasons why conflicting parties and external actors accept or even favor such inclusive and asymmetric arrangements regarding rights and obligations. The question to what extent agreements on the separation of armed forces or the exchange of goods produced in disputed territories may be considered legally binding is also raised. The chapter defends the thesis that the recognition implied in such formalized relations with contested states does not suspend political and legal contestation.

The way that Abkhazia, Transnistria and North Cyprus were — or were not — involved in ceasefire and trade agreements will be compared. Although these three cases demonstrate a significant variety of characteristics, the selection is small. For that reason, a comparison of the positions of the conflicting parties in different settings and the type of agreements they reached regarding status resists generalization. The conclusions of the chapter reflect on this selection and, more particularly, the consequences that a different selection may have on the comparison.

For each of the cases, the negotiations on the agreements, as well as the agreements themselves, are analyzed. This includes the way that implementation is conceived under the agreement, although not implementation as such. Such a focus allows a comparison of the recognition and non-recognition policies of the conflicting parties regarding status and identity.

The present analysis does not give equal attention to the ceasefire and trade agreements in each of the three cases. For instance, in the Abkhazia case, more attention is given to the recognition and non-recognition policies in the ceasefire agreements than in the trade agreements. In the case of Transnistria, the opposite is true. And the policies of recognition and non-recognition of Moldova and Transnistria regarding trade are more complex than in the case of Cyprus, even though North Cyprus managed to achieve a higher status as a trade partner of Cyprus. The descriptive analysis of the various ceasefire and trade agreements, therefore, varies in length.

This chapter is divided into six sections. Following the introduction, the concepts of policies of recognition and policies of non-recognition are outlined in section two. These concepts are developed as descriptive tools. Their use in the analysis of the normative positions of the conflicting parties, as well as the difference between these concepts and the normative concept of misrecognition and the normative principle of non-recognition, are explored.

In the third section, the concept of a contested state is defined, highlighting the intersubjective dimension of state relations and disputes. A comparison is made with the concept of a *de facto* state. It will be demonstrated that the distinction between these two concepts in political science finds a parallel in international law in the distinction between a declaratory and a constitutive approach to statehood. This section includes a further explanation of how contested states may achieve some form of legal recognition on a non-state level.

The fourth section addresses the status question in terms of policies of recognition and non-recognition in the cases of ceasefires in Abkhazia (1994 and 2008), Transnistria (1992) and Cyprus (1974). This allows for a better understanding of these policies, as well as a better understanding of how status and identity interrelate in each of these cases. The cases are not analyzed in chronological order, but rather in respect to the status that the contested states managed to achieve. The same approach to the ordering of cases is applied in section five, which offers an analysis of the agreements regarding trade—or the lack thereof—in the conflicts over North Cyprus, Transnistria and Abkhazia.

The sixth and final section of this chapter compares the contested nature of the recognition and non-recognition achieved in these types of mutual agreements and offers a conclusion. It compares how each of the contested states has been included in ceasefire or trade agreements, and which status they achieved or avoided. This section also compares the extent to which such differences reflect particular power differentials among the conflicting parties and forms of subordination between them. Finally, it explores the potential for research on a broader comparison between conflicts on secession involving contested states.

2. Policies of Recognition and Non-Recognition

A descriptive use of the concepts of recognition and non-recognition, as intended in this chapter, allows for a better understanding of the mutual interrelationship between status and identity. Regarding policies of recognition, contested states attempt to construct state identity as a source of self-respect and dignity[2] through the affirmation of equal status with the central government, and central governments through the affirmation of their authority over contested states. Both contested states and central governments attempt to destroy the source of state identity of the other party through a policy of non-recognition. Contested

---

2 On state identity see Fearon 1999: 33–35.

states deny the authority of the central government over them and claim status equal to the central government. Such equal status is denied by the central government. Status and identity are defined here, first in terms of self-perception, then in terms of the perception by the other conflicting party, and, eventually, in terms of how both conflicting parties want themselves and the other party to be perceived by external actors. Status and identity are equally crucial to conflicting parties, but the involvement of contested states in the negotiation and signing of ceasefire or trade agreements is primarily about status.

Policies of recognition and non-recognition express the normative positions of parties directly involved in a conflict of secession. These policies are aimed at the correction of a state of affairs that is perceived as a severe injustice. Mutual accusations generally include the denial of national self-determination, aggression, breaches of territorial integrity, ethnic cleansing and foreign occupation. The authorities of contested states identify their past status with oppression and consider this irreconcilable with their state identity. For the authorities of a central government confronting breakaway, policies of recognition and non-recognition are primarily aimed at the restoration of the *status quo ante*, which means territorial integrity and the subordinated status of the breakaway territory.

The descriptive use of the concept of a policy of recognition — or non-recognition — differs from its use in normative political theory. In the latter, the concept of recognition refers to a process of emancipation through the realization of the self. Recognition is then considered to be positive. In this chapter, recognition has a broader meaning. The parties involved in a conflict over secession may associate their policies of recognition with such a positive meaning, but this is not necessarily the case. They may very well resist policies of recognition from other parties for normative reasons.[3]

---

[3] This particular approach to recognition and non-recognition of status and identity is in line with Hegel's view on the master/slave relationship. Each of the conflicting parties affirms its status and identity through the negation, even attempts at the annihilation, of the status and identity of the other (Duquette 2001; McQueen 2011; Siep 2014; Ikäheimo 2014). Each of the parties strives for

A further distinction must be made between a policy of non-recognition and the concept of misrecognition. Normative political theory builds up a contrast between, on the one hand, recognition that is associated with due respect for identity and rights, and, on the other hand, misrecognition (*Verkennung* in German), whose defining characteristics are the lack of due respect through subordination or other relations that threaten or distort the identity of a subject. Misrecognition is here defined as a form of injustice (Bedorf 2010: 137–149; Daase et al. 2015: 7–9; Hsieh 2019b). From the point of view of a contested state or a government confronting secession, a policy of non-recognition is not unjust or a misrecognition, but, to the contrary, the refusal to recognize what is unjust. This, then, is perceived as a form of resistance against injustice.

Similarly, the descriptive concept of a policy of non-recognition, as used in this chapter, differs from the normative principle of non-recognition found in international law. The latter is about the duty not to recognize situations where *ius cogens* norms have been violated (Brownlie 1963: 410–423). This principle is applied, for instance, in certain cases of foreign occupation and annexation. Such a principle turns a policy of resistance against severe breaches of international law — the creation of a new state through illegal occupation, for example — into an obligation of non-recognition. It is then no longer within the discretionary power of the state to recognize such a state. Resistance becomes a duty (Berkes 2017: 12; Talmon 2005: 125; Lauterpacht 2013: 431; Coppieters 2018b: 352). In contrast, the descriptive concept of a policy of non-recognition, as used in this chapter, refers to the policies of the conflicting parties regarding the status and identity they do not want to be associated with or that they do not want to be attributed to the other. Such a policy is always fueled by

---

recognition of the self through the non-recognition of the other. Hegel's metaphor indicates that the relationship may imply dominance and subservience, up to the point of recognizing such relationship as constitutive of one's own identity.

normative considerations, but its analysis is not necessarily normative.

Regarding the literature on international relations, this chapter's descriptive analysis of the mutual tensions between the specific objectives of policies of recognition and policies of non-recognition builds on studies of counter-secession policies (Ker-Lindsay 2012).[4] The concepts of a counter-secession policy and a non-recognition policy can both be used in a descriptive analysis, but the latter is more abstract and allows for a different kind of analytical precision than the former. The concept of counter-secession is more broadly conceived. It is not only about non-recognition, but also about recognition—efforts to re-establish state authority over a lost territory, for instance.

The literature on the European Union's (EU's) policy of "non-recognition and engagement" also must be taken into account (De Waal 2018; Caspersen 2018; Coppieters 2017; Coppieters 2019). The present analysis differs from such descriptive analysis of the role of an external actor by focusing on the relationship between the two conflicting parties, and by considering engagement as a form of recognition.

The need to overcome the exclusive focus on the recognition of statehood by including other objects of recognition is in line with more recent international relations literature on contested states, such as the examination of the efforts of Taiwan to establish economic relations with other countries (Hsieh 2019a) or of the EU to "normalize" the relations between Serbia and Kosovo, on the basis that these relations are neutral regarding the question of statehood (Visoka & Doyle 2015).

In confrontation with breakaway states, central governments do not have a common view regarding non-recognition policies. This corresponds to the general observation that states do not have any formalized normative doctrine on the recognition or non-

---

4   International relations theory has widely used the concept of recognition in analyzing international conflicts such as those between revisionist and status quo states or those following from the search for great-power status and prestige (Haacke 2005: 191–192; Strömbom 2014; Daase et al. 2015; Hayden & Schick 2016).

recognition of other states (Coppieters 2018a; Coppieters 2019). Confronted with a secessionist crisis, they will generally invoke principles such as territorial integrity or national self-determination, but such references do not make their recognition and non-recognition policies fully explicit. Such formalization would impose unnecessary constraints on freedom of action. For instance, formal policy guidelines or normative frameworks risk being counterproductive in the search for compromises through the use of diplomatic instruments or, alternatively, in the search for the best way to confront the adversary.

Similarly, contested states generally do not defend a clear formal position regarding recognition and non-recognition. When participating in negotiations, contested states are themselves often in doubt as to which status they should pursue or the kind of status they want to achieve in an agreement. They often change their recognition and non-recognition policies over the course of the conflict in which they are involved. Moreover, the contested states examined in this chapter have substantially different policies and normative claims in this respect. While North Cyprus considers itself independent, it would also be satisfied with political equality within a federation. Transnistria defends a quite complex position: it strives for independence and for unity with Russia, but also accepts participating in negotiations that are led by the Organization for Security and Cooperation in Europe (OSCE) and based on the principle that it can only obtain special status within Moldova, which is a concession that Abkhazia never accepted.

Status and identity are themselves powerful motivators in conflicts over secession, but other interests also must be considered in an analysis of policies of recognition and non-recognition. Negotiations of a ceasefire and a trade agreement involve discussions among the conflicting parties on whether particular security or economic interests are to be held in common. Regarding trade relations, the literature on power differentials (Chen 2011) and the distinction between absolute and relative gains, or between symmetric and asymmetric forms of interdependency (Barbieri 2005), allows for a better understanding of the tension between recognition and non-recognition policies.

3. Contested States

Abkhazia, North Cyprus and Transnistria are contested states. This descriptive concept underlines the disputed nature of their claim for statehood (Geldenhuys 2009; Papadimitriou & Petrov 2012). A contested state is not recognized by the state from which it is breaking away and is also disputed by a significant part of the international community. This focus on the intersubjective dimension of state disputes makes it more appropriate for research on international relations—for instance, research on counter-secession policies (Ker-Lindsay 2012)—than the political science concept of a "*de facto* state," which is more widely used in the literature.[5] In its judgement about the objective existence of statehood, the latter concept focuses on the intrinsic criteria of statehood. This includes effective control over a territory and its population and the capacity of a polity to establish relations with other states. The concept of *de facto* statehood does not focus on the intersubjective dimension of recognition and non-recognition on the international level. It corresponds to the declaratory view of statehood in international law, which considers the reality of a state as being based on the presence of a number of intrinsic characteristics (such as its capacity to establish foreign relations) and independent from its recognition by other states (the establishment of effective diplomatic relations). The concept of a contested state, in contrast, is in line with the constitutive view, as it considers the lack of recognition *of* a state as constitutive of the contestation of its existence *as* a state. This constitutive view does not neglect the criteria for statehood that refer to the indigenous

---

[5] According to Scott Pegg "A de facto state exists where there is an organized political leadership which has risen to power through some degree of indigenous capability; receives popular support; and has achieved sufficient capacity to provide governmental services to a given population in a specific territorial area, over which effective control is maintained for a significant period of time. The de facto state views itself as capable of entering into relations with other states and it seeks full constitutional independence and widespread international recognition as a sovereign state. It is, however, unable to achieve any degree of substantive recognition and therefore remains illegitimate in the eyes of the international society" (Pegg 1998: 26).

capacity to exercise state power—such as the possibility to establish diplomatic relations—but sees their practical fulfilment as contested. It thus remains attentive to the question of contestation of these criteria and of statehood through non-recognition.

A lack of diplomatic recognition implies uncertainty, according to the constitutive standards for statehood that involve international status for entities controlling a particular territory and its population. Such doubt or even contestation about the objective existence of a state is raised within the scholarly community, as well. In contrast to the declaratory view of statehood in international law or the concept of a *de facto* state in political science, where it is assumed that scholars may objectively deduce the existence of statehood from the observation of a number of key characteristics of statehood, the constitutive view of statehood in international law and the concept of a contested state imply scholarly contestation of the statehood of an entity in parallel with its contestation by the international community of states.[6]

In a secessionist conflict, contestation is mutual. Neither of the parties in a conflict involving a contested state recognize the claims of the other party regarding its own statehood. The state authority of both conflicting parties is, therefore, contested, but to a different degree. There is a considerable difference in the nature of the contestation taking place at each pole of the dyadic relation. The central government of the state from which a part of the territory has separated does not recognize the breakaway entity as a state. It does not consider that the territorial boundaries with this entity constitute international boundaries. From their side, the authorities of the seceded entity contest the constitutional right of the state from which they have broken away (or attempted to break away)

---

[6] Deon Geldenhuys limits the definition of a contested state to this first characteristic (Geldenhuys 2009: 7). According to Ker-Lindsay, the concept of contested state "neatly captures the full political and legal problems faced by these territories." From the perspective of the declarative position regarding statehood, the contestation only refers to the lack of agreement or even willingness among states in the international community to offer recognition to the state in question, but, from the perspective of the constitutive position regarding statehood, the contestation goes further than that: "the point of contestation is whether or not they are actually states" (Ker-Lindsay 2012: 20).

to exercise control over their territory. But they do not contest its statehood as such.[7] The term contested state takes this qualitative difference in the type of non-recognition into account and refers exclusively to the breakaway entity.

The present chapter focuses on the dyadic relations between the conflicting parties, without neglecting the importance of the recognition and non-recognition policies of external parties such as patron states and large powers. The conflicting parties take external actors as relevant judges of their respective claims. External actors have their own interests to defend regarding the international status of a breakaway territory, and their own international status and identity may — in the case of patron states, for instance — even become central to the disputes, turning a secessionist into a geopolitical conflict. A contested state may strengthen its position — and its status and identity — by securing partial recognition for itself. However, an increase in the number of recognitions does not necessarily end the contestation. United Nations (UN) membership generally suspends it, but this is not always the case.[8] From the perspective of conflict resolution, the contestation over independent statehood only comes to an end through recognition by the state from which the contested state has broken away.

The concepts of recognition and non-recognition allow consideration of mutual agreements involving a contested state that are not necessarily related to statehood, such as ceasefire and trade agreements. Similarly, participation in negotiations over such agreements is not necessarily based on statehood, and this is even the case if the negotiations are dealing with the question of common statehood or reintegration. In all such cases, representatives of contested states are not considered by the other conflicting party as having the legal capacity to underwrite international treaties.

---

7 Turkey refuses, however, to recognize Cyprus, as it considers that the breakup of the Republic of Cyprus in 1964 invalidates the claim of the Greek Cypriot government to represent the Cypriot state, which was recognized internationally four years earlier, in 1960 (see Leigh 1990).

8 The UN membership of the two Germanys and the two Koreas can be mentioned in this context.

However, it is generally accepted in international law that ceasefire agreements can be signed by non-state armed groups and a signatory to a trade agreement does not necessarily have to be a state. Representatives of contested states can, in such a case, be recognized. In turn, these representatives do not consider their counterpart as having state authority over the territory they are themselves in control of. The latter policy of non-recognition finds expression in ceasefire agreement articles dealing with the separation of forces. The acknowledgement of the validity of such an agreement that sets out the rights and obligations of the signatories thus implies a kind of mutual yet asymmetrical recognition. Recognition, then, still refers to a particular status with specific legal and political consequences.

The ceasefires analyzed in this chapter are referring to a moment in time where the breakaway entities did not necessarily proclaim their sovereign and independent status. Nonetheless, the present chapter takes into account that the armed conflicts have profoundly affected — and accelerated — the state building process of these entities. The concept of a contested state is, therefore, appropriate to describe them in a still early stage of state building.

The legal literature on ceasefire agreements is highly relevant for an analysis of responsibilities and obligations. The Abkhazian and Transnistrian armed forces can, for instance, be described as non-state armed groups. This means that their leaders are not recognized as representing state authorities. In contrast, the present chapter describes such military leaders as representing contested states, from the perspective of political science. Each of these two concepts — non-state armed group and contested state — is addressing problems that are proper to its discipline. The legal concept of a non-state armed group is useful to demonstrate, in the context of ceasefire agreements, that it is possible to attribute a specific legal status implying rights and duties to armed forces that are not under the control of a recognized state. By contrast, the political science concept of a contested state is useful for analyzing the ways in which statehood is not only disputed on the battlefield, but also in processes of recognition and non-recognition of status.

4. Ceasefire Agreements

A. Georgia and Abkhazia

The traditional practice of mediation in armed conflicts prescribes the inclusion of all armed groups in ceasefires as a necessary condition for their successful implementation. Governments involved in a military conflict with a contested state are unwilling, however, to increase the legitimacy of their adversary through any formal status in negotiations or agreements. However, they may be forced to recognize such status in order to end a military conflict when they are on the losing side.

After its military defeat in the 1992–1993 war and retreat from Abkhazia, Georgia had to enter into negotiations with the Abkhaz *de facto* authorities (Cohen 1999; Francis 2011). Mutual agreements involving Russia and the UN were expected to pave the way to an international political solution, including the return of the Georgian population that had fled the territory. Abkhazia wanted to negotiate these agreements on equal terms. Georgia tried to avoid such equality by presenting the conflict as an intra-state conflict in Abkhazia itself. At the first round of UN-led talks in Geneva at the end of 1993, it argued for a leading role in the negotiations for the so-called Abkhaz "government in exile"[9] — a government composed of former Georgian officials from Abkhazia representing the population that had been obliged to flee the territory (Francis 2011: 129). Georgia claimed that this government was *de jure* the only legitimate authority. This non-recognition policy aimed at delegitimizing the representative status of the *de facto* Abkhaz authorities, whose status had been enhanced by their military victory. However, the attempt to have either direct negotiations among the representatives of the two communities in Abkhazia or, alternatively, to have a separate representation at the negotiations for the government in exile failed. The negotiations were eventually held between the Abkhaz representatives, on the one hand, and the

---

9   A government in exile normally resides in a foreign country, which is not the case for this government, at least not from a Georgian point of view. Nonetheless, this term has been widely used over the years, including by Georgian media.

Georgian representatives—including those of the government in exile—on the other.

These negotiations led to the signature of a "Memorandum of Understanding" on December 1, 1993, which detailed measures to be taken to favor a comprehensive peace settlement. It was signed on equal terms by the parties, as was a common "Declaration on Measures for a Political Settlement of the Georgian-Abkhaz Conflict" and a "Quadripartite Agreement on Voluntary Return of Refugees and Displaced Persons," which were both signed on April 4, 1994. Russia and international organizations such as the UN, the UN High Commissioner for Refugees (UNHCR) and the Conference for Security and Cooperation in Europe (CSCE) confirmed their presence under these two documents. The "Agreement on a Ceasefire and Separation of Forces" was signed in Moscow on May 14, 1994.[10] It included a clause on the non-use of force and a list of guiding principles for the separation of armed forces. It was signed, just as the previous ones, on equal terms by the representatives of Abkhazia and Georgia, without any reference to their official position.

The ceasefire—as with the other agreements signed among the sides—internationalized the conflict. Russia, which had taken a mediatory role in the conflict, did not sign this particular document. The agreement included an appeal to the Heads of States of the Commonwealth of Independent States (CIS) for the creation of a collective peacekeeping force (PKF) and to the UN Security Council to support a monitoring role for UN military observers (United Nations Observer Mission in Georgia, UNOMIG). The presence of the CIS PKF would have to favor the return of refugees and internally displaced people (IDP) to Abkhazia.[11]

Georgia's signature under the ceasefire agreement implied a recognition of Abkhazia's *de facto* authorities as being in military

---

10 The documents signed in the period 1992–1994 by Georgian and Abkhaz representatives include agreements, common communiqués, declarations and proposals. Among them, no less than three ceasefire agreements were signed—and successively broken—before the end of the 1992–1993 armed conflict. The main documents can be found in Cohen (1999).
11 The PKF was nominally CIS, but in practice Russian.

control of the disputed territory. Contrary to the first ceasefire agreement signed in the first weeks of the war on September 3, 1992, here there was no reference to the objective of the restoration of Georgia's territorial integrity (Francis 2011: 127). The ceasefire did not indicate any obligation for the Abkhaz side to disarm, requiring only that "all volunteer formations made up of persons from beyond the frontier of Abkhazia shall be disbanded and withdrawn" (Cohen 1999: 69). All prescriptions regarding the deployment of weapons were valid for both sides. The clause on the non-use of force implied that Georgia would have to rely exclusively on negotiations to re-establish its territorial integrity.

How should we analyze this asymmetric arrangement from the perspective of a mutual recognition and non-recognition and as compared with prescriptions found in the legal literature dealing with this topic (Bell 2006; Public International Law & Policy Group 2013)? The Abkhaz authorities had obstinately refused to let the Abkhaz government-in-exile have any separate representation at the negotiating table (Francis 2011: 129). This means that the non-recognition policies of the Georgian government failed to have the government-in-exile recognized as a party to the conflict within Abkhazia. It further failed to deny the Abkhaz authorities equal status in the negotiations. On the other hand, the Abkhaz authorities were successful in their recognition policies (regarding their own representativeness and equal status to the Georgians) and non-recognition policies (regarding their refusal to have the Abkhaz government-in-exile recognized as a separate party to the negotiations).

The risk that the signature of the Abkhaz authorities under a ceasefire would be challenged later by the Georgian government or other parties and that the agreement would, therefore, not be considered legally binding was not to be excluded. The validity of agreements where one of the sides is not recognized as a state is a key problem addressed in the legal literature on ceasefires and peace agreements (Bell 2006: 380–381; Public International Law & Policy Group 2013: 6–8). In order to minimize the risk of contestation, a number of pragmatic rules are generally used to enhance the acceptance of agreements as legally valid and, consequently, enhance the chances of implementation. Such a pragmatic approach can be found in the 1994 ceasefire agreement.

First, this document was precisely drafted in respect to the rights and responsibilities of the parties (for instance, in the clauses on the separation of forces and the presence of weapons) and expressed an evident intention by the signatories to be bound to the agreement. The agreement also clearly circumscribed the role of third parties—i.e., the CIS and the United Nations Security Council (UNSC). It did not refer directly to the obligations of the parties outside the military context, but this was not necessary. Obligations of this kind—regarding the return of refugees and IDPs, for instance—were included in the two April 4, 1994 documents that were signed previously, as already mentioned.

Second, the document gave a crucial role to third parties in keeping the peace in Abkhazia. The CIS peacekeeping force would, according to the agreement, make their "best efforts to maintain the cease-fire" and its observation. This force and the UN military observers were further assigned a supervisory and monitoring role. These real but limited tasks are in line with prescriptions in the literature on the optimal role of third parties in a situation that is only weakly regulated by the rules of international law and, consequently, characterized by a lack of effective enforcement mechanisms. Their main role here is increasing the political costs of non-compliance (Public International Law & Policy Group 2013: 7). This was surely the case for the 1994 agreement: at the time, it could indeed be expected that the risk of refusal by one of the conflicting parties to comply with an agreement to be monitored by the CIS and the UNSC was high.

This ceasefire implied not only recognition by the parties of their equal status in the framework of the agreement, but also their acceptance of a number of mutual rights and obligations regarding its implementation. They further agreed to the principle of the non-use of force and of having the CIS and UNSC play a supervisory role in the regulation of the conflict. The common appeal by the conflicting parties to the international organizations (the CIS and UN) to secure the peace indicates, as described in the legal literature (Bell 2006: 378), that the agreement went clearly beyond the internal constitutional order and addressed the international dimensions of the conflict.

The ceasefire was in line with the Abkhaz policy of non-recognition regarding the military presence of Georgia on its territory. Georgia, being defeated militarily, did not have the means for an effective non-recognition policy for the purposes of this agreement. It was not able to include any obligation for the Abkhaz side to disarm or to recognize Georgia's territorial integrity. The war had significantly weakened Georgia's international status, and this also affected its self-confidence and sense of justice. Its military defeat led to a victim identity, particularly in regard to the flight and expulsion of IDPs from Abkhazia. It would, for years to come, call for the international community to come to its rescue, in order to restore its territorial rights and those of the Georgian community from Abkhazia. The Abkhaz victory, in contrast, was a source of pride and self-confidence for the contested state. Its victory in September 1993 is commemorated yearly by a military parade in the Abkhaz capital of Sukhum/i.[12]

A very different geopolitical setting prevailed in August 2008. At that time, France had the presidency of the EU and took the role of mediator in the negotiations to end the Russian-Georgian war. It facilitated the signing of a ceasefire agreement. It was, in contrast with the 1994 ceasefire, an agreement among states, where the signatures of the leaders of South Ossetia and Abkhazia were added later (Phillips 2011: 8). This had a higher chance of being considered valid, compared to the kind of agreement where one of the sides was exclusively represented by a contested state, but it lacked precision—the international negotiations on security mechanisms, for instance, were postponed until a later date.

One of the major divergences between Russia and Georgia in the negotiations for the ceasefire agreement was about the way future negotiations should handle the international status of Abkhazia and South Ossetia. The Russian government defended open-ended negotiations and supported the inclusion of the

---

12 Georgians use the English transliteration Sukhumi, whereas Russians and Abkhaz prefer Sukhum.

following sentence in the ceasefire agreement: "Opening of international discussions on the future status and the modalities of lasting security in Abkhazia and South Ossetia." This stress on the international character of the negotiations aimed at overcoming Abkhaz resistance to a discussion of the status question. Before the war, the Abkhaz authorities had always refused to discuss this question within the framework of Georgia's territorial integrity. The lack of any reference to the principle of territorial integrity as a condition for status talks would allow for Abkhaz participation.[13] The French supported the view that international discussions could keep the future of Abkhazia and South Ossetia open and prevent their recognition by Russia (Asmus 2010: 206–207). The Georgian government opposed such open-ended discussions. According to its policy of non-recognition, the lack of explicit reference to the status of Abkhazia within Georgia would enhance the legitimacy of secessionist claims. It proposed the following formulation: "Opening of international discussions on the modalities of lasting security in Abkhazia and South Ossetia, based exclusively on the decisions of the UN and the OSCE"[14] (Kramer 2008). Russia rejected this alternative, and both parties eventually agreed on the following formulation, which became the basis of the future Geneva International Discussions: "Opening of international talks on the security and stability arrangements in Abkhazia and South Ossetia" (Phillips 2011: 8).

The absence of an international framework to discuss the status of Abkhazia and South Ossetia seems to have facilitated or at

---

13 The Russian proposal was in line with a German roadmap for peace developed just before the war aiming at deescalating the conflict. In July, 2008, the German Minister of Foreign Affairs Steinmeier had proposed, with the support of other Western governments and Russia, to have open-ended negotiations, and for the same reasons, the active participation of Abkhazia. Berlin did not consider such a position as contradicting their policy of non-recognition, as they would further refuse to recognize Abkhaz independence (Coppieters 2018a: 999).

14 The original Russian proposal was as follows: "Ouverture de discussions internationales sur le statut futur et les modalités de sécurité durable en Abkhazie et en Ossétie du Sud," whereas the Georgians proposed "Ouverture de discussions internationales sur les modalités de sécurité durable en Abkhazie et en Ossétie du Sud, basées sur les seules décisions de l'ONU et de l'OSCE" (see the reproduction of this French document in: Kramer 2008).

least accelerated Russia's recognition of Abkhazia and South Ossetia as independent states on August 26, 2008. Russia had several motives to reconsider its previous position on non-recognition, but the launching of international status negotiations would have created a number of constraints to doing so. Russia would at least have had to wait for the obvious failure of the talks before recognizing the two entities.

Russia and Georgia's heads of state put their signatures on documents with slightly different wordings. Dmitry Medvedev signed a Russian version referring to the "security *of* Abkhazia and South Ossetia", whereas Mikheil Saakashvili put his signature on a French text referring to the "security *in* Abkhazia and South Ossetia." The French president Nicolas Sarkozy signed both texts as a witness (Phillips 2011: 8). Abkhazia and South Ossetia were not involved in the negotiations. The six-point ceasefire did not even name these entities, referring to "pre-conflict positions" (*"lieux habituels de cantonnement"*) instead. It also did not mention their armed forces — referring exclusively to Georgian and Russian forces (Phillips 2011: 8). The fact that these contested states could not participate in the negotiations and that their signatures were added after those of the state leaders expresses a weak form of recognition of their role in solving the conflict.

A follow-up agreement to the one of August 15 was signed on September 8, 2008, by the Russian and the French presidents, after Russia's recognition of Abkhazia and South Ossetia (Civil Georgia 2008). It contained a more detailed description of the measures to be implemented, with the aim of enhancing the binding character of the ceasefire. The agreement referred directly to Abkhazia and South Ossetia and described the tasks of the OSCE, the UN, and European Union Monitoring Mission (EUMM). Russia supported this follow-up agreement, as it did not consider it as contradictory to its recognition of Abkhazia and South Ossetia. President Dmitry Medvedev then declared at the press conference that Russia's decision to recognize them was "final and irreversible."

As compared to the 1994 ceasefire, the agreements of 2008 expressed a significant shift in the interaction between Georgia and Abkhazia regarding their recognition and non-recognition policies, their status and its implications for identity. The way that Abkhazia was included in the 2008 arrangement profoundly differed from the approach in the 1994 ceasefire. The Abkhaz authorities were not part of the 2008 negotiations, even though there were no legal hurdles to their participation. The 1994 ceasefire demonstrated, in contrast, that it had been possible to sign such an agreement on equal terms with Georgia. This shift cannot be explained by a lack of active participation by the Abkhaz armed forces in the 2008 war. Their military significance was far less than in the 1992–1993 war, but they still had been successful in expelling the Georgian forces from Kodor/i Gorge[15] with Russian support.[16] The marginalization of Abkhazia in the negotiation process leading to the ceasefire was not due to military but rather political considerations. In contrast to the 1994 setting, Georgia had been confronting Russia. Georgia, France and Russia considered it sufficient for the three states to agree on the terms of a ceasefire. Through their signatures, Abkhazia and South Ossetia then had to give additional guarantees as to the agreement's implementation. This approach did not give them any say, but it was still in line with the pragmatic rule of having all armed formations included in a ceasefire.

The lack of direct interaction with Georgia in the process of negotiating the ceasefire weakened Abkhazia's status and legitimacy. Abkhazia did not have any active role in producing an agreement indicating its specific rights and duties. The responsibility to end the military conflict on its territory was left to Russia, as Abkhazia's protector's state. Such diminished status was, however, counterbalanced by Russia's recognition of Abkhazia's statehood in August 2008. Abkhazia could then claim that its recognition gave it a totally new status under international law. It was now at least partially recognized by the international community. In Russia and Abkhazia's perception, this would strengthen its legal and political status in the negotiations. Indeed,

---

15 Georgians use the English transliteration Kodori, whereas Russians and Abkhaz prefer Kodor.
16 The Kodor/i Gorge was, up to that time, the only region of Abkhazia still under Georgian control.

it made it far more difficult for Georgia and its Western allies to impose decisions on Abkhazia through the means of international organizations—or, alternatively, to isolate Russia within these organizations in attempts to impose their non-recognition policies. The UNSC, for instance, was now openly divided regarding the application of the principle of territorial integrity to Georgia and, thus, unable to prescribe conditions for the deployment of peacekeeping forces or observers in Abkhazia; Russia would veto any Western proposal that would not respect the rights of Abkhazia as an independent state. UNOMIG had to leave Abkhazia (Coppieters 2015) and the observers from the EUMM did not receive the authorization from Sukhum/i to enter it. Abkhazia was also able to sign interstate treaties with Russia regarding its military presence on its territory.

Abkhazia perceived its enhanced status as a result of its steadfast refusal to compromise. Abkhazia considered itself freed once and for all from foreign occupation and colonization. The ties with Russia were described as a strategic partnership, based on sovereign equality. Abkhazia's new self-confidence as a result of the recognition of its independence by Russia found direct expression in economic expectations: the house prices in Sukhum/i rose significantly after Russia's recognition (Nazarenko 2014).

Georgia, in contrast, confronted with an even more radical loss of control over the breakaway territory, hardened its policy of non-recognition after the August war. It considered Russia's actions as an act of revenge against Georgia's efforts to join the NATO alliance in line with its Western identity (Asmus 2010: 50). The format of negotiation for the ceasefire strengthened Georgia's view that Russia was not only a direct party to the conflict in Abkhazia and South Ossetia—a role that Russia has always denied—but that it was actually an occupying force. Georgia addressed all the issues that were to be raised at negotiations (security, trade and human rights) in the framework of occupation. Russia was, for instance, now considered to have specific legal responsibility for human rights violations in Abkhazia. This was a very different discourse than the one that prevailed after the 1992–1993 war, when Tbilisi considered the Abkhaz authorities to be entirely responsible for the failure to respect agreements on the return of IDPs and refugees, and when it held the international community—including the Russian authorities—to account. The discourse on occupation further expressed Georgia's principled stand in its refusal to accept the loss of its territories (Asmus 2010: 50). This stance gave it a kind of self-respect against the backdrop of military defeat: Georgia had not been defeated militarily by Abkhazia or South Ossetia, but by Russia.

Abkhazia was considered by Georgia to be a territory occupied by Russia. This position would make it even more difficult for Abkhazia to participate in negotiations on an equal footing. Georgia even refused to acknowledge the Abkhaz participants as *de facto* representatives of Abkhazia in the Geneva International Discussions. This represented a radical shift in the negotiating position of Georgia as compared to the period before the August 2008 war. Georgia asserted that the Abkhaz participants could only speak in their personal capacity as individual 'experts.' The Abkhaz participants accepted this demand in order to participate in the negotiations, but they did so at the price of having the formal status of the Georgian representatives in the working groups not acknowledged as well (Ministry of Foreign Affairs of the Republic of Abkhazia 2013).

The delegations' lack of representativeness meant that they had little incentive to make the negotiations fruitful, and this complicated the conclusion of legally binding agreements. This mutual non-recognition of the representative status of the parties to the negotiation made it difficult to initiate confidence-building measures. Expectations of reciprocity were low. This made attempts to create institutional forms of cooperation or common security mechanisms more difficult for many years to come.

B. *Moldova and Transnistria*

The ceasefire agreement of July 21, 1992, to end the fighting in Transnistria was signed exclusively by the representatives of the Republic of Moldova and the Russian Federation. Contrary to the 1994 ceasefire in Abkhazia, there was, to speak in formal terms found in the legal literature (Bell 2006: 390), no mix of state and non-state signatories, which meant that there was also no full correlation between the signatories of the treaty and the parties to the conflict. The fact that the signatories had the same international legal status strengthened the legal status of the agreement, in line with the prescription in the legal literature that "those who wish to frame agreements clearly as treaties can best do so by framing them as between state parties only" (Bell 2006: 386). The ceasefire, thus, did not imply the same kind of recognition of the breakaway authority as would later be the case in the 1994 ceasefire in Abkhazia.

However, the document still allowed the *de facto* authorities to play a role in its implementation. It prescribed a halt to all armed activities and the withdrawal of troops and military equipment to allow for the creation of a security zone to separate the two parties. A Joint Peacekeeping Force (JPKF) was set up. It was initially composed of mainly Russian troops and later of Russian, Moldovan and Transnistrian battalions and companies. The belligerent parties were, thus, fully integrated into the peacekeeping. The JPKF had to protect bridges and prevent armaments from being brought into the security zone that separated the two sides. Transparency was enhanced by the presence of 40 military observers from Moldova, Transnistria, Russia and Ukraine.

The *de facto* status of the Transnistrian authorities was further strengthened through their participation in the Joint Control Commission (JCC), together with Moldova and Russia. The JCC had to supervise the ceasefire by commanding the JPKF. Its role included preventing breaches of the ceasefire agreement and restoring the ceasefire in cases of its violation. Transnistria's inclusion in the JCC fostered its commitment to the implementation of the agreement between Russia and Moldova, even without any signature.

The inclusion of the two belligerent parties in the peacekeeping operation had political consequences regarding the resolution of the conflict. The seeking of consensus within the JCC avoided the destabilization of the security arrangement, but it also reinforced the *status quo* by limiting transparency and mediation initiatives. It has, for instance, been difficult for the parties to exchange information on the security situation.

In terms of identity, those Moldovans who considered the conflict with Transnistria as a proxy conflict with Russia found confirmation of this interpretation in the terms of the ceasefire: Why did Moldova sign it exclusively with Russia if the Transnistrians were not Russian pawns? (Hill 2012: 52). Transnistria, in contrast, claimed that it was an international actor in its own right, and that it was capable of contributing to the regulation of this conflict.

C. Cyprus and North Cyprus

The August 1974 ceasefire in Cyprus was, in contrast to the ones in Georgia and Moldova, not based on an agreement among the conflicting parties but on a unilateral decision by Turkey to halt the advancement of its troops. Turkey had started the first military invasion of the island on July 20, 1974, placing a major part of Cyprus under its control. The first round of peace talks followed in Geneva on July 25, 1974. These talks were exclusively held by Turkey, Greece and the United Kingdom. These states were committed, according to the 1960 Treaty of Guarantee, to protect the constitutional order and security of the island. In a second round of talks, on August 8, the circle of participants was enlarged to include representatives of Greek and Turkish Cypriots. The negotiations failed. The second invasion started on August 14, 1974 (Ker-Lindsay 2005: 14). The Turkish forces enlarged the territory under its control. It halted the progress of its military operations through a unilateral *de facto* ceasefire two days later.

The lack of a precisely formulated ceasefire agreement has complicated the fulfillment of the mandate of the UN Peacekeeping Force in Cyprus (UNFICYP) since then. The UNFICYP was given a supervisory role regarding the deployment of the Cyprus National Guard in the south and the Turkish Cypriot and Turkish forces in the north. A large buffer zone was established, extending about 180 kilometers across the whole island (about 3 percent of the whole territory) to separate the opposing forces (United Nations 2002).

Unlike the ceasefires in Abkhazia and Transnistria, the armed conflict in Cyprus only ended through the unilateral decision of an external actor. On the basis of the 1960 Treaty of Guarantee it had signed with Cyprus, the United Kingdom and Greece, Turkey could claim to be one of the guarantor states of Cyprus that had the right to re-establish, if necessary, order on the island. In terms of identity, Turkish and Greek Cypriots developed a discourse focusing on the justice of their respective causes — either as a victim of oppression and liberated by Turkey's brotherly support, or as victim of occupation counting on the support of the international community.

5. Trade Agreements

A. North Cyprus

The majority of the Greek Cypriot community in Cyprus rejected the UN plan for the reunification of Cyprus in 2004. Consequently, the Turkish Cypriot community could not accede to the EU. The EU proposed a number of measures to avoid the isolation of North Cyprus and to prepare it for its future reunification with the south. On April 29, 2004, the Council of the European Union issued a trade regulation — the so-called Green Line Regulation — for the transportation of goods between north and south. The Turkish Cypriot Chamber of Commerce received the authorization to issue certificates of origin. This allowed goods produced in the north to be traded with the south. The Council made this decision just a few days before the formal accession of the Republic of Cyprus to the EU, but not against its will. The fact that the Chamber of Commerce had been founded in 1958, before the division of Cyprus, made it a legitimate institution for this purpose in the eyes of the Greek Cypriot government. Direct trade between North Cyprus and the EU, however, remained excluded.

The regulation of trade between north and south is significant in political but not in economic terms. In 2018, the value of this regulated trade between the two parts of the island amounted to only 4.8 million euros (European Commission 2019). The low level of trade from south to north (1.1 million euros in 2018) is largely a consequence of the status question: North Cyprus asks customs duties to be paid on goods coming from the south, as it regards the border to be an international one. However, according to the

Republic of Cyprus and the EU, the border is not international. The goods exported to the north are, therefore, not exempt from value added tax (VAT), in contrast to goods that are exported outside the EU (Mirimanova 2015a: 53; Coppieters 2017: 41–42).

This arrangement is an interesting compromise in terms of recognition. The Greek Cypriot leadership recognized the Turkish Cypriot Chamber of Commerce as a legitimate authority to issue trade documents, and the Turkish Cypriot side acknowledged that it had a subordinate role in an asymmetric arrangement, where all trade with the EU had to pass through the south of Cyprus.

The Turkish Cypriots also hoped to enhance their status regarding trade through the regulation of direct trade with the EU, but all attempts in this direction have failed, despite the support they received from the European Commission. The Republic of Cyprus and the majority of the European Parliament opposed such a trade liberalization, as it would imply that the EU would grant North Cyprus the status of a separate legal entity (Coppieters 2017: 43).

B. Moldova and Transnistria

The Moldovan strategy has been to obtain concessions from the Transnistrian regime through outside pressure, enforcing a non-recognition policy in the economic field in particular. Transnistria, previously a relatively well-developed industrial region in the Soviet Union, has no access to export markets other than through Ukraine or Moldova. In 2005, Chisinau, with active support from the EU and in cooperation with the Ukrainian authorities, introduced border and customs controls for Transnistrian goods, with the aim of forcing Transnistrian export companies that want to trade with the EU or Ukraine to register in Chisinau in order to obtain the necessary customs papers (Popescu & Litra 2012). This policy — where Transnistrian companies were forced to engage in trade with the EU as if they were Moldovan — was difficult to accept from the perspective of Transnistria's non-recognition policies. However, the threat that all exports to the EU would be halted gave it no other choice. It had to accept the use of Moldovan certificates of origin to export its goods to the EU. Around 2,000 Transnistrian companies were registered in 2019. Companies trading exclusively with Ukraine, small companies and individual entrepreneurs managed to avoid such registration.

The Moldovan policies created tensions with Transnistria, although not enough to prevent a partial rapprochement (European Commission & High Representative of the European Union for Foreign Affairs and Security Policy 2013). An intensification of trade links was favored by the change of government in Transnistria in December 2011, when Igor Smirnov, who had held the presidency for two decades, was defeated by Yevgeny Shevchuk. Train traffic between Moldova and Ukraine through Transnistria resumed in April 2012. Transnistria's external trade with the EU benefited from the customs tariff introduced as a result of Moldova's participation in the EU's Autonomous Trade Preferences (ATP) regime (Konończuk & Rodkiewicz 2012). Moreover, the EU established direct links with Transnistrian authorities, organizing seminars on EU policy and training sessions on trade regulations.

However, at no point did the partial improvement of relations with Chisinau and Brussels reduce Transnistria's preference for further integration with Russia—including leaning towards the Eurasian Economic Union. The severe economic recession in Transnistria caused by the Russian-Ukrainian war in 2014—which made it more difficult to use Ukraine as a transit route to Russia— increased its financial dependence on Moscow, strengthening its eastward political orientation. The EU rejected Transnistria's demand to be considered a full negotiating partner on an equal basis as Moldova. Transnistria, for its part, refused to participate actively in the negotiations between the EU and Moldova on a Deep and Comprehensive Free Trade Area (DCFTA). The DCFTA was included in the Association Agreement between the EU and Moldova of June 27, 2014. It was due to replace the EU's ATP regime with Moldova, which had allowed Transnistria to receive preferential treatment regarding trade, and which was due to expire at the end of 2015. As a non-recognized entity, Transnistria would not be able to participate in the ATP on its own. The loss of a preferential treatment due to remaining outside the DCFTA would have led to a substantial increase in its export tariffs. Brussels presented the choice to Transnistria as an "either/or" decision.

A compromise was found in November/December 2015 (Calus 2016; Secrieru 2016). The agreement between Transnistria and Moldova did not mention the DCFTA, but used a more ambiguous formula, referring to trade facilitation measures. Under the agreement, the DCFTA would be implemented on the "entire territory" of Moldova from January 1, 2016, onwards (EU-Republic of Moldova Association Council 2015). Thus, Transnistria would join the DCFTA before having introduced the appropriate legislation and, in exchange, would lift its trade barriers for EU products within a period of two years and comply with World Trade Organizations (WTO) regulations.

This compromise was in the interest of all parties and reflected the power differentials between them. A fall in Transnistria's exports to the EU would not have benefited any of the parties. Russia was not interested in diminishing Transnistria's westward trade, as it would then have to compensate for the loss by giving additional economic support to Transnistria. The EU, for its part, was interested in a rapprochement between Moldova and Transnistria. Having closer economic links with the breakaway republic—which would increase Transnistria's long-term dependence on the EU and its capacity to reintegrate into Moldova—seemed more important than the creation of a common legal framework for overseeing the implementation of the DCFTA regulations in the immediate future. The EU was ready to accept that it would not be able to monitor the required legal reforms in Transnistria in the initial stages of implementation of the agreement. From the Transnistrian (and also the Russian) perspective, the fact that this process was reversible facilitated its acceptance. Moreover, Transnistria managed to save face, due to the fact that the details of the agreement were not disclosed: its officials claimed that the agreement resulted from direct bilateral negotiations with Brussels where, as they said, they convinced their counterparts of the correctness of their position (Infotag 2015).

The proportion of Transnistrian goods destined for the EU market increased as a result of this agreement (Popsoi 2016; Montesano, Van der Togt & Zweers 2016). Moreover, the OSCE facilitated the signing of a large number of protocols on various forms of cooperation between Chisinau and Tiraspol (European Commission & High Representative of the European Union for Foreign Affairs and Security Policy 2018). However, Transnistria has also repeatedly accused the EU and Moldova of imposing an economic blockade and forcing it to accept terms it would otherwise have rejected.

The European Union pushed Transnistria to fulfill the DCFTA requirements and strives to monitor its implementation. Despite positive steps forward in terms of practical cooperation between Moldova and Transnistria, the positions of both parties regarding their status and identity remain confrontational on the rhetorical level. Moldova recognizes Transnistria as a trading entity, but not as an equal trading partner, with Transnistria unwillingly accepting a status of subordination to Moldova. In addition, Moldova and Transnistria do not recognize each other in terms of their respective political identities.

C. Georgia and Abkhazia

The parties in the Georgian-Abkhaz conflict never prioritized economic gains. A rare exception is a hydraulic power station that has been in operation since 1992–1993 for the benefit of both sides; its hydro-technical facilities are located in Georgia and its control panel in Abkhaz territory (Basaria 2011: 18). Trade has otherwise been characterized by confrontation. Abkhazia has forbidden trade with Georgia since 2007, whereas Georgia's 2008 law on occupied territories made all economic activities with and in Abkhazia without Tbilisi's authorization illegal. However, the authorities on both sides have turned a blind eye to several forms of trans-border commerce, including the "suitcase trade" by local inhabitants. In 2015, the overall volume of trade was estimated to be in the range of 7 to 15 million U.S. dollars (Mirimanova 2015b: 12, 15). Abkhazia's economy is marginal for Georgia, except for the Georgian regions along their common border. Abkhazia's commerce with Georgia is less important than its trade with Russia, but still substantial for its economy, despite the fact that it is not legally regulated.

When Russia applied for WTO membership, it had to obtain the agreement of Georgia—a WTO member. Both parties agreed in 2011 on a complex set of regulations, where both contested territories were turned into "trade corridors" for Russian and Georgian goods. A Swiss company accountable only to the Swiss government would monitor the movement of goods. This was in line with Georgia's objective of having international mechanisms put in place to control trade with the breakaway entities (Jamnews 2018). Neither Abkhazia nor South Ossetia were given any active role in negotiating this agreement. The two territories were defined through a set of geographic coordinates, which led to firm protest in Abkhazia and South Ossetia (Mirimanova 2015b: 14). They did not consider this lack of legal status acceptable and considered the fact that their territory was turned into a trade corridor an insult to their national identity—and this not only by their adversary, but also by their closest ally.[17] They demanded full participation and equal status in negotiations on the creation of trade routes through their territory.

The idea of restoring rail links between Russia and Armenia through Abkhazia and Georgia has been widely discussed over the years, including in terms of economic costs and benefits (Mirimanova 2013). This would necessitate a specific compromise on customs and border controls, which is difficult to achieve in the framework of the non-recognition policies of the two conflicting parties. They define the benefits of such cooperation mainly in terms of relative, not absolute, gains. The Abkhaz authorities fear, for instance, that asymmetric trade patterns would make them politically dependent on Georgia.

The question of trade regulation has continuously been put on the agenda in Georgia and Abkhazia, but it meets with political resistance on both sides. Abkhazia does not consider the increase of its trade with Georgia a good political option, as this would make

---

17 At the time of writing, this agreement has not yet been implemented.

it more dependent on Tbilisi. The lack of trade regulation is largely explained by the fear of becoming economically dependent on Georgia, which may later force Abkhazia to make political concessions in exchange for economic benefits.

From the Georgian perspective, there is a readiness to give products from Abkhazia access to Georgian markets. However, Abkhaz producers then would have to accept trading with documents issued by Georgia. These documents would not indicate any country of origin but still include a minimum amount of information regarding the personal identity of the producer (full name and city). The Georgian authorities presented such a procedure as "status-neutral labelling" (OC Media 2018). The Abkhaz goods exported to the EU would, however, receive a Georgian certificate of origin. This plan—which was unveiled in April 2018—is fully in line with the Georgian recognition and non-recognition policies. It recognizes the right of individual Abkhaz producers to trade internationally and also their right of not having to choose the Georgian nationality to do so. This is made possible by these so-called neutral documents—documents delivered by the Georgian authorities without mentioning nationality. This procedure does not involve the Abkhaz authorities. However, the Abkhaz authorities deny that such status is "neutral," as it is granted by Georgia.[18] They rejected this proposal.

The regulation of trade implies a resolution of certain status questions, but it also addresses problems of identity. Abkhaz and Georgian entrepreneurs both see certain advantages in trade regulation, including the strengthening of their respective national identities. Abkhaz businesspeople are of the opinion that the regulation of trade would improve the political relations of their state with its neighbor. This would strengthen its security and independence. Georgian traders, in contrast, are convinced that Abkhazia's trade with the economically more advanced Georgia could convince them of the need for reintegration and help to restore Georgia's territorial integrity (Mirimanova 2018: 4 & 10).

---

18 This proposal is based on the Georgian practice of issuing "neutral" travel documents, which are for the same reason rejected by the Abkhaz authorities.

Thus, both parties expect that the mutual recognition of Georgia and Abkhazia as trade partners would best serve their respective political objectives.

6. Comparisons and Conclusions

The ceasefire agreements analyzed in this chapter have ended open violence in military conflicts involving "non-state armed groups" — as they are designated in international humanitarian law — or "contested states" — as they are designated in this political analysis. The contested states did not have the same military weight in the different cases analyzed. The non-state armed forces fighting for the Abkhaz cause against pro-government troops in 1992–1993 were in the vast majority constituted by Abkhaz, but also included volunteers from the North Caucasus. The role of non-state armed groups fighting against the central government was likewise substantial in the Transnistrian war of 1990–1992, even if the Russian military forces stationed in the territory remained militarily predominant (Hill 2012: 51–52). The Abkhaz troops were effectively operating on their own territory in the case of the Georgian-Russian war of 2008. In contrast, Turkish Cypriot armed forces played a marginal role in supporting the offensive of the Turkish troops in Cyprus in August 1974.

In all these three cases, the state opposing secession was severely defeated. However, the contested states did not contribute to these defeats to the same degree. The role they played in the military operations — as compared to that of their patron states — differed greatly, and this difference was reflected in the way they were included in the ceasefire negotiations and agreements. Inclusion took place in three different ways. The first type was full participation in the ceasefire negotiations, as representing one of the sides in the armed conflict. In the second type, the contested state did not participate in the negotiation of the ceasefire agreement but, instead, gave its formal support through its signature. In the third type, the contested state did not participate in the negotiations and did not have an opportunity to express its support for the agreement through its signature, but still fully participated in the mechanisms for its enforcement.

Each of these roles expresses a specific power differential among the conflicting parties, is attached to a different status in the negotiations and in the agreement and is linked to different rights and obligations in its implementation, as well as different forms of recognition and non-recognition.

This typology can be applied to the three cases under consideration. The first type applies to the 1994 ceasefire agreement in Abkhazia. This was, in legal terms, an agreement negotiated and signed by the representatives of the non-state armed forces on an equal footing with the representatives of the state from which they were breaking away. The contested state was not part of the mechanisms to monitor its implementation or restore security in case of violation of the ceasefire. The Georgian authorities failed to impose the participation of representatives of a "legitimate" Georgian government of Abkhazia as an autonomous actor in the negotiations.

The second type applies to the ceasefire agreement that ended the Georgian-Russian war of 2008. Georgia was defeated for a second time in 2008 and expelled from the Kodor/i gorge—the small bit of Abkhaz territory it still controlled—but this happened in a military conflict with Russia, an interstate conflict where the Abkhaz military forces played a real but secondary role. Abkhazia did not participate in the negotiations leading to its ceasefire agreement, but its signature was added afterwards, in order to bind it to its implementation. As a signatory, it was formally included on equal terms with Georgia. Russia failed, however, to add the question of the international status of Abkhazia to those of security and humanitarian issues in the international negotiations in Geneva, and the ceasefire did not include any clause that would indicate a specific formal status for Abkhazia in the Geneva International Discussions.

The third type applies to the 1992 ceasefire agreement between Russia and Moldova. Transnistria did not negotiate and was not a co-signatory to this agreement, but it was formally granted a position equal to the two signatories in the JCC responsible for its implementation.

The August 1974 ceasefire in Cyprus was unilaterally imposed by the Turkish side. This case cannot be subsumed under any of the three types of inclusive ceasefire agreements described above. It excluded, by definition, any formal involvement by North Cyprus. It was up to the interposing peacekeeping force of the UN to interact with the Turkish Cypriot authorities in order to implement the ceasefire.

Power differentials played a crucial role in determining the status of the contested states in the trade agreements analyzed in this chapter—or, alternatively, in explaining the failure to reach such agreements. Their status is very much a function of their degree of dependence, not only on the state from which they are breaking away, but also on the patron state. In the case of North Cyprus, the authority of its chamber of commerce to issue its own certificates of origin for goods produced on its territory was recognized by Cyprus and the EU in 2004. Such a status has not been granted to any similar institution linked to the authorities of Transnistria or Abkhazia. The Georgian proposal to have Abkhaz traders bring their goods to the Georgian market with "status-neutral" labeling has been rejected by Abkhazia.

The DCFTA and the Green Line Regulation were both designed and implemented by the EU. Transnistria has high economic expectations of the EU, and North Cyprus also has high political expectations. Abkhazia, in contrast, avoids any economic dependence on Georgia or the EU. It has never shown any interest in Georgian proposals to increase its trade with the EU through the DCFTA—proposals that were always linked to concessions in the political field. Abkhazia remains entirely dependent on its Russian ally. It has to accept this dependence, even if Russia may occasionally go against its policies of recognition and non-recognition regarding Georgia. Abkhazia could not avoid the lack of any formal status in the bilateral agreement between Russia and Georgia on the conditions for Russia's WTO membership—a lack of status that it considered insulting in terms of its own identity.

The involvement of external powers in the Treaty of Guarantee of 1960 for Cyprus established international guarantees of its constitutional order. This internationalization of the Cypriot conflict strengthened the position of the Turkish Cypriot community, as it facilitated Turkey's unilateral intervention. However, the status and identity conflict between the two Cypriot communities was also internationalized through the integration of the island into the EU, which, in contrast, reinforced the position of the Greek Cypriot community.

Similarly, the internationalization of the conflict over the status of Abkhazia changed the relationship between the two parties. Both parties hoped that the peacekeeping role granted to the international organizations (the CIS and UN) in the 1994 ceasefire agreement would enhance their own position. However, it was Abkhazia that managed to gain the most from the presence of Russian peacekeeping forces on its territory, and it managed to get its independent status recognized by Russia in 2008. Georgia, on the other hand, has tried to gain some leverage over the Russian military and economic presence in Abkhazia through the deployment of the EUMM along the boundaries with Abkhazia and through the creation of international mechanisms to monitor the movement of goods over the Russian-Abkhaz border.

Transnistria and Moldova are also making use of international support to foster their policies of recognition and non-recognition. Moldova had to accept equal status with Transnistria in the JCC that oversees the peacekeeping forces in Transnistria. By contrast, Transnistria had to accept a subordinate status to Moldova in order to be part of the DCFTA, although it did not have to publicly acknowledge the disparity. Regarding the internationalization of these three conflicts, the contested states can count on military support from their patron states to strengthen their status and identity, whereas the states confronting secession can count on the EU's trade policy in advancing their policies of recognition and non-recognition. The small size of the contested states analyzed in this chapter means that they do not have sufficient political clout to push for membership to any international economic organization. For Abkhazia and Transnistria, this is even the case for economic organizations that are dominated by Russia, such as the Eurasian Economic Union.

As already indicated earlier, one of the conflicting parties may have to accept a particular status or identity for itself or for the other party, even if it considers that status or identity unjust, or even if it contradicts its policy of non-recognition. Such a concession does not negate the possibility of countering such a status or identity at a later time. Each of the three cases here illustrates these kinds of shifts in the conflictual process on status. The contested states Abkhazia and Transnistria were, for instance, able to impose equal status in a ceasefire agreement or its implementation, but the state they were confronting would not allow them to reach such status in agreements on trade regulation.

It may be concluded that the concept of recognition, together with non-recognition, is well suited to describe the disputes among conflicting parties regarding their status and identity. The analysis of the ceasefire agreements in this chapter has shown that a constitutive approach to statehood has to take into account its intrinsic characteristics—such as the degree of control over a territory and its population—in analyzing the conditions under which particular forms of recognition take place, as well as the power differential which results from external support, among other things. The fact that Abkhazia was granted equal status to Georgia in the 1994 ceasefire has to do with the high degree of control it had achieved over the Abkhaz territory and its population—a degree of control that was higher than Transnistria achieved in 1992 or the Turkish Cypriots in 1974.

The formal character of the status question allows for a direct comparison among all three cases, as is also the case regarding the military role of contested states in achieving victory, or the degree of economic dependence in assessing the relationship of forces in trade agreements. Such a comparison is far more difficult to achieve on the level of identity, which is largely a question of self-awareness and self-description.

The number of cases in this study is limited. A broader selection of cases would surely enrich the comparison with new descriptive analysis. The 1994 ceasefire that ended the fighting in

Nagorno-Karabakh was signed by the representatives of Azerbaijan and Armenia, as well as by the military commanders of the breakaway entity. This is, to a certain extent, similar to the ceasefire between Russia and Georgia in 2008. The 1992 ceasefire in South Ossetia had the same formal character as the one signed the same year in Transnistria: an interstate treaty (in the former case, between Russia and Georgia) that did not bear the signature of representatives of the contested state and that regulated its involvement in the control of its implementation. The second Minsk agreement of 2015 on Eastern Ukraine carried the signatures of representatives of the contested states. Regarding the 1999 war in Kosovo, the NATO-led peacekeeping Kosovo force KFOR made a specific ceasefire agreement with the Kosovar Liberation Army on June 20, 1999, in order to guarantee its demilitarization (NATO 1999).

In contrast to Cyprus and Transnistria, there was no formal regulation of trade through an agreement in any of these other cases — and there is not even any trade between Nagorno-Karabakh and Azerbaijan. A major exception is the role of trade agreements in the Kosovo conflict, in the framework of Serbia and Kosovo's integration within European structures, and with far reaching implications for their respective status and identities. In that case, Serbia had to accept equal status with the contested state of Kosovo as a condition for its further integration with the EU. This acceptance goes against its non-recognition policy, as was also the case for Transnistria and North Cyprus when they had to accept a subordinate status in trade agreements to reach the same goal. In addition, there were intensive trade relations between Georgia and South Ossetia up to the 2003 Rose Revolution, although without any formal regulation.

Each of the parties involved in these conflicts has its own recognition and non-recognition policies to address these issues. Georgia, which has been fighting on two fronts against secession, even developed simultaneously yet different recognition and non-recognition policies in regard to Abkhazia and South Ossetia. A comprehensive and detailed analysis of the kind of mutual recognition achieved in these cases and the kind of recognition and non-recognition policies pursued by the parties would not challenge the thesis of the contested nature of recognition in secessionist conflicts, but rather enrich its understanding.

Bibliography

Asmus, R. D. (2010). *A Little War that Shook the World*. New York: Palgrave.

Barbieri, K. (2005). *The Liberal Illusion: Does Trade Promote Peace?* Ann Arbor: The University of Michigan Press.

Basaria, V. (2011). The Inguri Hydropower Station: Why This Model of Trans-Inguri Economic Cooperation Remains the Only One. In *Regulating Trans-Ingur/I Economic Relations: Views from Two Banks*, N. Mirimanova and O. Pentikainen (eds). International Alert, July 2011, 18–21, http://www.international-alert.org (accessed 1 October 2019).

Bedorf, T. (2010). *Verkennende Anerkennung: Über Identität und Politik*. Frankfurt/M.: Suhrkamp.

Bell, C. (2006). Peace Agreements: Their Nature and Legal Status. *The American Journal of International Law* 100 (2): 373–412.

Berkes, A. (2017). "Status Neutrality" of International Organizations: A Mission Impossible with Regard to Self-Proclaimed Separatists Entities? In European Society of International Law, *Conference Paper Series*, Conference Paper No 2/2017.

Brownlie, I. (1963). *International Law and the Use of Force by States*. Oxford: Clarendon Press.

Calus, K. (2016). The DCFTA in Transnistria: Who Gains? *New Eastern Europe* (15 January 2016), http://neweasterneurope.eu/old_site/articles-and-commentary/1861-the-dcfta-in-transnistria-who-gains (accessed 1 October 2019).

Caspersen, N. (2018). Recognition, Status Quo or Reintegration: Engagement with de facto States. *Ethnopolitics* 17(4): 373–389.

Chen, D.P. (2011). *Liberal Peace across the Taiwan Strait? The U.S. Strategic Ambiguity Policy in the Era of Economic Cooperation Framework Agreement (ECFA)*. Paper presented at the 2011 Annual Meeting of the American Political Science Association, September 1–4, 2011, http://papers.ssrn.com/sol3/papers.cfm?abstract_id=1903025 (accessed 1 October 2019).

Civil Georgia. (2008). New Agreement in Force, *Civil Georgia*, 8 September 2008, https://old.civil.ge/eng/article.php?id=19435 (accessed 1 October 2019).

Cohen, J. (ed.). (1999). A Question of Sovereignty. The Georgia-Abkhazia Peace Process. *Accord*, Issue 7, http://www.c-r.org/accord/geor-ab/accord7/index.shtml (accessed 1 October 2019).

Coppieters, B. (2015). The United Nations Observer Mission in Georgia (UNOMIG) in Abkhazia (August 1993–June 2009). In *The Oxford Handbook of United Nations Peacekeeping Operations*, J. A. Koops, N. MacQueen, T. Tardy and P. D. Williams (eds). Oxford: Oxford University Press, 443–453.

Coppieters, B. (2017). The EU's policies towards contested states. In *Secession and Counter-secession. An International Relations Perspective*, D. Muro and E. Woertz (eds). Barcelona: CIDOB, 12/2017, 37–43, https://www.cidob.org/en/articulos/monografias/secession_and_counter_secession/the_eu_s_policies_towards_contested_states (accessed 1 October 2019).

Coppieters, B. (2018a). Four Positions on the Recognition of States in and after the Soviet Union, with Special Reference to Abkhazia. *Europe-Asia Studies* 70 (6): 991–1014.

Coppieters, B. (2018b). 'Statehood', 'De facto Authorities' and 'Occupation': Contested Concepts and the EU's Engagement in its European Neighbourhood. *Ethnopolitics* 17(4): 343–361.

Coppieters, B. (2019). Engagement without Recognition. In *The Routledge Handbook of State Recognition*, G. Visoka, J. Doyle & E. Newman (eds). London: Routledge, 241–255.

Daase, D., Fehl, C., Geis, A. & Kolliarakis, G. (eds). (2015). *Recognition in International Relations: Rethinking a Political Concept in a Global Context*. Basingstoke: Palgrave Macmillan.

De Waal, T. (2018). *Uncertain Ground: Engaging with Europe's De facto States and Breakaway Territories*. Washington, DC: Carnegie Endowment for International Peace, https://carnegieeurope.eu/2018/12/03/uncertain-ground-engaging-with-europe-s-de-facto-states-and-breakaway-territories-pub-77823 (accessed 1 October 2019).

Duquette, D.A. (2001). Hegel's Social and Political Thought. *Internet Encyclopedia of Philosophy*, https://www.iep.utm.edu/hegelsoc/ (accessed 1 October 2019).

European Commission. (2019). *Report from the Commission to the Council*. Fifteenth Report on the Implementation of Council Regulation (EC) No866/2004 of 29 April 2004 and the Situation Resulting from its Application Covering the Period 1 January until 31 December 2018, COM (2019) 323 final, https://ec.europa.eu/info/sites/info/files/annual-report-2018-implementation-green-line-regulation_en.pdf (accessed 1 October 2019).

European Commission & High Representative of the European Union for Foreign Affairs and Security Policy. (2013). *Joint Staff Working Document: Implementation of the European Neighbourhood Policy in the Republic of Moldova. Progress in 2012 and Recommendations for Action.* SWD (2013) 80 final, 20 March 2013, https://eur-lex.europa.eu/legal-content/EN/TXT/PDF/?uri=CELEX:52013SC0080&from=EN (accessed 1 October 2019).

EU-Republic of Moldova Association Council. (2015). Decision No 1/2015 of the EU-Republic of Moldova Association Council of 18 December 2015. *Official Journal of the European Union,* L 336/93 23 (December 2015), https://eur-lex.europa.eu/legal-content/EN/TXT/PDF/?uri=CELEX:22015D2445&from=EN (accessed 1 October 2019).

Fearon, J.D. (1999). *What is Identity (as we Now Use the Word)?,* https://web.stanford.edu/group/fearon-research/cgi-bin/wordpress/wp-content/uploads/2013/10/What-is-Identity-as-we-now-use-the-word-.pdf (accessed 1 October 2019).

Francis, C. (2011). *Conflict Resolution and Status. The Case of Georgia and Abkhazia 1989–2008.* Brussels: VUB Press.

Geldenhuys, D. (2009). *Contested States in World Politics.* Basingstoke: Palgrave Macmillan.

Haacke, J. (2005). The Frankfurt School and International Relations: On the Centrality of Recognition. *Review of International Studies,* 31(1), 181–194.

Hayden, P. & Schick, K (2016). *Recognition and Global Politics. Critical Encounters between State and World.* Manchester: Manchester University Press.

Hill, W.H. (2012). *Russia, the Near Abroad, and the West: Lessons from the Moldova-Transnistria Conflict.* Washington: Woodrow Wilson Center Press & Baltimore: The John Hopkins University Press.

Hsieh, P. L. (2019a). The Quest for Recognition: Taiwan's Military and Trade Agreements with Singapore under the One-China policy. *International Relations of the Asia-Pacific* 19 (1): 89–115.

Hsieh, P. L. (2019b). *Rethinking Recognition and Non-Recognition: Taiwan's Bilateral and Plurilateral Agreements.* PhD Dissertation, Vrije Universiteit Brussel.

Ikäheimo, H. (2014). *Anerkennung.* Berlin/Boston: De Gruyter.

Infotag. (2015). Transnistria has Persuaded EU not to Cancel Preferential Trade Regime—MFA. *Infotag,* 8 December 2015, http://www.infotag.md/rebelion-en/214263/ (accessed 1 October 2019).

Jamnews. (2018). The Fate of Georgian-Russian Transit Trade through Abkhazia and South Ossetia. *Jamnews*, 21 May 2014, https://jamnews.net/georgia-and-russia-discuss-potential-transit-corridor-through-abkhazia-and-south-ossetia/ (accessed 1 October 2019).

Ker-Lindsay, J. (2005). *EU Accession and UN Peacemaking in Cyprus*. Basingstoke: Palgrave Macmillan.

Ker-Lindsay J. (2012). *The Foreign Policy of Counter Secession*. Oxford: Oxford University Press.

Konończuk, W. & Rodkiewicz, W. (2012). Could Transnistria Block Moldova's Integration with the EU?'. *OSW Commentary* (23 October 2012), https://www.osw.waw.pl/en/publikacje/osw-commentary/2012-10-23/could-transnistria-block-moldovas-integration-eu#_ftn1 (accessed 1 October 2019).

Kramer, A.E. (2008). Peace Plan Offers Russia a Rationale to Advance. *New York Times*, 13 August 2008, https://www.nytimes.com/2008/08/14/world/europe/14document.html (accessed 1 October 2019).

Lauterpacht, H. (2013). *Recognition in International Law*. Cambridge: Cambridge University Press.

Leigh, M. (1990). The Legal Status in International Law of the Turkish Cypriot and the Greek Cypriot Communities in Cyprus (20 July 1990). *Republic of Turkey, Ministry of Foreign Affairs*, http://www.mfa.gov.tr/chapter5.en.mfa (accessed 1 October 2019)

McQueen, P. (2011). Recognition, Social and Political. *Internet Encyclopedia of Philosophy, IEP*, https://www.iep.utm.edu/recog_sp/ (accessed 1 October 2019).

Ministry of Foreign Affairs of the Republic of Abkhazia. (2013). Irakli Khintba Gave a Press Conference on the Results of 23rd [sic] Round of the Geneva Discussions, 4 April 2013, *Ministry of Foreign Affairs of the Republic of Abkhazia*, http://old.mfaapsny.org/en/information/?ID=1019 (accessed 1 October 2019).

Mirimanova, N. (ed.). (2013). Rehabilitation of the Railways in the Southern Caucasus. *International Alert*, October 2013, https://www.international-alert.org (accessed 1 October 2019).

Mirimanova, N. (ed.). (2015a). Regulation of Trade across Contested Borders: The Cases of China/Taiwan, Serbia/Kosovo and Cyprus. *International Alert*, April 2015, https://www.international-alert.org/publications/regulation-trade-across-contested-borders-en (accessed 1 October 2019).

Mirimanova, N. (2015b). Abkhazia: Regulations for Trade with Disputed Statehood. *Politorbis*, 60(2): 9–16, https://www.eda.admin.ch/dam/eda/mehrsprachig/documents/publications/Politorbis/Politorbis%2060_dfe.pdf (accessed 1 October 2019).

Mirimanova, N. (2018). Opening the 'Ingur/i gate' for Legal Business: Views from Georgian and Abkhaz Private Companies. *International Alert*, March 2018, https://www.international-alert.org/publications/opening-inguri-gate-legal-business (accessed 1 October 2019).

Montesano, F.S., Van der Togt, T. & Zweers, W. (2016). The Europeanisation of Moldova: Is the EU on the Right Track? *Clingendael Report* (July 2016), https://www.clingendael.org/sites/default/files/pdfs/Clingendael%20Report%20The%20Europeanisation%20of%20Moldova%20-%20July%202016.pdf (accessed 1 October 2019).

NATO. (1999). Undertaking of Demilitarisation and Transformation by the UCK, 20 June 1999. *NATO's role in Kosovo: Basic Documents*, https://www.nato.int/kosovo/docu/a990620a.htm (accessed 1 October 2019).

Nazarenko, S. (2014). A Housing Nightmare in Abkhazia, *Böll Stiftung: South Caucasus*, 16 January 2014, https://ge.boell.org/en/2014/01/16/housing-nightmare-abkhazia (accessed 1 October 2019).

OC Media. (2018). Georgia Unveils 'Unprecedented' Peace Initiative for Abkhazia, South Ossetia. *OC Media*, 4 April 2018, http://oc-media.org/georgia-unveils-unprecedented-peace-initiative-for-abkhazia-south-ossetia/ (accessed 1 October 2019).

Papadimitriou, D. & Petrov, P. (2012). Whose Rule, Whose Law? Contested Statehood, External Leverage and the European Union's Rule of Law Mission in Kosovo. *Journal of Common Market Studies* 50(5): 746–763.

Pegg, S. (1998). *International Society and the De Facto State*. Aldershot: Ashgate.

Phillips, D. L. (2011). *Implementation Review: Six-Point Ceasefire Agreement between Russia and Georgia*. Washington: The National Committee on American Foreign Policy and the Institute for the Study of Human Rights, https://www.ncafp.org/2016/wp-content/uploads/2011/08/implementation-review-russia-and-georgia-aug2011.pdf (accessed 1 October 2019).

Popescu, N. & Litra, L. (2012). Transnistria: A Bottom-Up Solution, *Policy Brief 63, European Council on Foreign Relations*, London, 25 September 2012, http://www.ecfr.eu/publications/summary/transnistria_a_bottom_up_solution (accessed 1 October 2019).

Popsoi, M. (2016). Transnistria: Change of Leadership, But Not Policy. *Eurasia Daily Monitor*, 13(198), 16 December 2016, https://jamestown.org/program/transnistria-change-leadership-not-policy/ (accessed 1 October 2019).

Public International Law & Policy Group. (2013). *The Ceasefire Drafter's Handbook: An Introduction and Template for Negotiators, Mediators, and Stakeholders*. Washington, May 2013, https://static1.squarespace.com/static/5900b58e1b631bffa367167e/t/5b730a224fa51ab1083c22bb/1534265892577/PILPG+Cease-fire+Drafter%27s+Handbook+%28Including%2BTemplate%2BCease-fire%2BAgreement%29-2.pdf (accessed 1 October 2019).

Secrieru, S (2016). Transnistria Zig-zagging towards a DCFTA. *PISM Policy Paper* 4:145 (January 2016).

Siep, L. (2014). Hegel on the Master-Slave Relation. *Fifteen Eightyfour – Academic Perspectives from Cambridge University Press*, 2 May 2014, http://www.cambridgeblog.org/2014/05/hegel-on-the-master-slave-relation/http://www.cambridgeblog.org/2014/05/hegel-on-the-master-slave-relation/ (accessed 1 October 2019).

Strömbom, L. (2014). Thick Recognition: Advancing Theory on Identity Change in Intractable Conflicts. *European Journal of International Relations* 20(1): 168–191.

Talmon, S. (2005). The Constitutive Versus the Declaratory Theory of Recognition: *Tertium non Datur*? *British Yearbook of International Law* 75(1): 101–181.

United Nations. (2002). Cyprus Background UNFICYP. Peace and Security Section of the Department of Public Information in cooperation with the Department of Peacekeeping Operations, http://www.un.org/Depts/DPKO/Missions/unficyp/unficypB.html (accessed 1 October 2019).

Visoka, G. & Doyle J. (2015). Neo-Functional Peace: The European Union Way of Resolving Conflicts. *JCMS: Journal of Common Market Studies* 54(4): 862–877.

The World-System and Post-Soviet *De Facto* States[1]

Mikhail Minakov

Today most of the Earth's land surface and its populations are governed or controlled by states. The state, as a form of complex political and socio-economic organisation, has become dominant globally in the last few centuries. Inter-state relations have developed into a complex world-system with its own rules, dynamics and 'ecology.' This world-system has three elements — interpreted in terms of the metaphor of core and centre: (1) an influential core dominating the international legal-political and economic order, (2) a politically and economically influenced periphery, and (3) a semicore/semiperiphery striving for global or regional influence. The elements are unequally correlated and hierarchically bonded (Prebish 1950; Wallerstein 2004; Gotts 2007; Agh 2016). There have been attempts by a number of international and intergovernmental organisations to create international law and globally followed rules granting inter-state equality. Despite this, states, their populations and their economies differ in terms of quality of life, productivity, political influence and their role in global exchange. The core states and the peripheral polities are usually described as interdependent in political, economic and cultural terms, thus constituting some sort of ecological system of global, local, and regional interdependence.

However, stable non-recognised states (NRS) remain outside this interstate system's description. These are peripheral, even with regard to the least influential peripheral states. My key question here is what kind of group do these states constitute in world-system?

---

[1] This chapter is based on research that was done with the support of German Academic Exchange Service at the Institute for European Studies, European University Viadrina, and Ukrainian Research in Switzerland Program at the University of Basel.

To answer this question, I will apply the core-periphery model to their case. In this chapter, I argue that non-recognised states represent an *extreme periphery,* the fourth element of today's world-system. I use the term *extreme periphery* to signify a group of states that employ extreme measures to enter the class of normal periphery because these states (1) do not enjoy full or partial recognition by other recognised states and members of international relations, (2) do not participate—or if they do participate, participate minimally—in the global economy (because of sanctions against them), (3) have populations face much bigger socio-economic and biopolitical limitations than in any other part of the world, and (4) need an additional source of legitimacy, usually provided by some fully recognised state (sponsor state[2]) for their survival.

Out of many de facto states existing today around globe, I will test the class of extreme periphery on the six non-recognised polities that emerged in post-Soviet Eastern Europe. After the collapse of the Soviet Union, people engaged in three waves of secessionist processes with the aim of creating new states. The first wave, between 1989 and 1994, started with a number of secessionist movements: some representing the title populations of fifteen Soviet republics; some being smaller movements in the interests of the ethnic groups of Soviet 'nationalities.' When the USSR was dissolved in December 1991, and up until the Budapest Memorandum (1994)[3], within the territory of the USSR, fifteen fully recognised independent states were established (Armenia, Azerbaijan, Belarus, Estonia, Georgia, Kazakhstan, Kyrgyzstan, Latvia, Lithuania, Moldova, Russia, Tajikistan, Turkmenistan, Ukraine and Uzbekistan) and four NRS (Abkhazia, Nagorno-

---

2   I use the term of sponsor state here as a generic synonym to other related terms like 'patron state,' 'patronal state,' 'supervising state', etc.
3   This is the international agreement of 1994, according to which Belarus, Kazakhstan, and Ukraine refused nuclear weapons (that remained on their territories from Soviet times) in return for a guarantee of their borders and territories. The guarantors of the memorandum were Russia, USA and UK; France and China were guarantors with reservations. The full text version of the memorandum is accessible here: http://www.centrepir.org/media/content/files/12/13943175580.pdf (accessed on 3 October 2019).

Karabakh, South Ossetia, and Transnistria) (Hale 2005: 57; Broers 2013: 60; Gammer 2014: 40; Bianchini & Minakov 2018: 299).

The second wave, 1994–2008, was connected with the Russian centre's fight to control its territories and the acceptance of a new federal treaty by all federal lands, including Chechnya, Dagestan, Ingushetia, and Tatarstan. During this period, Ukraine coped with secession attempts in 1994/5 in Crimea and in 2004/5 in Donbas (Hale 2005: 57–9; Gammer 2014: 41/2). The Georgian government politically reintegrated Adjara and started preparations for the military reintegration of Southern Ossetia in 2004–8. The regions of Transnistria and Nagorno-Karabakh turned into zones of 'frozen conflict'. There were no new significant secession movements in other post-Soviet states in this period.

The end of anti-secessionist operations in Russia gave rise to the third wave of post-Soviet secessionism (ongoing since 2008, as at the date of publication of this chapter). The Russian-Georgian war of 2008 led to the strengthening and partial recognition of South Ossetia and Abkhazia. In the six years that followed, Russia annexed Crimea and launched systemic support for secessionist movements in South-Eastern Ukraine. The latter strategy helped to establish two new breakaway regions in Eastern Donbas: 'DPR' and 'LPR'). As a result, since 2014, there has been an increased network of six post-Soviet NRS with a population of over 4 mln people and a history of over a quarter of century of existence.

So these states constitute and group of interconnected phenomena in the history of state-creation and state-building. Most of these states proved to be stable political units with their own role in world-system. As I stated above, I argue that the post-Soviet *de facto* states (DFS) constitute an example of extreme periphery, and namely extreme periphery to the Western core. This extreme peripheral status means that political, economic, social, legal and economic processes in these polities do not happen in the same way as they would do in any other peripheral state, and they do so against the will and interests of the Western core and their patronal states. Thus, the usual interdependency and struggle of core and different semicores and peripheries here is more striking; and thus these DFS have to use extreme measures of security, political and economic measures for survival and development. It leads to the need to add a fourth class to the existing three classes which make up Wallerstein's 'core-peripheries' scale: the *extreme periphery* class.

1. Methodology

1.1. Core-Periphery Differentiation.

Ever since 1950-ies, the metaphor of core/centre and periphery has framed the vision of historians, social and political scholars, diplomats, politicians, as well as practitioners of international development. This vision stems from the observation of global inequalities in different times, among different states. Raúl Prebisch, Andre Gunder Frank and Samir Amin, who was among the first scholars to use core-periphery analysis, looked at the differences between core and periphery nations in terms of economy, production and politics (Prebisch 1950, 1981; Frank 1967; Amin 1976). These authors all applied core-periphery metaphor to a new social reality that grew up in the place of a once global imperial/colonial system. Administrative, political and military tools of metropolitan dominance over colonies had become history by the 1970s; however, inequality persisted. Their approaches were summed up in the world-system approach of Immanuel Wallerstein and his followers.

According to the contemporary world-system approach, core and periphery have specific characteristics that have a tendency to change over time, due to inter- and inner-state processes (Wallerstein 2004; Arrighi et al. 2012; Agh 2016). Immanuel Wallerstein defined the main features of core and peripheries as "the degree of profitability of the production processes", role of monopolies in production and international exchange, where peripheral states lose in economic and political exchange (Wallerstein 2004: 28). Core states are defined as benefiting economically from unequal exchange, and in the 20th century, they were mainly Western states and the USSR (before 1989–91). Core states are innumerous and constantly safeguard their superior position through international law, economic and political means.

The strong states that contain the biggest share of core-specific processes focus on protecting their monopolies. Consequently, periphery states are politically and economically weaker than the core nations; they are internally less stable and more dependent on the core in economic and political terms. The weakness of these states impedes their ability to win from global exchange (Wallerstein 2004; Agh 2016).

However, between the two poles of global exchange, there is a dynamic group of ascending semiperipheral and/or descending semicore states. The semicore/semiperipheral states are under constant pressure from core states; the semicore states put pressure on peripheral states, and do whatever possible, through the use of economy, politics and military action, not to slip into the periphery and enter the core state class (Wallerstein 2004: 29ff). Basically, these are states that either exhausted themselves due to the lasting effect of monopolies (like the USSR), or that just started the cycle of power and wealth concentration through monopolisation (like post-Soviet Russia, or modern Turkey) (Kick et al. 2000; Kick & Davies 2001).

There are other states that do not fit into the three above categories. Among them, (1) 'external areas' that maintain social and economic divisions of labour, independent of the capitalist world economy (USSR, China, North Korea etc) (Wallerstein 1974); (2) areas controlled by the antisystemic movements that are national liberation movements using the nationalist logic of 19th century capitalism to destroy old states and create new ones by dressing "political claims in cultural clothing" (Arrighi et al. 2012: 1, 25). While the first group has decreased since the 1990s, when Russia and China became important parts of the capitalist world-system, the second group continued their antisystemic action.

By the second decade of the 21st century, the role of culture became even more visible in the core-periphery analysis. Core states were seen as centres of cultural hegemony (Rokkan 1967, 1970; Said 1978; Arrighi 1999; Baer et al. 2013; Griffiths & Arnove 2015). These studies show how world-system core states dominate not only through economy and politics, but also through culture and language of legitimacy. A centre imposes hierarchies of identities on the peripheral populations and tends to destroy or subordinate local identities through the centralised use of transnational administrative, economic and education systems, mass media and other propagandistic uses of power and/or cultural practices.

From this perspective, the term 'extreme periphery' designates those groups and/or communities who are not included within the hierarchy of identities established by the core but manage to sustain their identity in spite of the core's policies.

Based on the theoretical and methodological approaches outlined above, I summarise the following key characteristics of core, semicore/semiperipheral, peripheral and extreme-peripheral states:

Table 1.   Core-Periphery Characteristics

	Economic	*Political*	*Cultural*
Core	<ul><li>quasi-monopolies</li><li>benefit from unequal exchange</li><li>suppression of competition</li><li>high level of added value</li><li>minimal poverty</li></ul>	<ul><li>non-questioned political influence</li><li>decisive impact on inter- or national legislation and political order</li></ul>	<ul><li>producers of cultural product</li><li>definers of identities' hierarchies</li><li>centres of education and scholarship with strong impact on legitimacy definitions</li></ul>
Semicore/ Semiperiphery	<ul><li>quasi-monopolies competing with core</li><li>bigger role of competing economy</li><li>lower level of added value</li><li>considerable poverty</li></ul>	<ul><li>questioned political influence</li><li>sporadic impact on international legislation and political order</li><li>political competition with core in certain regions for control over peripheries</li></ul>	<ul><li>mixed production and consumption of own and core's cultural output</li><li>subjects of biggest pressure from core-defined identities' hierarchies</li><li>sporadic influence in global education and scholarship</li><li>weak impact on global legitimacy definitions</li></ul>
Periphery	<ul><li>production with minimal added value</li></ul>	<ul><li>minimal political influence outside country</li></ul>	<ul><li>consumers of core's cultural product and</li></ul>

	• imposed competition • widespread poverty	• strong impact of core and semicore inside country • adaptation to regional order	identities' hierarchies • consumers of education and scholarship products of the core and semicore • sporadic impact on legitimacy definitions
Extreme periphery	• production with minimal value added • weakest party in competition • under international economic sanctions • widespread poverty, usually dependent on some sponsor state's economy	• minimal political influence • mainly in resistance to the centre and parental state[4] • the subject of a strong impact of core and semicore states (especially sponsor state)[5] • adapting to order established by others • striving for the status of normal peripheral condition	• consumers of and resisters to the core's cultural products and the hierarchical identities of the parental state • consumers of and resisters to the education and scholarship products of the core and semicore • no impact on legitimacy definitions

I will now review the status of post-Soviet NRS across these characteristics to verify my hypothesis that these constitute a special case of extreme periphery in the contemporary Western-dominated world-system.

---

4   I use the term 'parental state' to designate a recognised state from which the non-recognised state or territory has seceded; from the moment of secession onwards, the parental state has limited *de facto* sovereignty over its territory and population, which results in non-recognition *vis-à-vis* the breakaway region and its political, economic and demographic structures. The parental state usually uses international law (sanctioned by the core states) to impose sanctions against the non-recognised state (and in some cases, against its sponsors).

5   I use the term 'sponsor state' here to designate a recognised state that supports breakaway region and sponsors its development into a non- or partially recognised state through economic, political, and other means. The sponsorship is provided to help the non-recognised state survive the challenges of surviving the economic limitations and security challenges imposed from the core and the parental state.

1.2. Definition of Non-Recognised States (NRS).

Before I analyse post-Soviet NRS further, I would like to take a closer look at different types of state organisations.

Over centuries, states developed into 'sovereign states.' In his archaeology of contemporary states, Charles Tilly offered the following set of criteria for the 'sovereign state': it is the political entity that (became dominant in Europe after 1500 and in other regions at a later stage, and) (a) controls a well-defined territory, (b) is relatively centralised, (c) differs from other sets of institutions and organisations functioning in the same lands, and (d) has "a monopoly over the concentrated means of physical coercion within its territory" (Tilly 1992: 23). The 'stateness' is measured by "formal autonomy, differentiation from non-governmental organizations, centralization, and internal coordination," and presence of "an organization employing specialized personnel which controls a consolidated territory and is recognized as autonomous and integral by the agents of other states" (Tilly 1992: 12). Thus the functions of state, according to Tilly are (1) war-making (elimination of external threats outside of own territories), (2) state-making (elimination of internal rival forces), (3) protection (elimination of potential threats to the controlled population) and (4) extraction (collection of taxes or revenue that provides a state to secure the means of fulfilling the previous three functions) (ibid., 12). Later functionalists have basically agreed with these criteria (e.g. Ghani & Lockhart 2008: 3).

Practitioners of international relations agree with the above functional definitions as well; however, they add one more feature of contemporary state: recognition. Thus, they refer to Article 1 of the 1933 Montevideo Convention on the Rights and Duties of States, where the "capacity to enter into relations with the other states" is ascribed as a necessary characteristic of stateness. Recognition is a formal indicator of such capacity and is key for stateness (Daase 2015; Ker-Lindsey 2017; Coppieters 2018).

To understand the phenomenon of NRS we should bear in mind these five characteristics of a state: (1) defence from external threat of a population living on a certain territory; (2) full control over populations on a given territory through elimination of internal rivals; (3) provision of the state's exclusive administrative, justice and other services to the population on its territory; (4) collection of taxes and other resources necessary for state's functionality and reproduction; (5) participation in the international order and in inter-state relations. According to these, NRS do not fulfil the fifth criteria. Should they qualify as states at all, then?

In realistic terms, NRS constitute state-like organisations that vary from almost-states to stateless communities. According the recent studies of NRS and DFS around the world, there are three basic types of those: (1) *as-if states*, that is, internationally recognized states which are therefore fully-fledged actors on the international scene, but cannot perform the basic functions of a state such as controlling their territory or holding a monopoly on the use of force in their area; (2) *almost-states*, that is, para-state organisms that have managed to gain de facto independence from the home country and aspire to the status of a full-fledged state, but are not recognised by the international community; and (3) *black spots*, that is, areas that do not aspire to independence, while yet remaining beyond the control of any state authorities and are administered by local organized crime, clan, or religious groups (Stanislawski 2008: 367; Pełczyńska-Nałęcz, Strachota & Falkowski 2008: 371). These degrees, measured according to the previously defined list of the five functionalities of a sovereign state, include the specificities as described in Table 2.

Table 2. Degrees of NRS

	Defence of territory from external threat	Full control over internal populations	Provision of state's exclusive services	Collection of resources necessary for state's functionality	Recognised by other subjects of international relations
As-if state	no	no	no	no	yes

De facto state/ almost-state/ para-state	yes	yes	yes	yes	no (sometimes partially recognised)
Black spots	partially	partially	partially	partially	no

The analysis of post-Soviet polities across the three definitions of NRS and five state functions shows that post-Soviet NRS, including Abkhazia, Nagorno-Karabakh, South Ossetia, and Transnistria, are almost-states/para-states, i.e. DFS lacking international recognition and thus unable to enter into international relations with other states.

Henceforth in this paper, I will use NRS and DFS as synonyms for the less-often-used 'almost-states/para-states'. All of these terms refer to state-like organisations that implement the first four functions in a more or less complete form but generally lack external recognition by *de jure* states. I will also use the temporal dimension for differentiating 'break-away territory' from DFS/NRS offered by Pål Kolstø: the authorities of a break-away territory have to "persist in this state of non-recognition for more than two years" (Kolstø 2006: 725/6). This two-year term, however, is quite arbitrary and should be used *cum grano salis*. I agree that the two-year period of existence means that a state-like organisation has sufficient human, military, and financial resources to resist (a) the attempts of a parental state to reintegrate the seceded community and (b) the pressure of the core states as international order guarantors on leaders of the breakaway territory. The ability to maintain such resistance implies the presence of some political and military force that can control population and territory. Nonetheless, it does not imply that this secession is achieved by a legitimate political and legal entity that has the right to recognition. So, in this study, I use the two-year period only as additional factor in defining NRS. All six post-Soviet NRS that are analysed in this paper fulfil these criteria.

Now that de facto/non-recognised states have been described, I will apply these descriptions to the post-Soviet NRS and test the hypothesis that they can be classified as the extreme periphery of the contemporary world-system.

1.3. Data on Non-Recognised States.

To conduct this research, I not only used published materials by other researchers and analytical centres, but also information from diplomats, journalists, security staff and other people involved in talks, monitoring or other missions in the Southern Caucasus, Moldova and Ukraine in 1992–2018. Literary sources described in the second part of this paper are referred to conventionally; the interviews are referred to by code letter and number, e.g. a#, d#, j#, m#. A detailed description of the interviewees can be found in Table 3 below.

Table 3. Interviewed experts having first-hand experience and knowledge of the situation in post-Soviet NRS

Professions of interviewees	Number	Place/period of involvement with NRS	Periods when interviews were conducted	Terms on which interview is given
Diplomats (participants of talks, diplomatic observers, UN staff) (coded as d1–d9)	9	Armenia, 1993–7, 2009–11; Georgia 1992–2002, 2008–9; Moldova, 1990–8, 2004–10, 2015–18; Ukraine, 1993–5, 2005–10, 2014–18	2008–10, 2014–18	Anonymous
Monitoring specialists, security background (OSCE,	7	Armenia, 1993–9; Georgia,	2008–10, 2014–18	Anonymous

EUBAM) (coded as m1–m7)		1992–6, 2008–9; Moldova, 1995–9, 2008–10, 2015–18; Ukraine, 2008–10, 2014–18		
Journalists/reporters (5 from Western media, 3 from Russian media) (coded as j1–j8)	8	Armenia, 1993–5, 2017–18; Georgia 1992–6, 2008–9; Moldova, 1990–94, 2004–7, 2015–16; Ukraine, 1993–5, 2014–18	2014–18	Off-record
International NGO activists (coded as a1–a8)	8	Georgia 1994–6, 2008–9; Ukraine, 2014–18	2014–18	Off-record

The interviews and data collection were based on the cognitive interviewing method. A cognitive interview is (a) the collection of information in a conversation with a person who understands the aim of the conversation, during which (personal and/or acquired collective) memories about the past are recalled and reflected upon (Fisher & Geiselman 1992: 12–13), and, at the same time, (b) the interviewer's self-reflection, testing his/her/their own methods and premises, of the question set and his/her/their honesty in clarifying the goals of the research in the course of conversations with their respondents (Willis 2015: 16). Although this method is related to reflexive sociology and its qualitative research methods, as well as contemporary investigatory practices of witness interrogation, for me, as an academic researcher, this method is also a refined practice of sincere conversation between people who have information not described in official reports or avoided by academic publications. The result of my conversations with many interlocutors has been an opportunity to better understand the situations in which people in conflict-torn societies find themselves.

I found the cognitive interview method to be a particularly good tool in helping me move towards this.

The set of interview questions was reviewed and clarified several times, which is also a part of the method (Willis 2015, 5ff). However, the basic questionnaire structure remained the same, namely: 1) How did NRS' populations survive sanctions in economic terms? 2) What were the ties between populations of seceded territories and parental states, and how did they change over time? 3) How did political identities emerge and develop in NRS, and what were the roles of local authorities, parental states and sponsor states in the process? 4) How did state-building proceed in the NRS; what were its common features? 5) What were the expectations of the Western/Russian governments *vis-à-vis* NRS, and how did these expectations change over time?

With the above-described conceptual apparatus and sources, I can test the hypothesis that post-Soviet NRS can be classified as the extreme periphery of the contemporary world-system.

2. Post-Soviet Non-Recognised States (NRS)

In December 1991, the Soviet Union was dissolved *de jure*. The *de facto* dissolution, however, had already started in the Perestroika period, when the Baltic countries, as well as Georgia, Azerbaijan and Moldova announced their sovereignty and decided to not to participate in the referendum of 1991 and the Novo-Ogarevo process that involved the signing of a new Union treaty. After the attempted *coup d'état* in August 1991, the remaining republics within the former USSR saw an opportunity to leave the Union. In December 1991/January 1992, fifteen newly established states in Eastern Europe and Northern Eurasia were in the process of formation and receiving international recognition.

However, not only did the secessionist movements of the Perestroika era feature within Soviet republics' 'nationalities'; they also featured within smaller ethnolingual groups (Soviet *nationalities*) that did not have their own republics at the end of the 1980s but had some level of autonomy and self-governance. Among them are the Nagorno-Karabakh Armenians in Azerbaijan SSR, the

Tatars and Chechens in the Russian SFSR, the Ossetians and Abkhazians in the Georgian SSR, and the Russophone populations of the Moldavian SSR (Transnistria) and the Ukrainian SSR (Crimea). Over time, these movements engaged in their own state- and nation-building attempts. These secessionist movements—unlike those of the Soviet republican nationalities—did not lead to the creation of *recognised* states.

As at the end of December 2018, the post-Soviet states that did not have international recognition included six NRS in different stages of creation (see Table 4).

Table 4. Key Characteristics of Post-Soviet NRS

	Population	Territory (km²)	Period of existence	Internationally recognised territory of parental state	States that recognise the non-recognised state
Abkhazia/Apsny	240,750[24]	8,660	appx. over 25 years	Georgia	*recognised states*: Russia, Venezuela, Nicaragua, Nauru and Syria *non-recognised states*: South Ossetia, Transnistria, Nagorno-Karabakh and 'DPR'
'Donetsk People's Republic' ('DPR')	2,299,120[25]	n/a	appx. over 4 years	Ukraine	No
'Lugansk Peoples Republic' ('LPR')	1,475,841[26]	n/a	appx. over 4 years[27]	Ukraine	No

24 According to: Abkhaz census 2011.
25 See: DNR 2017.
26 See: LNR 2017.
27 DPR and LPR have signed an agreement on federation, which should be kept in mind. Also, in November 2017 there was a coup in LPR supported by DPR, which shows inequality of relations in this 'federation'.

Nagorno-Karabakh/ Artsakh	150,932[28]	11,500	appx. over 25 years	Azerbaijan	no
South Ossetia/Alania	53,532[29]	3,900	appx. over 25 years	Georgia	*recognised states*: Russia, Venezuela, Nicaragua, Nauru and Syria *non-recognised states*: South Ossetia, Transnistria, Nagorno-Karabakh and 'DPR'
Transnistria	475,665[30]	4,163	appx. over 25 years	Moldova	no

---

28 Data from the 2015 census (source: The Demographic Handbook of Armenia 2016).
29 Data from the 2015 census: Tibilov 2016.
30 See: Kratkie Predvaritelnyiie Itogi… 2017.

According to this data, over 4 mln people (4,267,840) live in six post-Soviet NRS, two out of which have partial recognition, and several more are recognised by other NRS.

2.1. The Economic Specifics of Post-Soviet NRS.

Post-Soviet NRS developed in conditions of international sanctions and blockades by patronal states and their allies. In economic terms, international sanctions against NRS created incentives for local populations to encourage their leaders to reintegrate with the parental states. In a number of interviews with diplomats and security staff involved in talks between parental states and NRS in the first half of the 1990s, there was a widely shared expectation from Western parties (and in some cases from Moscow) that economic sanctions — and the hardships they cause populations and power groups — would force the authorities in NRS to seek opportunities to compromise with the parental states' governments (Lynch 2002: 833; Kolstø 2006: 724ff; Broers 2015: 288; d1, d2, d4, m1, m3).

These sanctions were intended to create such economic conditions that would force the breakaway communities and regions to return to their parental states. From my interviews with international diplomats who participated in the conflict settlement in Georgia, Azerbaijan and Moldova, I understand the rationale of the first wave of sanctions to have been based on the idea that economic hardships would inspire the authorities in NRS to be more open to economic integration with their parental states. At least two interviewees concluded that they underestimated the value of group identity and the fresh memory of the mutual violence that prevented the expected scenario from being fulfilled. All of them later recognised that economic sanctions made the everyday lives of people living in NRS much harsher than in other post-Soviet countries, as they enforced warlords' power and ethnonational consolidation. It also contributed to DFS depending more on their sponsors for support: Armenia (in the case of Nagorno-Karabakh) and Russia (in all of the remaining cases) (Kolstø 2006: 725; d1, d2, d3, d4, d5).

The first reaction of the ruling groups and the wider populations to post-conflict sanctions was to create unofficial and informal economic institutions and cross-border ties. Over time, these evolved into an economic model specific to the extreme periphery. The extreme periphery model was formed as a result of the need to survive under a regime of sanctions. The model is typical for most NRS, including Abkhazia, South Ossetia, Nagorno-Karabakh, and for the eastern Donbas territories after 2014. People in all of these territories had to survive when borders between the parental state and other neighbours who supported international sanctions were closed for trade and transportation. The behavioural model of the sponsor state also changed from agreeing with the sanctions at first to subsequently denying them, and resuming economic cooperation with NRS. Due to the fact that the Abkhazian economy is studied best and there is enough data about its economic system for analysis, I will describe it as both (1) a specific case of survival under strict international economic sanctions and (2) a generic model for most NRS' economies that were subjected to such sanctions.

Abkhazia, one of the wealthiest regions of the USSR, after the crisis of Soviet planned economy (1990/91) and by the end of Georgian-Abkhazian conflict (1992-93) was extremely impoverished. As a result of ethnic conflict, ethnic cleansing, and the mass emigration of ethnic Georgians, it had lost approximately half of its population (Dale 1997: 100; Kolossov & O'Loughlin 1998: 153). During the 1992-93 war, at least half of its industrial and tourist complexes were destroyed (Derluguian 1998: 262-3). It was only logical for the international parties involved in the conflict settlement to expect that the risk of the economic isolation would force the leaders of the Abkhazian rebels to agree on reintegration with Georgia.

However, in 1993-94, the Abkhazian authorities and populations acted in a way that the West, Georgia and Russia did not envisage (Gegeshidze 2008: 68-70). Economic life moved into the 'shadow', promoting corruption, organised crime and smuggling networks inside Abkhazia, as well as on the Abkhazian-Georgian front line and the border with Russia (Oltramonti 2015:

292ff). For security reasons, as well as wanting to force the Abkhazian authorities to comply with the peace plan, Georgia (in 1993) and Russia (in 1994) closed their borders to the movement of goods, finance, transport, and—to some extent—people (Zverev 1996: 177). For example, the Russian government prohibited all Abkhazian men between the ages of 16 and 60 years from entering its territory during the period of the first Chechen war (ibid., 178).

The sanctions regime harshened in 1996 when the Commonwealth of Independent States banned transport, financial, telephone, and trade ties with Abkhazia at state level. Gradually, Soviet documents (passports, IDs, etc) expired, resulting in the reduction of opportunities for members of the Abkhazian populations to travel legally across the Russian border and the Georgian front line (Markedonov 2010; Broers 2015; Oltramonti 2015).

In addition to Russian and CIS sanctions, other international prohibitions were imposed on Abkhazia. According to the list provided by Archil Gegeshidze, five further elements contributed to Abkhazia's isolation. (1) UN Security Council resolution 876 (UNSCR 1993) issued "to prevent the provision from their territories or by persons under their jurisdiction of all assistance, other than humanitarian assistance, to the Abkhazian side and, in particular, to prevent the supply of any weapons and munitions." (2) The Georgian government's decision to close the port of Sukhumi and establish a maritime blockade in Abkhazian offshore waters. (3) The Georgian government's decision not to open up Sukhumi airport to international flights, as well as (4) The closure of the Trans-Caucasian railway through Abkhazia. (5) The ban, by Tbilisi, on almost all economic cooperation with Abkhazia (with one exception: the joint operation of the Inguri power station) (Gegeshidze 2008: 68).

According to statements in several interviews and to published research (Markedonov 2010; Oltramonti 2015; m1, m2, j3, a1, a3), economically, Abkhazia was deindustrialising, deurbanising and ruralising fast. Private gardens and small farms—both in the capital, Sukhumi, and in other cities—provided households with necessary food supplies. Connections between rural and urban populations intensified (Oltramonti 2015: 293). For at least a decade, the collection and smuggling of scrap metal became one of the businesses controlled by the Abkhazian authorities; this scrap metal was illegally transported to Russian and Turkish metallurgic plants (Oltramonti 2015: 294; m1, m2). The passionate collection of scrap metal added to deindustrialisation since the scrap metal was often taken from equipment from non-working plants. These processes had the political and ideological consequences of spreading neotraditionalism and ethno-conservatism, that in turn supported warlordism and ethnonationalism in Abkhazia (Derluguian 2007: 169/70).

Illegal trade and smuggling became a central means of delivering goods and services that were officially and internationally banned. Since the shadow economy was growing also in Russia and Georgia, the Abkhazian informal trade networks were finding partner shadow economic structures that were booming in the neighbouring countries (Aslund 2002: 89ff; Oltramonti 2015: 293-95). In three interviews, information was provided by eye witnesses on everyday bribery on the Abkhazian-Georgian dividing line and Abkhazian-Russian border in the 1990s (m2, d1, d3). Accordingly, under the sanctions, the shuttle trade networks with Georgia, Russia and Turkey became the dominant means of trade for Abkhazia. And the change in Russian policy towards sanctions in 1999-2003 did little to change the centrality of this type of trade: up until 2003, smuggling prevailed in cross-border trade with Russia. It remains dominant in trade with Georgia and Turkey (m1, m2, d1, d3; Eissler 2013: 126; Oltramonti 2015: 293/4).

By 1999, the political economy of Abkhazia was structured in such a way that informal economic mechanisms provided the basis for the country's development. Political institutions had to play a double role: formal and informal. Formally, the authorities followed officially sanctioned rules and norms; informally, they controlled and gained from the shadow economy.

Figure 1. The Shadow Economy in Georgia and Russia (1994–2015)

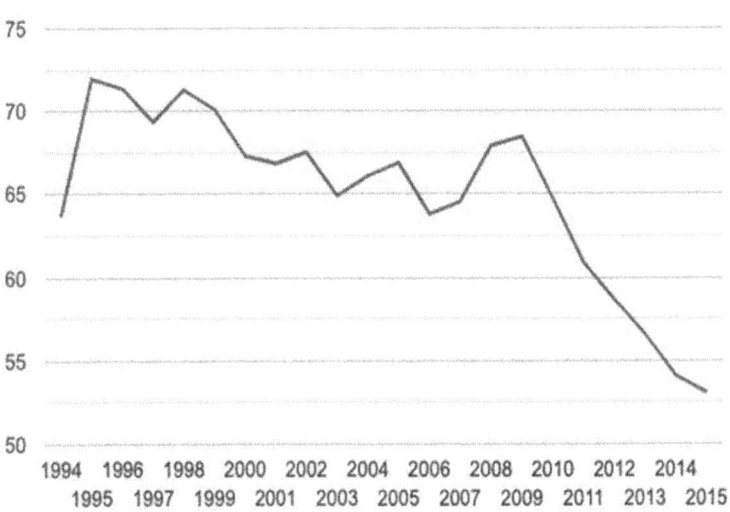

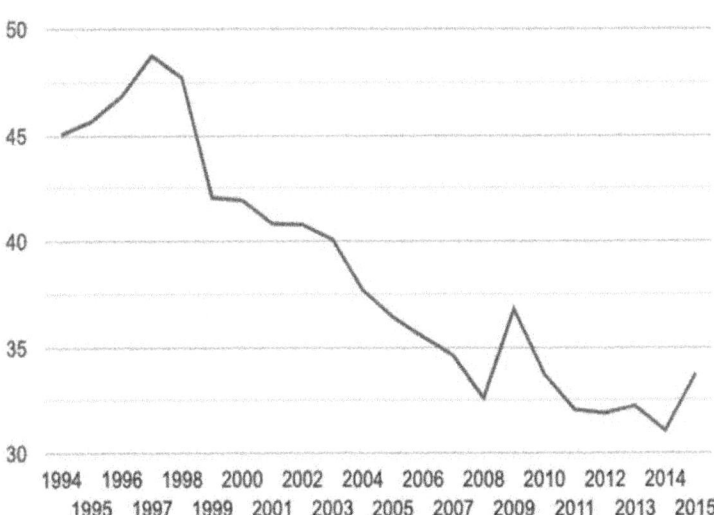

Data source for the tables: https://www.theglobaleconomy.com/rankings/shadow_economy/

There is no specific data for the Abkhazian shadow economy. However, as two security staff interviewees who were in Georgia and Abkhazia in the mid- to late 90s stated, it was "much higher and much more systemic than in Georgia at the time" (i.e. 1994–99) (m2, m3; Kolossov & O'Loughlin 1998: 160). Based on the data in Figure 1, one may reasonably assume that in 1994–2000, the role of the shadow economy in Abkhazia was above 70% (the average level for Georgia in this period).

Between 1999 and 2003, the Russian government changed its policy towards Abkhazia and Georgia. The border with Russia was gradually opened for the movement of people, goods, natural resources and services (Diasamidze 2003, 349/50; Oltramonti 2015: 294/5). The Russian government started letting in members of the male population of Abkhazia; it also recognised documents provided by the Abkhazian authorities. By 2006, Russian and Turkish investments in transport infrastructure, tourism and natural resources delivery had reached sizeable levels (Closson 2007; Sepashvili 2004). In 2005, the tourist business brought in over fifty thousand tourists and earned Abkhazia about 50 mln USD (Lynch 2006: 49; Trier et al. 2010: 110). So, by 2008, when the Russian-Georgian war led to Russia's recognition of Abkhazian sovereignty and independence, Abkhazia already had its economy developed to a level that provided members of the local population to live better and the non-recognised state with some resources to sustain its existence.

However, this level of economic development was not sufficient to enable Abkhazian authorities to fully rely on their own economy and income from taxation. Being in an extreme situation, even by comparison with other post-Soviet peripheral countries, Abkhazia developed its economic, financial and tax institutions in a way that supported its elites and populations in their survival efforts and created a stable socio-economic model in which smuggling was extremely important. Government-controlled smuggling was no longer a crime in the non-recognised state; it became an institutionalised practice that defined the development of the *de facto* state under sanctions. Nonetheless, a stable and profitable shadow economy results in a lack of sufficient resources to support the existence of official institutes of power.

One of the consequences of this kind of economic development is the situation the Abkhazian government consistently finds itself in: it is unable to collect sufficient taxes for the proper functioning of the state. As was shown in the introductory part of this chapter, one of the four defining functions of a state is the collection of resources needed for the government operations. There are trustworthy statistics available for the GDP and the state income of Abkhazia only after 2010. According to this data, even after the 'normalization' of relations between Abkhazia and the Russian Federation, as well as after Russia's recognition of Abkhazia as a sovereign state in 2008, the country's government remains heavily dependent on Russia's financial support.

Table 5. Abkhazia's State Budget and Russia's Financial Support (in mln Rus. Rubles):

	2010	2015	2016	2017
Abkhazian GDP	20,777	28,569.2	30,292.2	30,397.1
State income total	4,676.1	6,343.1	10,071.9	10,200.9
Russia's financial support	approx. 5*	approx. 7*	10,530.2	10,713.0

Source: Information collected from the Apsny State Statistics Service website[31] (for 2016–17) and 'Abkhazia v tsyfrakh 2016' statistical report (for 2010–16).[32]
* deduced from the data provided.

According to this data, the Russian Federation provided approximately half of the Abkhazian state budget in 2010–17. It is quite plausible to assume that this support was not smaller in previous periods (for more information, see: Broers 2015).

---

31 Information from the following official resource, accessed on November 18, 2018, http://ugsra.org/ofitsialnaya-statistika.php?ELEMENT_ID=294] and [http://ugsra.org/ofitsialnaya-statistika.php?ELEMENT_ID=138.
32 See: Abkhazia v tsifrakh 2016.

In addition to direct budgetary support (as indicated in Table 5), there were other important ways in which Russia provided indirect economic support to Abkhazia. The International Crisis Group has long been monitoring this kind of support. For example, between 2010 and 2012, Russia invested about 350 mln USD in infrastructure projects in Abkhazia, and it planned to treble the amount in 2014–15 (Schreiber 2014). However, in 2018, the International Crisis Group issued a report in which it stated that — due to international sanctions on Russia (imposed since 2014) — the Russian government decreased its level of financial support to Abkhazia (and other NRS) (International Crisis Group 2018a, 2018b). While Russia's direct support continued, its indirect support of the Abkhazian economy was substantially cut. As the authors of the above report show, to cover the shortfall, Abkhazian economic players increased illegal trade with Georgia. This data proves that the extreme periphery model outlined here does not necessarily collapse if a sponsor state fails to deliver the necessary support to the authorities in NRS.

Thus, the economic model that Abkhazia developed between the post-conflict period and today, in spite of the changing roles of parental and sponsor states, is characterised by (1) the long-term prevalence of a shadow economy over the official one, (2) institutionalised informal trade ties that make sanctions ineffective, and (3) the dependency of state institutes and organisations on foreign sponsorship. The post-Soviet Abkhazian transition to a market economy took place in conditions of limited access to credits, and the insignificant reconstruction of its industrial potential; it was based on distorted economic practices that were even worse than those found in its parental state of Georgia.

As I stated above, the Abkhazian model is applicable to the cases of Nagorno-Karabakh (blockaded by Azerbaijan and Turkey, sanctioned internationally, sponsored by Armenia), South Ossetia (blockaded by Georgia, sanctioned internationally, sponsored by Russia), as well as 'DPR' and 'LPR' (blockaded by Ukraine, sanctioned internationally, sponsored by Russia).[33] Thus, the same

---

[33] These similarities are well described in: Gerrits & Bader 2016: 297–301.

three peculiarities fully apply to the first two cases, and are developing in the latter two (see: Mirimanova 2019: 2/3; von Twickel 2019: 25ff). Taking into account the size of 'DPR' and 'LPR' populations and industry, the level of Russia's support to them has reached 5.6 bln Euros per year (von Twickel 2019: 27) whilst the budget of the 'DPR' was 68 bln Roubles and that of the 'LPR' was 42 bln roubles in 2017 (ibid., 27/8).

In the case of **Transnistria**, one can see a different pattern of post-conflict development but with pretty much the same result in terms of economic model. Unlike the cases of Abkhazia, 'LPR' or 'DPR', the conflict in Transnistria was much less damaging, and much more internationalised. The clashes between Moldovan and separatist militias in 1990 and in 1992 led to Russia's decision to enter the conflict zone. The 14th Soviet (later, Russian) army entered the territory and stopped the bloodshed (Emerson & Vahl 2004: 170ff). During the period of talks in the first half of 1992, Russia denied OSCE-led peacekeeping forces the opportunity to enter the area. Thus, in July 1992, president Snegur had to sign a treaty relating to a Russian peacekeeping mission co-signed by President Yeltsin (Portela & Orbie 2014). Since then, the Republic of Moldova and the Transnistrian authorities have existed under conditions of frozen conflict with the strong presence of Russian, EU and US missions.

The Transnistrian economy developed without strict sanctions being imposed. The settlement and reconciliation process in 1993–2003 saved the Transnistrian population from the experience of the Abkhazian people. Where sanctions were imposed, these were mainly personal, not collective; issued against individual rulers, not against the population as a whole. For example, in 2003, the US and the EU attempted to encourage progress in a political settlement of the Transnistrian conflict, so restrictive measures were imposed on 17 leaders of the breakaway region. However, these sanctions "proved to be rather weak in achieving their goals" (Lehmkuhl & Shagina 2015: 66).

The Transnistrian economy developed without being cut off from Moldova, Ukraine and Russia. However, Transnistria's hardships were similar to those of the Moldovan and Ukrainian regions nearby. As Deon Geldenhuys points out, this region was economically very open for integration: about half of its exports (consisting of metal and mineral products, equipment, textiles and food) went to CIS countries, and another half to the Western markets (Geldenhuys 2009: 94ff).

Figure 2. Shadow Economies in Moldova, Russia, and Ukraine (1991/4–2015)

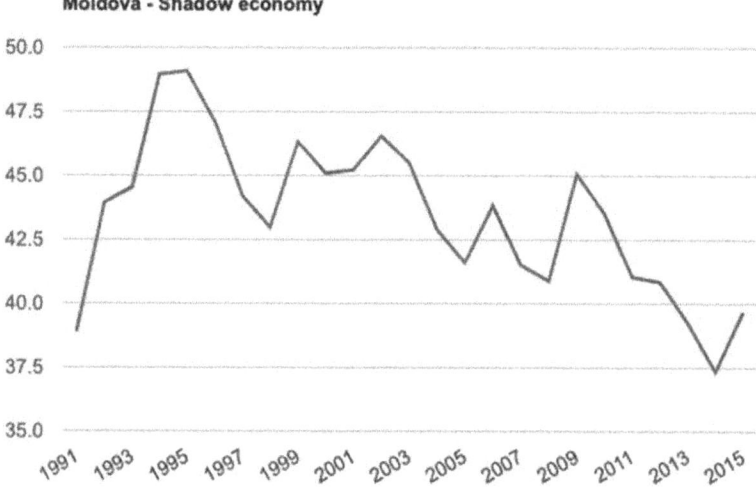

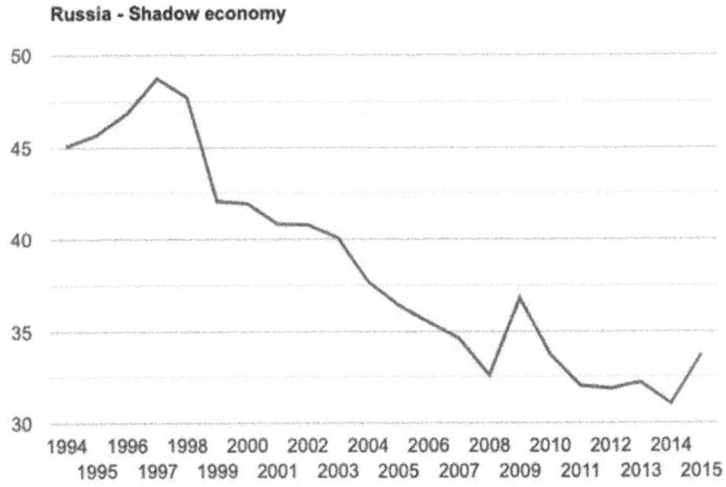

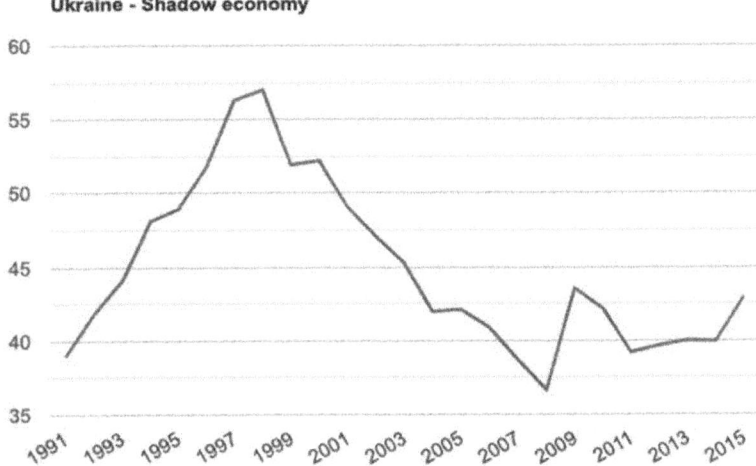

Data source for the tables: https://www.theglobaleconomy.com/rankings/shadow_economy/

In spite of much smaller sanctions, the Transnistrian economy developed in such a way as to be able to adjust to the vulnerabilities of the recognised states around it in 1993-2003. Smuggling, as a structural part of Transnistrian economy, had beneficiaries not only in this non-recognised state, but also in Moldova, Russia, and

Ukraine (Geldenhuys 2009: 99ff). According to the data in Figure 2, it is logical to assume, the Transnistrian shadow economy was well above average in Moldova and Ukraine. The vicinity of the port of Odessa and the fragile state of law and order in Moldova and Ukraine created a special smuggling industry in Transnistria by the early 1990-ies. This gave the Moldovan and Ukrainian governments a reason to act against such an economy in their neighbourhood.

In 2005, after the political change in Kiev, Ukraine and Moldova launched a programme of cross-border cooperation. With the Joint Declaration of 3 March 2006, all exports from Moldova to or via Ukraine needed to have Moldovan documentation (Chiveri 2016: 6). Furthermore, in 2005–2006, the EU, in cooperation with the Ukrainian and Moldovan governments, had to start a special border mission programme (EUBAM) to limit the damage that the smuggling was doing to EU economies.

It is interesting that Transnistrian authorities were eager to continue self-isolation. Attempts by Moldova, Ukraine and the EU to properly document trade in 2005, or to open up the Moldovan economy, including Transnistria (as in the AA/DCFTA of 2015 between the EU and Georgia, Moldova, and Ukraine respectively) provoked leaders of Transnistria to try to close the borders they shared with their parental state and to describe these acts at "military actions" (Chiveri 2016: 5, 13).

For over two decades, the Transnistrian economy has been based on funds created by the sale of Russian gas, cash remittances from migrants working abroad, and financial support from Moscow (Całus 2013: 1–3) which hindered the economy from becoming self-sufficient. At the same time, Moscow promoted the division of Transnistria from Moscow and Transnistria's closer economic integration with Moldova (ibid., 3, 7).

Yet state capacity-building depends largely on economic reconstruction. This aspect of state- and economy-building concerns not only social security for the population but also the government's budgetary income, including tax collection. In an effort to make their economy work, NRS create their own economic institutions and fiscal policies, independent from central states (Dembinska & Campana 2017: 4). Tiraspol established the

Transnistrian Republican Bank and issued its own currency in 1994 (Isachenko & Schlichte 2007: 20/1).

The official economy of Transnistria was import-oriented. In 2012, the value of products exported from Transnistrian companies was almost 700 mln USD, equivalent to approximately 70% of the Transnistrian economy. However, its foreign trade structure has obviously lacked diversity. 75% of all export revenues were generated by metallurgical and textile industries, as well as companies producing electricity. Exports were to mainland Moldova (250 mln USD), Russia (154.7 mln USD), Romania (103.1 mln USD) with some small amounts to Ukraine and Italy (Całus, 2013: 3).

Taking into account the data from Figure 2, it is logical to assume that Transnistria's shadow economy was the same as—or higher than—that of Ukraine and Moldova, which means it is unlikely that it dipped below 40%. Even though a shadow economy provides populations with the means of survival and provides considerable privileges to the elites, it hits NRS' governments and political institutions. In the case of Transnistria, the government was—and still is—unable to raise enough funds to fulfil its state monopolistic functions. So even in the Transnistrian case, where the economy was developing better than in Abkhazia, the government continued to depend on foreign sponsorship. For example, according to the Transnistrian law on the state budget in 2018, the government budget was approved with an income of 1,640,363,327 roubles and expenses of 3,238,556,806 roubles (Zakon PMR 2018). So the budget was approved with a deficit of 1,538,255,756[34] roubles (approx. 47% of the budget). The same level of dependency existed in 2013 (Całus 2013: 4). Contrary to the case of Abkhazia, there is no official data about the source of income to cover the state deficit, but it is an established fact that it was covered by the Russian government (Całus 2013: 5; j8, a7, a8, m6, m7). According to Kamil Całus, Russia supported the Transnistrian budget with approx. 27 mln USD annually between 2006 and 2012 (Całus 2013: 4). Also

---

34 This is the figure in the document, although mathematically the difference is 1,598,193,479 roubles.

there were additional subsidies that could have reached amounts ranging from 10–30 mln USD annually (ibid., 4/5).

Thus, in spite of rather different economic development conditions than those in Abkhazia, the Transnistrian economy also showed (1) the prevalence of a shadow economy, (2) institutionalised informal trade ties that make the sanctions regime ineffective, and (3) the dependency of its government on foreign sponsorship.

There is also a growing body of evidence that the extreme position of the NRS' economies are used by international criminal networks for production and transportation of drugs and weapons (Popescu 2005; Lynch 2002: 834ff; m6, m7, d7, d9). These sources confirm that NRS' leaders benefit from a criminal economy, which makes the possibility of them ruling in the interests of local constituencies highly questionable.

So my conclusion here is that NRS have entered a niche in the world-system where they survive under core-imposed sanctions by undermining the cooperation between the core and the states commonly seen as peripheral. A shadow economy, smuggling, participation in criminal economies, and a dependency on semicore (Russian) or peripheral (Armenian) foreign governments all allow the populations of NRS in general to survive economically, but to survive is not to thrive. These are exactly the *extreme measures* that the de facto authorities use for survival of their jurisdictions.

These societies, being in a constant situation of extreme survival from an economic point of view, are in the weakest position in terms of global economic competition. So, the Wallersteinian concept of unequal exchange here has its extreme example. The surplus-value from this type of exchange that NRS' populations are involved in goes either to shadow economic players in the sponsor and parental states, or to local warlords/elites (Broers 2015: 288). And this also has a strong impact on how the political systems and cultures of the NRS examined here have developed in their three decades of existence. The political systems specific to the extreme periphery will be analysed in the following section.

2.2. Political Systems of Post-Soviet NRS.

Post-Soviet NRS have been adapting not only their economies, but also their public and private institutions of power. Political systems in NRS developed in a way that, on one hand, tried to fulfil as many state functions as possible, and, on the other hand, to adapt to the need to be simultaneously responsive to the variety of needs of their own citizens, to the need to defend themselves from their parental states and the sanctioning global core, to preserve a complex connection with their sponsor states, and to develop as many international relations as they could, whilst functioning as unrecognised or partially recognised states. Accordingly, they developed institutions and organisations that met these conditions and needs.

In connection with the complex and contradictory conditions of their existence, post-Soviet NRS have invited discussion around the direction of their development. Pål Kolstø has argued logically that the future of NRS is fourfold. NRS would either (a) merge with the sponsor state, (b) become fully independent, or (c1) would return to the parental state in the status of a usual administrative unit or (c2) as a unit with special rights. He is among a group of scholars who see NRS as transitional, abnormal phases of state-building (Kolstø 2006: 734ff).

However, the longer NRS exist, and the more they proliferate in the post-Soviet region, the less evident their transitional nature becomes. At least from a mid- to long-term perspective, these states seem to be evolving into more stable model. This stable nature of the NRS' political systems is supported by studies by Daria Isachenko, Magdalena Dembinska and Aurelie Campana (Isachenko 2012: 3ff; Dembinska & Campana 2017: 2ff). For example, the latter correctly state that "we cannot but recognize that some de facto states have succeeded in building a form of authority sustained by a new political order and an infrastructural capacity over a contested territory. In essence, rather than viewing de facto states as atypical, deviant, temporarily limited black holes, we view them as dynamic political entities" (Dembinska & Campana 2017: 2ff). Furthermore, my own research shows that the dynamics of these polities implies dissemination of the institutional model of 'informal state' to other areas of conflicts in the post-Soviet and other areas (Minakov 2017b). E.g. the case of the creation of NRS in the Eastern Donbas that borrowed a lot from the experiences of Abkhazia and Transnistria. These have existed for over two years, survived several changes of rulers, developed some sort of local identity and evolved from irredentist situations into NRS. All of this adds to the argument that the post-Soviet NRS are a special case of the global periphery: the extreme periphery, rather than temporary political setups related to contested territories.

Concerning their responsiveness to their populations, the institutes of power in NRS show a certain level of responsibility regarding the basic needs of their citizens. Usually, as a result of conflict or some forms of nationalist mobilisation (whether ethnic, as in the case of Nagorno-Karabakh or Abkhazia, or civic, as in the case of Transnistria), NRS offer defence against the alleged 'aggression' of the parental states. Thus, the defence of their contested territory, which is one of a state's fundamental functions — even if it is unrecognised — coincides with the interest of the remaining populations in terms of their personal and collective security. To a large extent, post-Soviet NRS can fulfil this function with the use of military and diplomatic support from their sponsor states (Hale 2005: 56ff; Gammer 2014: 40). Thus, economic interests are not the only things that contribute to NRS' dependency on their sponsor states.

Another area where the local populations have their interests respected by NRS' authorities is local self-governance. According to data published by Freedom House, which has been monitoring political and civic liberties in Nagorno-Karabakh, South Ossetia, Abkhazia and Transnistria for over fifteen years, local administration and self-governance are areas where NRS exercise democratic control (Freedom House 2019). To some extent, elections function as a legal means for the elites' rotation in NRS' parliaments.[35] The same reports show that the legislatures had a say

---

35 However, the NRS parliaments have very little independence from the executive. At the same time, presidential elections in NRS are usually (with rare

during the changeover of presidents in Abkhazia and Transnistria. However, this role only develops in a state of emergency (Kolstø and Blakkisrud 2012: 142; Popescu 2006; Clogg 2008; Bakke et al. 2014; Dembinska & Campana 2017: 14).

Altogether, the data in Figure 3 shows that, in spite of all of their drawbacks, the freedom ratings of NRS can actually be better than those of their parent states (as in the case of Nagorno-Karabakh and Azerbaijan) or sponsor states (as in the cases of Abkhazia and Transnistria and Russia).

Figure 3. Freedom in the World Index (Armenia, Azerbaijan and Nagorno-Karbakh; Georgia, Russia, South Ossetia and Abkhazia; Moldova, Russia and Transnistria)

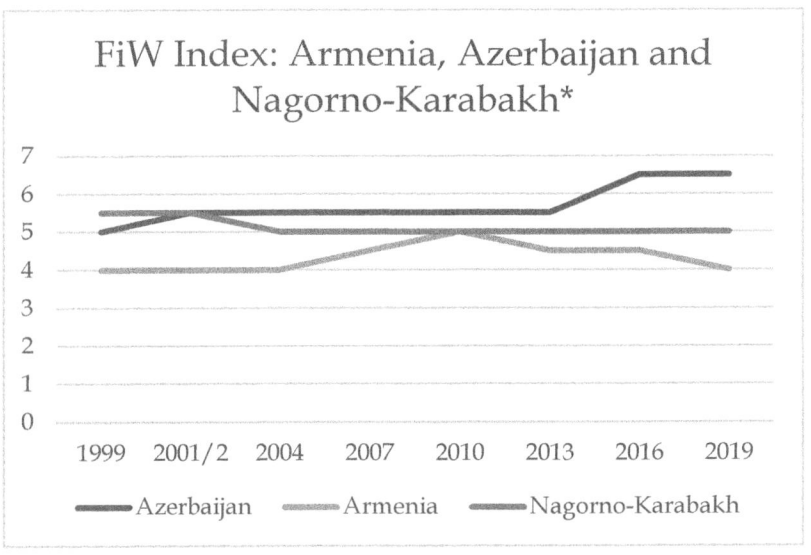

---

exclusions) manipulated and their results predetermined by sponsor state and local security structures that are inseparable from the security services and political elites of the sponsor state (Freedom House 2019; Isachenko 2012; Isachenko 2019).

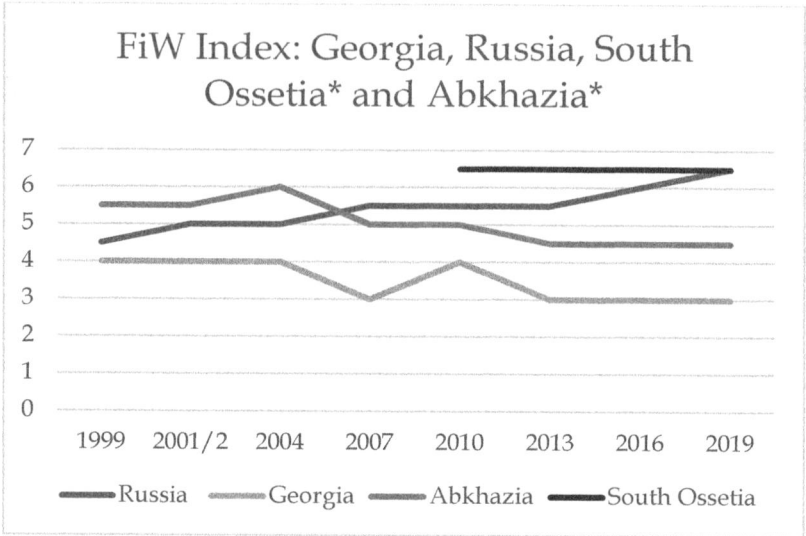

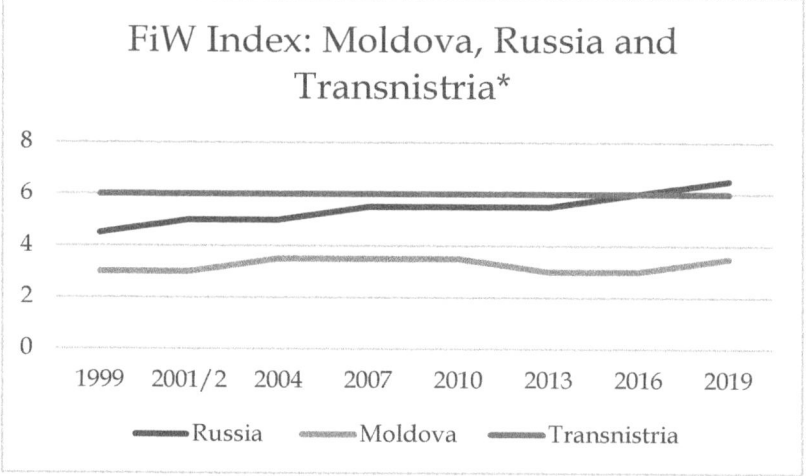

Source for all three tables: Freedom in The World Reports, 1998/9–2019. The higher the grade on the Y axes, the less free the country.
* marks the NRS with the disputed territories.

The six post-Soviet NRS of Abkhazia, Artsakh, South Ossetia, Moldova, Donetsk, and Lugansk are formally constituted as presidential-parliamentary republics.[36] The presidents of the NRS

---

36 See the following NRS constitutions: Konstitutsia Respubliki Abkhazia 1999;

oversee executives headed by a prime minister, a local army and security agencies. Informally, the president and their administration are power institutions that in usual, non-urgent situations are autonomous from any type of formal domestic parliamentary control. At the same time, they need to balance informal control by the sponsor state with local informal control by power groups and clans. The presidents control all types of military units on their territories (except for the sponsor state's troops, where applicable). They control the central budget and financial flows from the sponsor state, as well as the most profitable sectors of their formal and shadow economies. The analysis of the biographies of the presidents of the NRS featured in this study shows that—at least since 2000—they have all been connected either to sponsor states' security services or armies. Even though formally all NRS' presidents were elected to their positions, the elections were neither free, nor fair (Freedom House 2019; d6, d7, d9, m5, m6, m7, a7, a8).

So far, the relations described above between the key elements of the NRS' political systems look pretty much the same as in some post-Soviet periphery states. Indeed, in the NRS' political systems, there is no functional executive oversight of parliament, which pretty much resembles Russian or Azerbaijani political models. However, NRS' political systems differ in the establishment of a special informal institute of *kuratory* (caretakers), who represent sponsor states in NRS.

The *kuratory* are "officials tasked with making things work often bypassing, and sometimes competing with, formal institutions" who negotiate Russia's control over post-Soviet NRS (Isachenko 2019: 2). Between the mid-1990s, when the first *kuratory* appear in Russian foreign politics for Transnistria, and 2012, when they were an established form of cooperation with—and oversight by—sponsor states, these officials combined the status of

---

Constitution of the Republic of Artsakh 2006; Konstitutsia Respubliki Yuzhnaya Osetia 2016; Konstitutsia Pridnestrovskoi Moldavskoi Respubliki 2016; Konstitutsia Donetskoi Narodnoi Respubliki 2018; Konstitutsia Luganskoi Narodnoi Respubliki 2018.

Presidential Administration employees and, most often, affiliation with one of the security services, e.g. FSB or GRU (d6, d7, d9, m5, m6, m7, j 4, j5, a4, a7, a8; Isachenko 2019: 4ff). Among the most visible *kuratory* are Vladislav Surkov, Ramzan Kadyrov or Dmitriy Kozak (Pavlovsky 2016: 12/13; Wolff 2011: 866/7).

Usually, *kuratory* are multitasked officials who work within several 'republics'. For example, Surkov was concurrently 'taking care' of Abkhazia, 'DPR' and 'LPR' in 2014-18. In Abkhazia, he dealt with security, political and economic issues; in Donbas, with political and security issues only. Economic and social issues were taken care of by Kozak (Isachenko 2019: 5ff; Pavlovsky 2016: 3ff; Gerrits & Bader, 2016: 300–302; d6, d7, m5, m4).

According to available sources, to make sure that they could effectively oversee sponsored NRS, the *kuratory* were given exclusive control over 'directorates' which are formally parts of 'presidential' administrations in Abkhazia or Donetsk. However, these 'directorates' are autonomous from the formal heads of NRS: their staff are responsible for day-to-day communication with their Moscow-based bosses, monitoring the use of provided resources, the political situation in NRS, as well commenting on events in social and economic spheres.

It is important to point out that Nagorno-Karabakh is a special case in the relations between a sponsor state and NRS. Even though *kuratory* exist here, the sponsor state also has a strong long-term dependency on its client state. During 1990s, influential groups of Karabakhian and Armenian 'field commanders' evolved into the so-called 'Karabakh clan' that established non-formal control over most of the Armenian centres of power (Geldenhuys 2009: 101). This reciprocity of relations between sponsor and client states does not seem to exist in case of Russia (as sponsor state) and Abkhazia or Transnistria (as client states).

As 'importers' of political and security systems, NRS have another important non- or semi-formal power institution which brings together senior security and military staff members of the sponsor state and those of the non-recognised state (Blakkisrud & Kolstø 2011: 185; Gerrits & Bader, 2016: 305; Dembinska & Campana 2017: 4; ICG 2010; d1, d2, d4, d5, d8, d9, m1, m2, m5, m6, j1, j3, j4, j8, a1, a3, a4, a7, a8). During the 'hot phases' of the conflict periods of the early 1990s (in Nagorno-Karabakh, South Ossetia, Abkhazia and Transnistria), 2008 (in South Ossetia and Abkhazia) and 2014–15 (in Donbas) the stable model of a military command centre evolved. The centre usually includes local senior militia and security service officers and senior officers from the sponsor state. For example, in the case of 'DNR', the centre currently includes members of Russia's Armed Forces, and FSB and GRU officers who were officially 'on vacation' or 'in retirement' (*otpuskniki* and *otstavniki*—at different times, their number varied from 700 to 1,400) and local senior officers. This super-structure controlled the 'people's militia' facing Ukrainian Armed Forces on the front line, the Ministry of State Security (*MGB*) and security groups that function as police (Jarabik & Minakov 2016a, 2016b; Kudelia 2017: 214ff; Mirimanova 2019: 4; d9, m6, m7, j6, j8, a7, a8).

The Donbas 'republics' were modelled according to lessons learned from previous non-recognised-state-building processes, which allowed me to compose the following diagram which shows the major 'DPR' power institutes and the relations between them as at the end of July 2018. The diagram is based on the use of information from open sources and interviews with experts and insiders.[37]

---

[37] Open sources include reports in Ukrainian and Russian mass media, information from the websites of separatist authorities and published reports from the OSCE and EU (e.g. von Twickel 2019; Miriminaova 2019, etc), The State of the Donbass. A study of eastern Ukraine's separatist-held areas. Brussels: CEPS; less open sources included those who still live in Donetsk or visit the city often, and Ukrainian and international experts with proven knowledge of the situation in 'DPR' (d9, m6, m7, j6, j8, a7, a8).

Figure 4. Power structures in the 'Donetsk People's Republic', as at the end of July 2018

In this diagram, I demonstrate that the combination of *kuratory*, *head of state*, local 'cabinet,' 'parliament,' and security agencies have a certain vertical logic of power which involves cooperation between local and sponsor state agencies. While this diagram describes the situation in the 'DPR,' in general terms, it resembles the situation in Abkhazia, 'LPR,' South Ossetia, and Transnistria. In a way, this model summarises the post-Soviet non-recognised state-building experience.

The post-Soviet NRS are in regular communication with each other. Deon Geldenhuys analysed this communication in terms of the official meetings and stable cooperation between NRS' presidents, cabinets and ministries of foreign affairs (Geldenhuys 2009: 76ff). These states have permanent diplomatic relations, defence treaties and cooperation agreements; they recognised each others' independence by 2006 (ibid., 77). In 2007, these kinds of activities led to signing a 'Declaration on Principles of Peaceful and Fair Settlement of Conflicts on the Territory of Moldova, Georgia, Armenia and Azerbaijan'. This declaration showed that the 'extreme periphery' polities fully understand the sameness of their position in the world-system and strive to reach the status of the usual periphery (Deklaratsia 2007).

After the Russian-Georgian war of 2008, South Ossetia and Abkhazia attained the status of 'partially recognised states,' which showed that Pål Kolstø's option (b) is a desired aim for these entities. However, the partial recognition did not change much in real terms for either Abkhazia or South Ossetia. After the first wave of recognition (by Russia and Nicaragua in 2008, Venezuela and Nauru in 2009, and Syria in 2018), some states (like Vanuatu and Tuvalu) rescinded their recognition in 2013–14.

With the Russian-backed secessionist revolt in Donbas and the establishment of the 'DPR' and 'LPR', these new NRS were unofficially supported by the old NRS. There is a growing network of cooperation between separate ministries, industries and social organisations across the NRS, but mutual recognition between old and new NRS is not in place. For example, while the 'DPR' has recognised Abkhazia's sovereignty, Abkhazia does not recognise the 'DPR'. So, in spite of high levels of cooperation, post-Soviet NRS have their own logic of non-recognition.

Thus, in this section, on the one hand, I have provided arguments that support the view that post-Soviet NRS are peripheral polities based on their economic and political models. The descriptions of the NRS are summarised in Table 6.

Table 6. The Post-Soviet NRS' Economies and Political Systems, and their Roles in Core-Periphery Relations

	Economy	*Politics*	*C-P role*
Abkhazia/Apsny	• depends on Russia, • non-self-sufficient economy	• depends on Russia, • growing local volatility, • stablished state structure	• included in the world system as a non-competing economy and a competing political unit through Russia as semicore opposing core • extreme periphery with no clear perspectives of recognition or integration into Russia
'DPR'	• depends on Russia,	• depends on Russia,	• included in the world system as a non-competing economy and a

	• non-self-sufficient economy	• emerging state structures	competing political unit through Russia as semicore opposing core • blockaded by Ukraine • extreme periphery with no perspective of recognition or integration into Russia; some possibility of reintegration with Ukraine remains
'LPR'	• depends on Russia, • non-self-sufficient economy	• depends on Russia, • emerging state structures	• included in the world system as a non-competing economy and a competing political unit through Russia as semicore opposing core • blockaded by Ukraine • extreme periphery with no perspectives of recognition or integration into Russia; some possibility of reintegration with Ukraine remains
Nagorno-Karabakh/ Artsakh	• depends on Armenia, • weak, non-self-sufficient economy	• depends on Armenia, • history of long, strong political impact on Armenia, • established state institutions	• included in the world system as a non-competing economy and a competing political unit through Armenia as periphery obedient to EU/West and Russia • blockaded by Azerbaijan and Turkey • extreme periphery with no perspective of integration with Armenia, or of recognition
South Ossetia/ Alania	• depends on Russia, • non-self-sufficient economy	• depends on Russia, • established state structures	• included in the world system as a non-competing economy and a competing political unit through Russia as semicore opposing core • extreme periphery with no perspective of integration to Russia or Georgia, or of recognition
Transnistria	• depends on trade with Moldova and Ukraine and financial support from Russia, • non-self-sufficient economy	• depends on Russia, with sporadic local volatility, • strong state structures	• included in the world system as a non-competing economy and a competing political unit through Russia as semicore, opposing core • extreme periphery with no perspective of integration to Moldova or Russia, or of recognition

3. Findings and Conclusions

Above, I have provided arguments that demonstrate that the six post-Soviet NRS constitute a special type of state-like organisation that inhabits a certain niche in the world system. These NRS developed economically and politically under extreme conditions of limitations imposed on them by their parental states and by core states. Thus, these NRS evolved into extreme peripheral polities. Their formal economic and political institutions are weak. Their informal structures are much stronger than their formal institutions — or the same institutions in their parental states — and they are dependent on their constituencies, whilst being under the strong control of a sponsor state.

All of the post-Soviet NRS were established due to conflicts which led to the fragmentation of metropolitan states. In these conflicts, local populations and foreign states cooperated to help local authorities establish borders, military institutions, government structures and economic sectors. Parental states cooperated with the Western states (the core) to reverse fragmentation and re-establish control over the seceded communities. This cooperation established a number of specific relations between all of the elements of the contemporary world system: core, semicore/semiperiphery, periphery and extreme periphery. These relations are described in Figure 5.

Figure 5. Relations of Core, Semicore, Periphery and Extreme Periphery States in the Context of Post-Soviet NRS

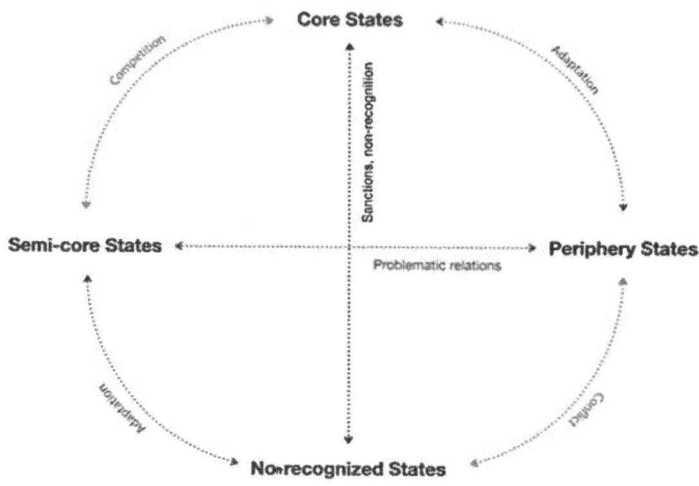

Accordingly, the NRS are under multilateral pressure. First, as violators of international law imposed and enforced by the core states, these *de facto* states are under sanctions and are not recognised as normal elements of the world-system. The core states are interested in the punishment of violators to prevent other antisystemic groups or regions with strong separatist movements from secession. Core states support paternal periphery states in their attempts of reintegration, however, with respect to international law (as in the Russian-Georgian war of 2008). Some core states compete with the semicore states and may impose sanctions not only on the NRS but on their sponsors as well (as, e.g., in the case of 'DPR' and 'LPR').

Secondly, all post-Soviet NRS exist under sanctions imposed by their parental states. The latter attempt to return seceded territories and communities, but usually lack the resources to do so by military force. The fact of secession puts the parental periphery states into a position of weakened polities unable to control all of the territory that is internationally recognised as theirs. The fact of secession provides radical parties in parental states with additional legitimacy which limits the opportunities of these states to explore more inclusive, West-like development, as well as their ability to join NATO or the EU.

Thirdly, the core and semicore states are in permanent competition for positions of influence in the post-Soviet peripheries. Sponsor semicore states like Russia gain leverage against pro-core parental states (Georgia, Moldova, Ukraine) in their plans to join NATO or EU. This competition makes the sponsor states invest a lot of resources into support of NRS and thus invest less in their own development, which, in turn, makes the semicore states less competitive with the core.

Fourthly, peripheral states adapt to the norms and practices offered by core states. In return, they expect their territorial integrity to be respected and expect support to be provided, in cases when some territories/communities try to secede. At the same time, relations between periphery states and the semicore state that functions as a sponsor state for seceded territories vary from military conflict, proxy war, and isolation from each other, to limited cooperation on some sectoral issues.

Finally, relations between a semicore state (functioning as a sponsor state) and NRS start with a process of two-way adaptation involving both parties, leading to the creation of formal and informal institutions that reconcile the different interests of the parties. The sponsor state provides security and financial support in return for loyalty and responsiveness to its national interests. The NRS import security and get support in different forms from their sponsor state. This cooperation, in at least two cases (Abkhazia and South Ossetia), has led to a partial recognition of NRS by their sponsor state. The sponsorship also means the provision of support to NRS populations in terms of travel and cultural ties.

The extreme periphery is thus a class of states that is transgressive in nature. States of this kind try to become legitimate part of the world-system and reach out for international recognition. However, as contradictory as it is, in order to survive they need to use 'shadow' economic and political strategies, and thus get the stigma of international outcasts. In this paper, I have looked at the extreme periphery from the perspective of NRS;

however, this class of state may involve other states, i.e. *as-if* states, *black spots* or failed states. None of these fulfil all state functionalities and thus need extreme measures for survival and development. However, the survival and development strategies contradict each other and keep the extreme periphery states in a transgressive position towards the world-system.

The above arguments provide us not only with a deeper understanding of the conditions in which the NRS exist, but also with evidence supporting the view that the threefold scheme of the core-, semicore/semiperiphery, periphery world system model needs updating. A fourth class should be added to the model: the extreme periphery class.

Bibliography

Abkhaz census. (2011). *The Abkhaz census in 2011*, 12 November 2011, http://www.apsnypress.info/news/chislennost-naseleniya-abkhazii-sostavlyaet-240-705-chelovek/?sphrase_id=7619 (accessed 1 October 2019).

Abkhazia v tsifrakh. (2016). *Abkhazia v tsifrakh 2016 goda. Upravlenie gosudarstvennoi statistiki Respubliki Abkhazia*. Sukhum: Lagvilava.

Agh, A. (2016). The increasing core–periphery divide and new member states: Diverging from the European Union's mainstream developments. In *Core-periphery Relations in the European Union*. London: Routledge, 145–157

Amin, S. (1976). *Unequal Exchange*. Brighton: Harvester.

Arrighi, G. (1999). *Chaos and governance in the modern world system*. Minneapolis: University of Minnesota Press.

Arrighi, G., Hopkins, T.K., Wallerstein, I. (2012). *Antisystemic movements*. New York: Verso.

Aslund, A. (2002). *Building capitalism: the transformation of the former Soviet bloc*. Cambridge, UK: Cambridge University Press.

Baer, H. A., Singer, M., & Susser, I. (2013). *Medical Anthropology and the World System: Critical Perspectives: Critical Perspectives*. Stuttgart: Praeger.

Bakke, K. M., O'Loughlin, J., Toal, G., & Ward, M. D. (2014). Convincing state-builders? Disaggregating internal legitimacy in Abkhazia. *International Studies Quarterly* 58(3): 591–607.

Balmaceda, M. (2013). Privatization and elite defection in de facto states: The case of Transnistria, 1991–2012. *Communist and Post-Communist Studies* 46: 445–454.

Bianchini, S., Minakov, M. (2018). State-Building Politics after the Yugoslav and Soviet Collapse –The Western Balkans and Ukraine in a Comparative Perspective. *Southeastern Europe* 42(3): 291–304.

Blakkisrud, H., & Kolstø, P. (2012). Yielding to the Sons of the Soil: Abkhazian Democracy and the Marginalization of the Armenian Vote. *Ethnic and Racial Studies* 17: 1–21.

Brenne, P. K. (2008). *External Contribution to De Facto State Building. Transnistria and the Outside World*. Oslo: Universitetet i Oslo, Masteroppgave ved Institut for Statsvitenkap.

Broers, L. (2013). Recognising politics in unrecognised states: 20 years of enquiry into the de facto states of the South Caucasus. *Caucasus Survey* 1(1): 59–74.

Broers, L. (2015). Resourcing de facto jurisdictions: A theoretical perspective on cases in the South Caucasus. *Caucasus Survey* 3(3): 269–290.

Całus, K. (2013). An aided economy. The characteristics of the Transnistrian economic model. *OSW Commentary* 108: 1–7.

Chiveri, V. (2016). Activity of the business community in the Transnistrian region in the conditions of the unsettled conflict, *Institute for European Policies and Reforms Policy Papers*, http://ipre.md/2016/06/23/study-activity-of-the-business-community-in-the-transnistrian-region-in-the-conditions-of-the-unsettled-conflict/?lang=en (accessed 1 October 2019).

Ciobanu, C. (2004). *NATO/EU Enlargement: Moldova and the "Frozen and Forgotten" Conflicts In Post-Soviet States*. Washington DC: United States Institute of Peace.

Clogg, R. (2008). The politics of identity in post-Soviet Abkhazia: managing diversity and unresolved conflict. *Nationalities Papers* 36(2): 305–329.

Closson, S. R. (2007). *State weakness in perspective: Trans-territorial energy networks in Georgia, 1993-2003* (Doctoral dissertation, London School of Economics and Political Science, United Kingdom).

Cojocaru, N. (2006). Nationalism and Identity in Transnistria. *Innovation* 19(3/4): 261–272.

Comai, G. (2017). The External Relations of the de facto States in the South Caucasus. *Caucasus Analytical Digest* 94: 8–14.

Constitution of the Republic of Artsakh. (2006). *Constitution of the Republic of Artsakh, 2006*, http://www.nkr.am/en/constitution-of-Artsakh (accessed 1 October 2019).

Coppieters, B. (2018). 'Statehood', 'de facto Authorities' and 'Occupation': Contested Concepts and the EU's Engagement in its European Neighbourhood. *Ethnopolitics* 17(4): 343–361.

Coppieters, B. (2018). Four Positions on the Recognition of States in and after the Soviet Union, with Special Reference to Abkhazia. *Europe-Asia Studies* 70(6): 991–1014.

Coppieters, B. et al. (eds.) (2011). *Europeanization and Conflict Resolution–Case Studies from the European Periphery*. Ghent: Academia Press.

Cornell, S.E. (2002). Autonomy as a source of conflict: Caucasian conflicts in theoretical perspective. *World politics* 54(2): 245–76.

Daase, C., Geis, A., Fehl, C., & Kolliarakis, G. (Eds.). (2015). *Recognition in international relations: Rethinking a political concept in a global context*. Frankfurt/M: Springer.

Dale, C. (1997). The dynamics and challenges of ethnic cleansing: The Georgia–Abkhazia case. *Refugee Survey Quarterly* 16(3): 77–109.

De Waal, T. (2013). *Black Garden: Armenia and Azerbaijan Through Peace and War*. New York: NYU press.

De Waal, T. (2018). *The Caucasus: an introduction*. Oxford: Oxford University Press.

Deklaratsia. (2007). Deklaratsia o printsipakh mirnogo i spravedlivogo uregulirovaniia gruzino-abkhazskogo, gruzino-osetinskogo, azerbaijano-karabakhskogo i moldo-pridnestrovskogo konfliktov (2007), *ofitsialnyi sait Ministerstvo inostrannykh del PMR*, http://mid.gospmr.org/en/node/150 (accessed 1 October 2019).

Dembinska, M., Campana, A. (2017). Frozen Conflicts and Internal Dynamics of De Facto States: Perspectives and Directions for Research. *International Studies Review* 1: 1–25.

Demographic Handbook of Armenia. (2016). *The Demographic Handbook of Armenia, 2016*, https://www.armstat.am/en/?nid=81&id=1847 (accessed 1 October 2019).

Derluguian, G. (1998). The tale of two Resorts: Abkhazia and Ajaria before and since the Soviet collapse. *Research Series-Institute of International Studies University of California Berkeley* 1998: 261–92.

Derluguian, G. (2007). Abkhazia: A Summary of Ethnic Conflict. In *Identity Conflicts: Can Violence be Regulated?* Jenkins, J. C., & Gottlieb, E. E. (eds.). New York: Transaction Publishers, 167–84.

Diasamidze, T. (2003). *Regional Conflicts in Georgia*. Tbilisi: Regionalism Research Centre.

DNR. 2017. Chislennost naseleniia Donetskoi Narodnoi Respubliki na 1 iiunia 2017 goda, *Glavnyi statistitcheskii komitet*, http://glavstat.gov dnr.ru/pdf/naselenie/chisl_naselenie_0617.pdf (accessed 1 October 2019).

Dreyer, I., Popescu, N. (2014). Do sanctions against Russia work? *European Union Institute for Security Studies*, 12.12.2014, https://www.iss.europa.eu/content/do-sanctions-against-russia-work (accessed 1 October 2019).

Eastwood, L. S. (1992). Secession: state practice and international law after the dissolution of the Soviet Union and Yugoslavia. *Duke Journal of Comparative and International Law* 3: 299-350.

Eissler, E. R. (2013). Can Turkey De-Isolate Abkhazia? *Turkish Policy Quarterly* Fall issue: 125-135.

Emerson, M., Vahl, M. (2004). Moldova and the Transnistrian conflict. In *Europeanization and Conflict Resolution–Case Studies from the European Periphery, Ghent: Academia Press and the Journal of Ethnopoliticsa and Minorities in Europe*, Bruno Coppieters et al. (eds). Ghent: Academia Press, 170-174.

Etkind, A. 2011. *Internal Colonization*. Cambridge, UK: Polity.

EUBAM. (2008). *European Union Border Assistance Mission to Moldova and Ukraine*. Odessa: Brochure.

Fischer, S. (ed.) (2016) *Not Frozen! The Unresolved Conflicts over Transnistria, Abkhazia, South Ossetia and Nagorno-Karabakh in Light of the Crisis over Ukraine*. Berlin: Stiftung Wissenschaft und Politik.

Fisher, R. P., Geiselman, R. E. (1992). *Memory enhancing techniques for investigative interviewing: The cognitive interview*. Boston: Charles C Thomas Publisher.

Frank, A. G. (1967). *Capitalism and underdevelopment in Latin America*. New York: New York University Press.

Freedom House. (2019). Freedom in The World Reports 1998/9-2019, *Freedom House website*, https://freedomhouse.org/report/freedom-world/freedom-world-2019 (accessed 1 October 2019).

Gammer, M. (2014). Separatism in the Northern Caucasus. *Caucasus Survey* 1(2): 37-47.

Gegeshidze, A. (2008) The isolation of Abkhazia: A failed policy or an opportunity? *Accord* 19: 68-70.

Geldenhuys, D. (2009). *Contested States in World Politics*. London: Palgrave Macmillan.

Gerrits, A. W. M., Bader, M. (2016). Russian patronage over Abkhazia and South Ossetia: implications for conflict resolution. *East European Politics* 32(3): 297-313.

Ghani, A., Lockhart, C. 2008. *Fixing failed states: A framework for rebuilding a structured world*. Oxford: Oxford University Press.

Gotts, N. M. (2007). Resilience, panarchy, and world-systems analysis. *Ecology and Society* 12(1): 30–47.

Griffiths, T. G., & Arnove, R. F. (2015). World culture in the capitalist world-system in transition. *Globalisation, Societies and Education* 13(1): 88–108.

Hale, H. E. (2005). The makeup and breakup of ethnofederal states: Why Russia survives where the USSR fell, *Perspectives on Politics* 3(1): 55–70.

Herd, G. P. (2005). Moldova and The Dniestr Region: Contested Past, Frozen Present, Speculative Futures? *Central and Eastern Europe Series*, 5.7.2005, https://www.files.ethz.ch/isn/97171/05_Feb.pdf (accessed 1 October 2019).

Hoch, T. (2011). EU Strategy towards Post-Soviet De Facto States. *Contemporary European Studies* 2: 69–85.

International Crisis Group, (2018b). Tracking Conflict Worldwide. Moldova, *Crisis Watch Database*, https://www.crisisgroup.org/crisiswatch/database (accessed 1 October 2019).

International Crisis Group. (2018a). Abkhazia and South Ossetia: Time to Talk Trade, *ICG Report*, 249, https://www.crisisgroup.org/europe-central-asia/caucasus/georgia/249-abkhazia-and-south-ossetia-time-talk-trade (accessed 1 October 2019).

Isachenko, D. (2012). *The Making of Informal States*. London: Palgrave Macmillan.

Isachenko, D. (2019). Coordination and control in Russia's foreign policy. *Third World Quarterly*, preprint, 1–17.

Isachenko, D., Schlichte, K. (2007). *The crooked ways of state-building: How Uganda and Transnistria muddle through the international system*. Berlin: Institute for Social Sciences.

Jarabik, B., & Minakov, M. (2016a). Ukraine's hybrid state, *Carnegie Endowment for International Peace*, 22(04) https://carnegieendowment.org/2016/04/22/ukraine-s-hybrid-state-pub-63417 (accessed 1 October 2019).

Jarabik, B., Minakov, M. (2016b) The Consolidation of Power in Ukraine: What It Means for the West", *Carnegie Policy Paper Series*, September 20, 2016, https://carnegieendowment.org/2016/09/19/consolidation-of-power-in-ukraine-what-it-means-for-west-pub-64623 (accessed 1 October 2019).

Ker-Lindsay, J. (2017). Secession and recognition in foreign policy. In *Oxford Research Encyclopedia of Politics*, https://oxfordre.com/politics/view/10.1093/acrefore/9780190228637.001.0001/acrefore-9780190228637-e-478 (accessed 1 October 2019).

Kick, E. L., & Davis, B. L. (2001). World-system structure and change: an analysis of global networks and economic growth across two time periods. *American Behavioral Scientist* 44(10): 1561–1578.

Kick, E. L., Davis, B. L., Lehtinen, M., & Burns, T. J. (2000). World-system position, national political characteristics and economic development outcomes. *Journal of Political and Military Sociology* 28(1): 130–42.

King, Ch. (2001). The Benefits of Ethnic War: Understanding Eurasia's Unrecognized States, *World Politics* 53(4): 524–552.

Kolossov, V., O'Loughlin, J. (1998). Pseudo-states as harbingers of a postmodern geopolitics: The Example of the Trans-Dniester Moldovan Republic. In *Boundaries, Territory and Postmodernity*, Newman, D. (ed.). London: Frank Cass, 151–176.

Kolstø, P. (2006). The Sustainability and Future of Unrecognized Quasi-States. *Journal of Peace Research* 43(6): 723–40.

Kolstø, P., & Blakkisrud, H. (2012). De facto states and democracy: The case of Nagorno-Karabakh. *Communist and Post-Communist Studies* 45(1-2): 141–151.

Konstitutsia Donetskoi Narodnoi Respubliki. (2018). *Konstitutsia Donetskoi Narodnoi Respubliki*, https://dnrsovet.su/konstitutsiya/ (accessed 1 October 2019).

Konstitutsia Luganskoi Narodnoi Respubliki. (2018) *Konstitutsia Luganskoi Narodnoi Respubliki*, https://nslnr.su/zakonodatelstvo/konstitutsiya/ (accessed 1 October 2019).

Konstitutsia Pridnestrovskoi Moldavskoi Respubliki. (2016). *Konstitutsia Pridnestrovskoi Moldavskoi Respubliki*, http://www.vspmr.org/legislation/constitution/ (accessed 1 October 2019).

Konstitutsia Respubliki Abkhazia. (1999). *Konstitutsia Respubliki Abkhazia*, http://www.apsnypress.info/apsny/constitution/ (accessed 1 October 2019).

Konstitutsia Respubliki Yuzhnaya Osetia. (2016). *Konstitutsia Respubliki Yuzhnaya Osetia*, http://www.parliamentrso.org/node/13 (accessed 1 October 2019).

Kratkie Predvaritelnyie Itogi. (2017). *Kratkie Predvaritelnyie Itogi Perepisi Naseleniia Pridnestrovia 2015 Goda*, accessed on line 12 November 2017, (http://gov-pmr.org/item/6831) (accessed 1 October 2019).

Kudelia, S. (2017). The Donbas Rift. *Russian Social Science Review* 58(2-3): 212–34.

Kukhianidze, A., Kupatadze, A., Gotsiridze. R. (2007). Smuggling in Abkhazia and the Tskhinvali Region in 2003–2004. In *Organised Crime and Corruption in Georgia*, Shelley, E. R. (ed.). London: Routledge, 324–45.

Lehmkuhl D., Shagina M. (2015). EU Sanctions in the Post-Soviet Space. In *The European Union and the challenges of the new global context*, Tache I. (ed.). Cambridge, UK: Cambridge scholars publishing, 52–85.

LNR. 2017. Chislennost naseleniia Luganskoi Narodnoi Respubliki na 1 iiunia 2017 goda, *ofitsialnyi sait Gosstata*, accessed online 13 November 2017, http://www.gkslnr.su/files/chisl_280617.pdf (accessed 1 October 2019).

Lynch, D. (2001). Managing Separatist States: a Eurasian Case Study, *Paris: ISS-WEU Occasional Paper* 32: 1–23.

Lynch, D. (2002). Separatist States and Post-Soviet Conflicts. *International Affairs* 78(4): 831–48.

Lynch, D. (2004). *Engaging Eurasia's Separatist States*. Washington DC: United States Institute of Peace.

Lynch, D. (2006). *Why Georgia Matters*. Paris: Institute for Security Studies.

Markedonov, S. (2010). *Radical Islam in the North Caucasus. Evolving threats, challenges, and prospects*. Washington DC: Center for Strategic and International Studies.

Marples, D. R. (2016). *The Collapse of the Soviet Union, 1985–1991*. London: Routledge.

Mikhelidze, N., Pirozzi, N. (2008). *Civil Society and Conflict Transformation in Abkhazia, Israel/Palestine, Nagorno-Karabakh, Transnistria and Western Sahara*. MICRON Policy Working Paper. Brighton, UK: MICRON.

Minakov, M. (2017a). Big Europe's Gap: Dynamic Obstacles for integration between EU and EAU. In *The Eurasian Economic Union and the European Union: Moving Toward a Greater Understanding*, A. Di Gregorio, A. Angeli (eds.). The Hague: Eleven International Publishing, 45–56.

Minakov, M. (2017b). Novorossiya and Transnationalism of Unrecognized Post-Soviet Nations. In *Transnational Ukraine? Networks and Ties that Influence Contemporary Ukraine*, Beichelt, T., S. Worschech (eds.). Stuttgart: ibidem, 2017, 65–88.

Mirimanova, N. (2019). *Economic disconnect and economic conundrum. Donbas private business on standby*. Geneva: Center for Humanitarian Dialogue.

Mirimanova, N., Klein, D. (2006). *Corruption and Conflict in the South Caucasus*. London: International Alert.

Ó Beacháin, D. (2012). The Dynamics of Electoral Politics in Abkhazia. *Communist and Post-Communist Studies* 45: 165–174.

Ó Beacháin, D. (2017). Electoral Politics in the De Facto States of the South Caucasus. *Caucasus Analytical Digest* 94: 3–7.

Oltramonti, P. G. (2015). The political economy of a de facto state: the importance of local stakeholders in the case of Abkhazia. *Caucasus Survey* 3(3): 291–308.

Pavlovsky, G. (2016). Russian Politics Under Putin. *Foreign Affairs* 95(3): 12–17.

Pełczyńska-Nałęcz, K., Strachota, K., Falkowski, M. (2008). Para-States in the Post-Soviet Area from 1991 to 2007. *International Studies Review* 10: 370–87.

Popescu, N. (2005). The EU and Transnistria: From Deadlock to Sustainable Settlement, *IPF Policy Brief*, http://www.policy.hu/npopescu/ipf%20info/IPF%201%20transnistria.pdf (accessed 1 October 2019).

Popescu, N. (2006). *Democracy in Secessionism: Transnistria and Abkhazia's Domestic Policies*. Budapest: CEU Center for Policy Studies.

Portela, C., & Orbie, J. (2014). Sanctions under the EU Generalised System of Preferences and foreign policy: Coherence by accident? *Contemporary Politics* 20(1): 63–76.

Prebish, R. (1950). *Problemas teóricos y práticos del desarrolo económico*. Santiago: Santos.

Prebish, R. (1981). Capitalism: the second crisis. *Third World Quarterly* 3(3), 433–440.

Protsyk, O. (2008). Representation and Democracy in Eurasia's Unrecognized States: The Case of Transnistria. *European Centre for Minority Issues Working Paper* 40: 1–23.

Reill, P. H., Szelenyi, B. A., (eds.) (2011). *Cores, Peripheries, and Globalization*, Budapest: CEU Press.

Rokkan, S. (1967). *Party systems and voter alignments: cross-national perspectives*. New York: Free Press.

Rokkan, S. (1970). *Citizens, Elections, Parties*. New York: McKay.

Roper, S.D. (2002). Regionalism in Moldova: The Case of Transnistria and Gagauzia. In *Ethnicity and Territory in the Former Soviet Union: Regions in Conflict,* Hughes, J., Sasse, G. (eds.). London: Frank Cass.

Said, E. (1978). *Orientalism*. London: Vintage Books.

Schreiber, W. (2014). The Hidden Costs of a Russian Statelet in Ukraine, *The Atlantic,* http://macmillan.yale.edu/sites/default/files/files/2014JournalismAward.pdf (accessed 1 October 2019).

Sepashvili, G. (2004). CIS Summit Reveals Rift in Russian/Georgian Relations. *Civil Georgia Report* 17: 1-12.

Stanislawski, B. (2008). Para-States, Quasi-States, and Black Spots: Perhaps Not States, But Not "Ungoverned Territories," Either. *International Studies Review* 10: 366–70.

Tibilov, I. et al. (eds). (2016). *Itogi Vseobshei Perepisi Naseleniia Respubliki Yuzhnaia Osetia 2015 Goda*. Tskhinval: Upravleniie Statistiki.

Tilly, C. (1985). War Making and State Making as Organized Crime. In *Bringing the State Back*, Evans, T., Rueschemeyer, D., Skocpol, T. (eds.). Cambridge, UK: Cambridge University Press, 169–87.

Tilly, C. (1992). *European States, AD 990-1992*. Cambridge, Mass.: B. Blackwell.

Trier, T., Hedvig, L., David, S. (2010). *Under Siege: Inter-Ethnic Relations in Abkhazia*. New York: Hurst.

UNSCR. (1993). *UN Security Council resolution 876*, 1993, http://unscr.com/en/resolutions/896 (accessed 1 October 2019).

von Twickel, Nikolaus (2019). *The State of the Donbass. A study of eastern Ukraine's separatist-held areas*, A special report for the European Comission, www.3dcftas.eu (accessed 1 October 2019).

Walker, E. W. (2003). *Dissolution: Sovereignty and the breakup of the Soviet Union*. London: Rowman & Littlefield.

Wallerstein I., (1974). *The Modern World-System: Capitalist Agriculture and the Origins of the European World-Economy in the Sixteenth Century*. New York: Academic Press.

Wallerstein, I. (2004). *World-Systems Analysis: An Introduction*. Durham and London: Duke University Press.

Willis, G. B. (2015). *Analysis of the cognitive interview in questionnaire design*. Oxford: Oxford University Press.

Wolff, S. (2011). A resolvable frozen conflict? Designing a settlement for Transnistria. *Nationalities Papers* 39(6): 863–70.

Zakon PMR. (2018). *Zakon Pridnestrovskoi Moldavskoi Respubliki "O respublikanskom biudzhete na 2018 god"*, 2018, http://www.vspmr.org/legislation/laws/zakonodateljnie-akti-pridnestrovskoy-moldavskoy-respubliki-v-sfere-byudjetnogo-finansovogo-ekonomicheskogo-nalogovogo-zakonodateljstva/zakon-pridnestrovskoy-moldavskoy-respubliki-o-respublikanskom-byudjete-na-2018-god-.html (accessed 1 October 2019).

Zarycki, T. (2007). An Interdisciplinary Model of Centre-Periphery Relations: A Theoretical Proposition. *Regional and Local Studies* (Special Issue): 110–30.

Zverev, A. (1996). Ethnic Conflicts in the Caucasus 1988-1994. In *Contested Borders in the Caucasus*, Bruno Coppieters (ed.). Brussels: Vubpress, 13–71.

Small State or Big Bargainer?
Azerbaijan's and Georgia's Agency in Russia's and Turkey's Near Abroad

Petra Colmorgen

Continuously challenged by threads from within and outside, Azerbaijan and Georgia are not perceived to be big bargainers on the international stage, but rather to be small states with limited options[1]. In a regional setting, this becomes particularly obvious when looking at the agendas of neighbouring Russia and Turkey. Their interests are not only directed at Azerbaijan and Georgia themselves, but the former imperial powers have specific relations to the secessionist entities[2] Karabakh, Abkhazia and South Ossetia as well. On one hand, both South Caucasian countries share those fundamental similarities as small parent states; on the other hand, they have shown rather diverse foreign policy objectives. Due to a complex and specific mix of internal and external factors, their room for manoeuvring and their results in achieving their goals have varied significantly as well. Azerbaijan could pursue its goal of independence from foreign interference successfully over time.[3] Georgia instead, could not achieve its main objective of integration into the Western systems. Emphasizing the ability to exert influence instead of focussing solely on the weakness of small states, it shall be therefore explored in this paper, how much foreign policy agency[4] parent states Azerbaijan and Georgia have as small states vis-à-vis their powerful neighbours Russia and Turkey.

---

1 I want to thank İnan Rüma and all other reviewers whose comments have greatly improved this manuscript.
2 The term secessionist territory/entity was given preference since this paper focuses on the perspective of parent states, but it is used synonymously to terms like break-away region, de-facto state or non-recognized state.
3 This article was written before the war between Armenia and Azerbaijan erupted again in September 2020. This escalation might impact the degree of Azerbaijan's agency in the future.
4 Agency is according to Brown understood in a broad sense as *"the ability to exert*

Agency of Small States

According to neo-realists, the notorious lack of resources and capabilities of the small (or weak) state leaves only limited options to react to bigger powers (Bailes et al. 2016: 12, Wivel 2016: 93, Kassab 2015: 60, Walt 1987: 22, Handel 1981: 36). But in reality, small states Azerbaijan and Georgia do not show uniform foreign policy goals and successes. While Azerbaijan's richness in natural energy resources puts Baku in a better bargaining position, this cannot be the only reason for its greater room of manoeuvring. As it will be shown, Baku pursues its goals successfully and is not exposed to an omnipresent external existential threat from bigger powers. Although, this is described to be the natural relation between small and big states according to neo-realists (Thorhallsson & Bailes 2017: 51f., Long 2016: 1, Maass 2009: 73, Mearsheimer 2003: 163, Elman 1995: 175).

Questioning the universality of neo-realist predictions regarding the behaviour of small states, a shift of emphasis towards each country's specific geographic, political and historical context plays a growing role in the literature (Gigleux 2016: 28, Wivel et al. 2014: 7f., Wohlforth 2010: 232). The question, whether small states are objects or actors in the international arena and how much room for manoeuvring and responsibility they have with regards to their own and other's fate receives increasing attention (Bueger & Wivel 2018: 171; Gibert & Grzelczyk 2016: 4; Gigleux 2016: 35; Long 2016: 3; Wivel 2016: 94; Neumann & Carvalho 2015: 9; Brown 2012: 1890). Therefore, the objective of this paper is to discuss, how Azerbaijan and Georgia can exert influence instead of focusing solely on their assumed weakness as small states. This shift of perspective shall be achieved through the application of a framework, which originates in the agency construct.

Agency is a broad concept and can be attributed to natural personas and social bodies alike (Hofferberth 2019: 129). In this context, it shall be understood as "the ability to exert influence"

---

influence". Brown, W. (2012). A question of agency: Africa in international politics. *Third World Quarterly* 33(10), 1889–1908.

(Brown 2012: 1892). Braun et al. suggest to concentrate on the function agency might have in order to describe a "practical achievement" (Braun et al. 2018). Another important aspect of agency is its emphasis of a relative character. Accordingly, the idea needs to be abandoned that agency is situated inherently in actors themselves but is rather a matter of relation (Hofferberth 2019: 127).

The term is academically disputed and has been criticised for its lack of analytical precision (Wight 2006: 178, Emirbayer & Mische 1998: 962). To draw a clear distinction between agency, autonomy and activism (as the opposite of passivism) seems to be an idle task, indeed. Hofferberth criticises, that International Relations theory did not add anything particularly meaningful to the agency debate, because it wrongly concentrated on the question, "which actors mattered in the world politics" (Hofferberth 2019: 129) — a question, which again aims mainly at structural differences between states. On the other hand, preference was given to this concept, because it provides the opportunity for a change of focus. Instead of looking at Georgia's and Azerbaijan's foreign policy solely as a function of external threat, or as a result of internal weakness, the paper's focus will be on their respective individual agency, that is to say, their ability to influence, which shall be discussed according to three proposed dimensions of agency:

Dynamic Dimension

Agency cannot be understood as a static achievement. Instead, any level of agency is rather a snapshot, which represents a current status. This is due to the fact that the degree of agency can change over time according to various events and developments (Hofferberth 2019: 138, Brown 2012: 1899). How can this dynamic aspect of agency be measured in a context of foreign policy? One indicator for the ability to act would be to assess, how foreign policy goals could be achieved over time. If the country shows a high degree of target attainment, its agency will be assessed accordingly to be high, if the target attainment is rather low, the ability to act will be assessed to be low. Both countries have formulated their fundamental long term foreign policy goals in their respective National Security Concepts. For Azerbaijan, independence from foreign influences is of key importance, whereas for Georgia, integration into Western alliances is a priority. In the first part of this paper, those goals will serve as the reference point to evaluate, which differences can be observed between Azerbaijan and Georgia, how they could achieve their targets over time, and how this can be related to their individual level of agency.

External Dimension

After having evaluated individual degrees of foreign policy target attainment in the first part, the paper continues with an assessment of agency limitations by others. The ability to exert influence has an external aspect as well, because agency materializes itself only in interaction with and potential curbing by others. Agency is therefore the result of a constant negotiation process with surrounding other actors (Braun et al. 2018; Wivel 2016: 92). Accordingly, Azerbaijan's and Georgia's respective agencies do not exist in a vacuum as well. They are influenced instead by other powers and their respective agendas. Russia and Turkey have been included into the discussion to enable an elaboration of this external dimension. In the second and third part of this paper, it will be therefore analysed, if and how those big neighbours limit Azerbaijan's and Georgia's agency.

Outcome Dimension

Like discussed, in the recent literature the neo-realist assumption of a small state's weakness, deficits and vulnerability is criticised. The focus had noticeably shifted towards emphasizing small states' opportunities (Wivel 2016: 94). One effect in this context is that an assumed lack of attributed agency for small states results in turn to consider the ability to exert influence as something predominantly good or desirable. Such an approach neglects that wrong vital decisions can be taken as well (Wivel et al. 2014: 14). Particularly Georgia's build up to the war in 2008 and its aftermath, which contradicts neo-realist small states expectations radically, can be analysed from this perspective (Lupu & Wivel 2014: 10). To ask, which outcome exerted influence might have, is therefore a crucial part of this analysis throughout all three parts of this paper. What if the responsibility lies with the small state and consequences of its agency are not positive, but negative? If a small state has agency, it might not use it in a constructive way to reach its goals. And while Azerbaijan proves to be successful in pursuing an independent foreign policy and can be therefore seen as an example of agency with a positive outcome, the Georgian case looks different. It can be observed, how the result of its ability to exert influence in 2008 might be interpreted as a form of agency with negative outcomes. It might be therefore not a lack of agency, which inhibits Georgia from reaching its foreign policy goal of integrating into NATO and EU persistently. Rather the negative outcome of its agency is one reason for failing to reach this aim. Finally, the very existence of secessionist entities on the territory of Azerbaijan and Georgia and the respective measures aiming at their reintegration did not achieve the aspired result, despite a very high level of executed agency by the parent state. While Azerbaijan favours punitive instruments like isolation and military threat, Georgia has enriched its options after the war in 2008 with non-punitive measures within the concept of engagement without recognition[5] (EWR). In this context as well, we might not be looking at a deficit of agency, but at a lack of positive outcome.

---

5   EWR covers a wide range of interactions and communication links between the parent state and the secessionist territories. Georgia applies EWR mainly in Abkhazia and provides free access to health services, education in Georgia and abroad as well as fostering mutual business cooperation (Gegeshidze & Haindrava 2011: 34f.).

Different Dynamics in Azerbaijan and Georgia

Azerbaijan: Independence from Foreign Influence for the Ruling Elite

Besides of solving the conflict in and around Karabakh, Azerbaijan's main foreign policy objective is independence according to its National Security Concept (Government of Azerbaijan 2007: 4). The independence objective is aspirational particularly for a small state but also given that Azerbaijan is encircled by countries with rather strong agendas in its immediate neighbourhood. Baku tries to achieve its goal through a balanced foreign policy approach, which can be described as principally pro-Russian, but not anti-Western (Gvalia et al. 2013: 126). Azerbaijan is keen on exploiting its advantages without any ideological subtext or aim for stable alliances (Morfini 2010: 147). Accordingly, the government has fostered oil deals with the US, UK, France, Russia, Turkey and Iran in order to create common material interests, which led to pro Baku standpoints in the respective countries (Dikkaya & Strakes 2017: 95f.).

Independence from foreign influence shall not be seen solely as the quintessence of Azerbaijan's general national interests, but as a crucial element in the interests of the ruling elites as well (Shirinov 2012: 2). First, there is a correlation between the degree of authoritarianism and the need to control key economic branches by the rulers. The more authoritarian the elites are, the more they need to control the economic output (Smith Stegen & Kusznir 2015: 103). While president Heydar Aliyev was an experienced leader in the post-Soviet space (Gül 2008: 58), his son Ilham performs a different and even more authoritarian style (Shirinov 2012: 2). Thus, for current Azerbaijan a higher degree of independence means more stability for the government. In that sense, Karabakh is also an important "source of national unity" (Waal 2019). Stabilising the regime, the enduring conflict with Karabakh diffuses pressure to reform. Accordingly, there is no incentive for the government to lower the intensity of the conflict (Radnitz 2019: 73).

Second, aiming for an independent foreign policy, Azerbaijan successfully tries to avoid asymmetric relations. One highly symbolic step in this respect is the Azerbaijani accession to the Non-Aligned Movement in 2011. Despite a noticeable rapprochement with Russia over time, there is no wish to enter the organizations, dominated by its northern neighbour. Unlike after independence, the country's ties with the Western institutions are characterized by growing self-confidence and scepticism. Ilham Aliyev faces the challenge to strike a balance between a principally pro-Western stand on one hand and abstaining from fully joining its organizations on the other hand (Strakes 2016: 294). The aim is to move away from institutional memberships that include the delegation of sovereignty to a multinational body, but to give preference to bilateral partnerships (Strakes 2016: 297, 2015: 3, Gvalia et al. 2013: 128). Baku would always present itself ready for economic cooperation, but does not show any interest in ideological influences from the West anymore (Shirinov 2012: 4). The cause and effect of this is that in recent years, Baku clearly distanced itself from the Western human right agenda. The elites do not see enough benefits in closer relation to the EU or further integration (Kakachia et al. 2018a: 287).

Accordingly, it could be argued that not only structural variables like the richness in resources shape Baku's foreign policy and enable it to aim for independent approaches, but that the ideas and interests of the elite play a crucial role as well (Gvalia et al. 2013: 130). If we look at the dynamic aspect of agency, the growing interest of the elite to avoid any interference in the state's affairs corresponds therefore very well with the foreign policy goal of independence. The increased success in pursuing this goal is therefore an indicator of increased agency of the state and its elites.

Georgia: Integration Illusion?

Georgia's foreign policy revolves around the question of integration. First, this is directed on the re-integration of Abkhazia and South Ossetia. It can be argued that Georgia has been more determined than Azerbaijan in pursuing the goal of restoration of its territorial integrity with several wars over the disputed territories since its independence from the Soviet Union (Ter-Matevosyan 2013: 331f.). On the other hand, the isolation of Karabakh had been more uncompromising in Azerbaijan, which is the most resolute parent regarding international isolation (Caspersen 2018: 378f.). Any access to Karabakh is prohibited and respectively punished by the government. Baku has banned Armenian names, imprisoned activists lobbying for a peaceful solution in Karabakh and aggressive state anti-Armenian rhetoric dominates the public discourse (Radnitz 2019: 67). Since in parallel Ilham Aliyev has increased military spending significantly, the probability of an attempt to regain control through military means persists (Blakkisrud & Kolstø 2012: 289).

Georgia instead became a more non-violent parent after 2008 with the primacy of peaceful means to restore its territorial integrity. This must be seen in the context of the impossibility to confront Russia militarily successfully over the issue (Ker-Lindsay 2014: 39). The application of measures in the framework of EWR shows ambiguous results, though and produces less win-win situations than anticipated. One limit is the insistence on prior approval of any international interaction with the secessionist entities. While this is no unusual practise for parent states per se, it limits the engagement of international actors such as the EU. Thus, on the expense of neglecting relations to Abkhazia and South Ossetia, the EU prioritises deepened cooperation with Georgia within the Eastern Partnership (Waal 2018: 27). The attractiveness of the Georgian EWR program for the secessionist entities is in doubt as well. The problem lies in principally different expectations on both sides. While the parent state aspires to prepare the ground for reintegration, the secessionist entity seeks self-determination (Caspersen 2018: 377). Accordingly, the introduced measures proved to be politically and socially difficult to be accepted by Abkhazians (Waal 2017: 3). To use the advantages of EWR produces a dilemma for the secessionist entities. If interaction with the parent intensifies, it becomes more difficult to portray the parent as a threat, it increases vulnerabilities through deepened interdependence and undermines sovereignty, since the parent state still dictates conditions for international cooperation (Caspersen 2018: 383). Let it be through punitive or non-punitive measure, attempts to isolate and control the secessionist territories and to avoid creeping recognition are strong in both parent states. Holding all cards, Azerbaijan and Georgia show a very high degree of agency in this respect. However, at the same time the results do not suggest that the exerted influence has a positive outcome, since Azerbaijan and Georgia stay estranged parents.

A second field of integration is Georgia's goal to integrate itself into the Western systems and "aspires to become part of European and Euro-Atlantic structures" according to its National Security Concept (Government of Georgia 2018: 5). Tbilisi's strong and persistent emphasis on full integration into the Western alliances differs strongly from Baku's pragmatic approach, which avoids any delegation of power. To seek alliance from the West and NATO to counterbalance the Russian influence is the fundamental direction of the Georgian foreign policy since 1995 (Abushov 2009: 197). Inevitably, Tbilisi's aspiration clashes with Moscow's interests and is a notorious source of conflict not only with Russia but this policy is also not welcomed by the secessionist territories Abkhazia and South Ossetia (Cooley 2017: 3f.). Garthon argues that it is "an illusion" to hope for the West to help Georgia restoring its territorial integrity no matter if the official rhetoric sounds otherwise (Gahrton 2010: 217). The cause lays in the desired effect. Neither the EU nor NATO is ready to stand by Georgia against Russia (Wivel 2016: 104).

One important aspect of the strategy for institutional rapprochement is the application of various discursive tools which are targeted at a national and an international audience. Despite the significant geographic distance to actual European countries, territorially closer identities serve as important Others for Georgia. To begin with, the country tries to escape identification with the turbulent Caucasian environment (Kakachia 2012: 6). Another important projection of otherness is the neighbouring Islamic world. Georgia understands itself as having been a part of a common cultural, European room till the 15th century. With the fall of Byzantium, Georgia got disconnected from the Christian world

(Beacháin & Coene 2014: 927). From then on, finding itself either under Ottoman or Persian occupation, the country's identity is formed in contrast to omnipresent Islam. Russian annexation, which started in 1801, was therefore seen as an opportunity to reconnect to the Christian West and its ideas despite sacrificing independence. With the Bolshevik Revolution and the subsequent loss of sovereignty to the Soviet Union, Communism served as an important Other again, isolating Georgia further from its Europeanness (Kakachia & Minesashvili 2015: 174). In the recent discourse, the most obvious Other is Russia, which is perceived to undermine not only Georgia's goals but to represent a political ideal, which contradicts the liberal Western progressiveness, Tbilisi feels itself to be part of. The authoritarian northern neighbour is perceived to follow and promote an obsolete model without ideological radiance or economic benefits (Kakachia & Minesashvili 2015: 177). Since independence, Tbilisi aspires therefore to leave Russia' sphere of influence and perceives Russia as its main threat, although to a softer extent after the change of government in 2012 (Oskanian 2016: 15). These described Others lead to a Georgian Self, which is located between traditional Orthodoxy and Western democracy.

This image was boosted during and after the Rose Revolution in 2003. The non-violent transition of power itself, its demands and aftermath were considered to be both: an expression of existing Georgian Europeanness and an aspiration for further Europeanisation (Beacháin & Coene 2014: 930). This emphasis on Georgia's European identity was hoped to be the key to integration into NATO and the EU (Kakachia & Minesashvili 2015: 171f.). Presenting itself as a shining example of democracy in the region, Georgia hoped to play an important role as a "norm entrepreneur"[6] in the area (Wivel 2016: 101). In Saakashvili's calculation, undemocratic Georgia under Shevardnadze would be the initial

---

6 Scandinavian small states have been originally described to act as such *"norm entrepreneurs"* on the international stage with respect to promoting sustainable development, peaceful conflict resolution and redistribution of wealth (Ingebritsen 2002: 20).

stone to fall in a regional domino effect. He was hoping that peaceful regime change would inevitably spread through the entire post-Soviet space and thus created a stable source of regional support and prestige among Western governments for Georgia's pioneering role (Oskanian 2016: 5). Another main assumption was that this democracy euphoria would eventually also spill over to Abkhazia and South Ossetia and would bring the territories back into Tbilisi's orbit.

In several economic, anti-corruption and democracy development aspects, Georgia unarguably championed over one or another former Soviet republic (Kakachia & Minesashvili 2015: 175). And while these successes need to be appreciated, starting from 2007 democratic ideals and realities began to diverge. The Saakashvili government faced accusations of high level corruption and authoritarian traits. Additionally, the aspired domino effect failed to appear, neither as a mass phenomenon in other post-Soviet states nor in its secessionist territories. Abkhazia and South Ossetia were not overly impressed by the democratization project and could not be lured back under Tbilisi's control (Oskanian 2014: 12). Neither the European identity narrative nor the "Beacon of Liberty" effect could help accomplishing Georgia's goal of integration into EU and NATO. For that reason, Georgia's agency in this respect must be assessed to be rather low.

Russia in the Region: Enemy or Role Model?

Azerbaijan and Georgia have to deal with Moscow's foreign policy ambitions and the consequences of its strong imperial heritage as well. This results in a particular relationship between Moscow and the newly independent countries around it—Russia's so called "Near Abroad". What springs to mind first is geography. Russia's Achilles' heel and chronic headache is its southern border in the North Caucasus with its own secessionist turmoil (Halbach 1999: 7). Azerbaijan and Georgia for its part were suspected to have supported North Caucasian rebels (Sadri 2003: 185). Moscow considers it therefore to be vital for its own security to have at least some degree of influence to keep the North Caucasus under its control (Oskanian 2013: 137) and to prevent conflicts from spreading to its own territory (Kelkitli 2017: 36).

Another motivation for Russia in the South Caucasus is to limit the influence of other actors. This is true for Turkey's and Iran's regional influence (Aslani 2010: 138, Cornell 2003: 331). Russia tries to limit Western and NATO influence, as well. The idea to lose the southern Caucasus as a buffer zone is deeply disturbing for Russia (Oskanian 2013: 137, Manutscharjan 2007: 59f.). NATO expansion and a spread of unfriendly regimes in its direct neighbourhood with democratization efforts in the form of coloured revolutions like in Georgia, challenged Moscow (Isachenko 2012: 139). Hill and Taspinar describe Russia in this respect as a "paranoid power" (Hill & Taspinar 2006: 15) Subsequently and starting with the war in Georgia, Moscow demonstrated that it is ready to take more assertive action, if it perceives its interests to be in danger (Rogstad 2017: 10, Freire 2010: 60).

Nonetheless, there are also material interests in the southern Caucasus. Russia does not only wish to influence the international energy market (Sadri 2003: 186), but fears to lose central Asia's and South Caucasus' energy reserves to the West (Oskanian 2013: 138). Moreover, the Russian government wants to generally strengthen its economic weight in the region through a strong role of Russian companies (Gül 2008: 54f.). Whether Russia's ambitions in the southern Caucasus are an expression of its neo-imperial ambitions is disputed. While Russia's behaviour and particularly its support for secessionists in Abkhazia and South Ossetia is called imperialist (Abushov 2009: 190), other authors emphasize the reactiveness of the Russian approach and the absence of a greater geostrategic plan (Tsygankov 2016: 233f., Markedonov 2015).

Moscow is interested to support friendly governments and to make life harder for unfriendly regimes (Siroky et al. 2017: 502). One of Moscow's most effective instruments in this respect is "controlled instability" (Kelkitli 2017: 37). Exploiting local conflicts with ethnic minorities, Russia is able to disrupt the building of nation states in its immediate neighbourhood, if necessary (Nodia 2017: 6f.). One crucial element in this respect is the "Russki Mir" concept as a very broad mobilisation tool. The "Russian World" is a fluid idea, which moves between the promotion of Russian language and culture abroad and the protection and management of the relation with compatriots in the neighbouring countries. It includes the understanding of a distinct Russian cultural space, which can be understood in contrast to imagined other concepts like "The West" (O'Loughlin et al. 2017: 7, Toal 2017: 243).

Through the support for the secessionist territories, Russia is able to use its influence to escalate or de-escalate the existing conflicts according to its needs. So far, Russia did not make use of "controlled instability" in Azerbaijan, mainly because it is recently most interested in stability there and also does not have or promote any Russian compatriots' agenda in Azerbaijan. The level of Russian interference in Georgia's affairs instead had been unparalleled among the post-Soviet states since Gorbachev (Cornell 2018: 233, 2014: 36, Hill & Taspinar 2006: 15f.). "Controlled instability" had been applied in many ways and the continuing Russian support for the secessionist territories guarantees further Russian military presence in the southern Caucasus (Abushov 2009: 204). This gives Russia unique leverage, which neither the West nor Turkey possess (Pestrecov & Babirov 2017: 5). It is important to recognize that these means are not used universally, but follow an individual local pattern and approach. While Crimea has been annexed, Abkhazia and South Ossetia have been recognized as independent states by Russia and a handful of other states, while Transdniestria had been denied such a status (Rogstad 2017: 6). Karabakh for its part is not recognized by Russia and does not receive any direct support from Moscow either (Cooley 2017: 3). A closer look at other foreign policy tools will support therefore the argument of a rather individual bilateral use of Moscow's instruments in Azerbaijan and Georgia respectively.

Azerbaijani-Russian Relations: Recent Selective Mimicry

Over time, the Azerbaijani attitude towards Russia has changed significantly. Today it is clear that Azerbaijan's foreign policy goal of reaching and maintaining sovereignty can be called accomplished, although the Soviet Union's initial reaction to Azerbaijan's attempt to reach national independence in 1990 was not welcoming at all[7]. Accordingly, there still exists mistrust towards Moscow to some extent in the government, but deep in society as well (Mehdiyeva 2011: 82). The anti-Russian public sentiments are rooted in the memories of several Russian interferences in domestic issues, namely the widespread suspicion, that Russia played a role in the coup d'etat in 1993 (Gül 2008: 58f., Manutscharjan 2007: 35).

However, today Russia is not seen as an acute threat to Azerbaijan's sovereignty anymore and both countries managed to move toward a more pragmatic partnership with strengthened economic ties. Baku understands and accepts Russia's interests in the region and tries to act accordingly through a "Non-irritating policy" towards Moscow (Valiyev 2014: 12). Moscow for its part is sceptical about Azerbaijan's general orientation towards Turkey and the West and particularly its cooperation with NATO. On the other hand, this does not lead to strong concerns in Moscow, because the increasingly authoritarian nature of the government puts Baku ideologically closer to its club of "Sovereign Democracies"[8]. Unlike the West, Russia does not voice any criticism over the repressive regime, which it considers to be its ally in the fight against the outbreak of coloured revolutions (Baev 2017: 74).

Nonetheless, the key issue in the Russian-Azerbaijani relations had been Moscow's support for Armenia (Gül 2008: 60). Russia is Armenia's main ally with massive direct and indirect general and military backing for Azerbaijan's arch-enemy (Musabekov 2012: 43). On the other hand, it is important to emphasize, that unlike on Georgian territory, Russia does not act as

---

7   The so called *"Black January"* was the violent oppression of the independence movement in Azerbaijan by the Soviet authorities after anti-Armenian pogroms in Baku.
8   The key feature of Sovereign Democracy is described by Lipman as the ability to *"act with little or no regard for the judgments of outsiders"*. She continues that international recognition and respect are still vital, but do not lead to less authoritarian behaviour (Lipman 2006).

a patron for Karabakh. The conflict is managed by Armenia and Azerbaijan and does not serve as a tool of manipulation or "controlled instability" for Russia. Accordingly, Russia does not limit Azerbaijan's agency in this respect. In fact, Russia treats Karabakh de jure as a part of Azerbaijan and it is accordingly excluded from the mutual defence agreement between Armenia and Russia. On the other hand, Armenia considers Russia's massive military presence as the main insurance against Azerbaijan (Halbach & Smolnik 2014: 6). In 2018 Azerbaijan and Armenia were among the top ten most militarized states according to the Global Militarization Index (Bonn International Center for Conversion).This is due to generous arm sales from Russia to both parties, which shall emphasize Moscow's neutrality in the Karabakh conflict (Bláhová 2019: 76, Antonopoulos et al. 2017: 373). Manutscharjan gives an anecdotal example of this "balanced" Russian arms trade, which did not favour one conflict party over the other: Moscow delivered jets to Azerbaijan to bomb Karabakh, while it simultaneously provided anti-aircraft missiles to Armenia to fight the Azerbaijani jets (Manutscharjan 2007: 34).

Unlike in other cases, Russia never made any use of mobilization of minorities or the claim of discrimination of the Russian speaking community. This might be also due to the fact that minorities such as Russians or Lezgins face indeed only minor problems nowadays because of an inclusive policy by the government (Cornell 2011: 351). Azerbaijan's interests in Russia are promoted by the diaspora and a powerful lobby (Chernjavskij 2013: 255). The big number of Azerbaijanis in Russia constitutes a tool for Moscow, too. Without membership in the Russia-led Eurasian Economic Union, Azerbaijani migrants and their status in Russia might be used to put pressure on Baku. Additionally, there is a significant anti-Azerbaijani public resentment in Russia, which mirrors general xenophobic tendencies and an aversion against the "Azeri Mafia"[9] in particular (Chernjavskij 2013: 252).

---

9   After monopolization of the fruit, vegetable and especially flower sale in the 1980ies, the Azerbaijani diaspora in Russia moved to other businesses, such as restaurants, casinos, car selling, drugs, control of markets with protection

The new pragmatic Azerbaijani attitude towards Russia can be observed in Azerbaijan's cautious reaction to recent conflicts with Russian involvement. The country has not voiced any strong criticism during and after the war in Georgia in 2008 (Valiyev 2011: 140). Azerbaijan has expressed its full support for the sovereignty of Ukraine, but it did not condemn Russia's action as well. Instead, Baku tried to use the crisis to its advantage, because alternative gas pipelines have been in demand and the sanctions and countersanctions against and from Russia have helped its own economy. Furthermore, Baku criticised the international double standards, whereby sanctions against Russia have been imposed due to the annexation of Crimea, while Armenia has never been sanctioned for its occupation of Karabakh (Valiyev 2014: 11ff.).

With the transition of power from father to son in October 2003, Putin's Russia started to serve as a role model and authoritarian tendencies were strengthened. "Putinisation" is omnipresent today in Azerbaijan with a powerful president in authoritarian and even dynastic rule, accompanied by a cult of personality (Gvalia et al. 2013: 129). The sovereignty of the state is seen as superior to any individual human right and any interference in those internal matters is rejected in Moscow and Baku alike. Regime change is no less feared by Ilham Aliyev than it is by Vladimir Putin (Markedonov & Suchkov 2015). Accordingly, Ilham Aliyev feels more comfortable with the Russian "interpretation" of democracy (Gvalia et al. 2013: 129). Imitating democratic institutions and mechanisms, Ambrosio calls this approach a "Potemkin democracy" (Ambrosio 2016: 103). Thus, the regime will shield itself against any foreign influence in its internal affairs. This results in the opportunity to accept different versions of local democracies on the expense of invalidation of universal democratic principles and human rights. On the other hand, it provides justification for assertive steps against any foreign influences, like the shutdown of NGO's (Cooley 2012: 112).

---

money (Iunusov 2003: 73). About 50 000 people out of the 2 million Azerbaijanis living in the Russian Federation (unofficial estimate) can be associated with criminal activities (Iunusov 2003: 74).

Especially the latter had been an export hit of the Russian Federation and respective legislation can be observed not only in Azerbaijan but for instance in Tajikistan and Kazakhstan, too (Owen et al. 2018: 296). Azerbaijan is considered to be an "early adopter" of NGO restrictions. Already in 2009, a law came into force, which made sure that organizations can only register as NGOs if they receive prior approval from the Ministry of Justice. In March 2013 NGO's were forbidden to receive any foreign funding over 185 Euro without approval. From that time onwards it was also mandatory to receive funds exclusively into a state bank's account (Hooper 2016: 13f.). From 2014 it became necessary that foreign donors receive prior agreement from the Ministry of Justice and that they need to open a local NGO branch (Levine 2016)[10].

It is important to note that Russia is not actively pushing its neighbours to adopt its model or legislation. The process of following Moscow's best undemocratic practice is highly voluntary. It could be argued that in Azerbaijan's case, its mimicry of Russian policies like the anti-NGO-law is also an expression of Baku's agency. Azerbaijan does not need to justify its course, neither domestically nor internationally. Baku's decision is not based on geopolitical considerations or any pressure from Moscow, but solely reflects the interests of the authoritarian elite to act without any foreign interference. Since contacts are on eye level, there is no need to distance itself from Russia, but it is the government's free choice to pick whatever fits its interest best. Consequently, Azerbaijan's agency is not limited by Russia. In the current situation, this results in a high degree of independence and no need for Russia to apply its arsenal of foreign policy instruments—a situation which looks completely different for Azerbaijan's neighbour Georgia.

---

10 For further details: (Guluzade & Bourjaily 2014).

Georgian-Russian Relations: Many Instruments, Many Storylines

The degree to which Russia interfered and interferes in Georgia's matters through various instruments is very high and undermines the realisation of Georgia's foreign policy goal of integration into the Western systems and effectively limits Georgia's agency. De Waal observes though that Georgia might not be one of Russia's top foreign priorities anymore. He argues that Moscow's focus has shifted within the Near Abroad towards Ukraine and that "There is little aggression versus Georgia today; it is definitely not comparable to what it was ten years ago" (Roehrs-Weist 2018). On the other hand, the Russian ban on direct flights to Georgia as a reaction to anti-government protests in Tbilisi in summer 2019, which were interpreted to be Russophobe by the Russian government, underlines the fragility in the asymmetric bilateral relations.

Looking at the Georgian Russian relations, Saakashvili's presidency stands out and the war in August 2008 and the aftermaths dominate regional and international politics since then. It needs to be emphasized that relations between Putin and Saakashvili had not been disastrous from the beginning. The first National Security Concept of Georgia under the Saakashvili government featured a relatively balanced approach towards Russia and avoided emphasizing bilateral conflicts (Ter-Matevosyan 2013: 335). Moscow for its part was rather restrained, too. Saakashvili's successful attempt to regain control over Adjara had been welcomed for instance (Huseynov 2016: 123). But those examples of an initially relaxed relation fade in comparison to the soon escalation of tension. Despite a steady deterioration in bilateral relations and noticeably growing Russian support for South Ossetia and Abkhazia, Saakashvili underestimated Russia's determination to act (Huseynov 2016: 123). Another source of misperception was the radiance he attributed to his liberal reforms and "part of the West"-narrative. Intensifying rhetoric about territorial integrity and taking measures to enforce it, like the isolation of South Ossetia from 2004 onwards, did not constitute an attractive alternative for the secessionist entities but alienated them even further (Waal 2008). In parallel, he overestimated the Western will to interfere and their determination to balance against the Russian influence (Oskanian 2016: 17).

Having not been able to reach his foreign policy goals and showing growing anti-democratic tendencies in domestic affairs, Saakashvili had to leave office in 2012. One of the most tragic twists in his presidency is that what constitutes the foreign policy priority became unreachable in the foreseeable future through his miscalculations. Precisely because of the changed situation after the war, despite all words, Georgia cannot be accepted into NATO soon (Huseynov 2016: 125). Can the failure of reaching the foreign policy goal of integration be understood accordingly solely as a lack of agency? Not necessarily, because it could be argued that exactly the presence of agency counteracted Georgia's aims. First, having violently challenged the status quo with Russia, Saakashvili demonstrated a surprisingly high level of agency, or "the ability to exert influence". This is particularly unexpected, given that Georgia is a small state with limited capabilities. The bargain was exceptionally big but it did not get accepted by the other players. And second: because his situational judgement was based on several misperceptions, this could not lead to a positive outcome, but the influence he exerted had highly destructive consequences for Georgian domestic politics, its relation to the outer world and the restoration of its territorial integrity. Saakashvili's aspiration to solve the conflict militarily was counterproductive and sustainably spoiled Georgia's already complicated relation to its secessionist entities (Blakkisrud & Kolstø 2012: 290). It led not only to worse relations with Abkhazia and South Ossetia, but to the self-inflicted impossibility of reaching its foreign policy goal of integration into the Western alliances as well.

Moscow for its part heavily limits Tbilisi's agency through a variety of instruments, ranging from traditional hard power during the war in 2008 to various other policies affecting the secessionist entities Abkhazia and South Ossetia directly, like passportization or borderisation[11], which started in 2009 in South Ossetia. One of Moscow's most important points of reference with respect to Abkhazia and South Ossetia is the "Russki Mir" concept. This points to a fundamental problem in the discussion of the Russian Georgian relations: there is a tendency to neglect the involvement of more than those two players. Instead, we look at no less than four actors, narratives and storylines. To deliver a profound analysis of different Georgian and Russian narratives about the developments since the dissolution of the Soviet Union or competing storylines about the war in 2008 is not within the scope of this paper.[12] Still, it is worth to give some room to different perceptions, especially from the perspective of the secessionist entities. Regarding the "Russki Mir" concept, fieldwork has suggested that there is a very high agreement from the inhabitants of Abkhazia and South Ossetia to belong to that civilizational space. Based on a survey from 2017, across all age groups (18 to over 60) more than 70% of the inhabitants of South Ossetia and even more than 80% of the Abkhaz population agree that their republic is part of the "Russki Mir" (O'Loughlin et al. 2017: 18). Additionally, trust in the Russian leadership[13] is very strong, too with almost 90% in South Ossetia and slightly smaller values for the Abkhazian population (Toal & O'Loughlin 2014). Those results show that South Ossetia and Abkhazia cannot share the Georgian Othering of Russia, which is promoted as an obligatory part of the Georgian identity and storyline.

Modelling the conflict solely as a Georgian-Russian one and contextualizing it geopolitically neglects a variety of local aspects. The demand for restoration of territorial integrity itself and the affirmation of this aim by the West might be problematic for two reasons. First, since its independence, Georgia never actually had

---

11 The term describes the erection of a state border fence around South Ossetia to physically separate the territory from the parent state Georgia. Along goes a criminalisation of crossings that line, which resulted in the detention of Georgians, for violations of the "border" (Kakachia et al. 2018b).
12 Toal offers a detailed overview of the different narratives (Toal 2008: 691).
13 When the survey was conducted, Dmitry Medvedev was president and Vladimir Putin served as Premier of the Russian Federation.

control over its entire territory, so restoration might not be the correct term. Second, by repeating and accepting this narrative, the West does support Georgia's maximum demand, which might be interpreted by Non-Georgians in Georgia as nationalistic and chauvinist (Toal 2008: 699). Intrinsic opposition to the West, NATO and EU might therefore not be surprising in South Ossetia and Abkhazia. Furthermore, massive isolation efforts have instead made Russian patronage inevitable (Ker-Lindsay & Berg 2018). Accordingly, the population in these territories rather welcomes Russian protection. It is additionally necessary and justified as well to criticise Russia for intensively using its leverage in these territories to its benefit. But this surely cannot be the only reason for the conflict. To stipulate the cause and effect of a reduced attractiveness of being a part of Georgia is not easy either. While Orttung and Walker see the omnipresent Russian threat and the unrest created by the uncontrolled territories as the reason for weak governance (Orttung & Walker 2015), Nodia looks at it the other way around. He emphasizes that it is "the failure of democratic and good governance reforms in Association Agreement countries", which influences, how strongly Russian influence can manifest itself (Nodia 2017: 27).

This points again to the question of the outcome of agency or more specific, who is to blame for the low level of Georgia's agency? Without doubt, using many of its foreign policy instruments against Georgia, Russia heavily restricts Georgia's agency. But on the other hand, the responsibility lies with Georgia as well to some extent. If Tbilisi continues to attribute the cause of its problems with the secessionist entities mainly to an external Other (Russia)[14] and the solution to an external Self (NATO, EU), the affected populations in South Ossetia or Abkhazia have not many reasons to look more favourably towards Georgia. Not everything can be blamed on Putin or be solved by the West. As long as the

---

14 In a "matroshka-esque" transmission of external attribution, Abkhazia blames the Georgian embargo to be solely responsible for its problems as well. This ignores Abkhazian mismanagement and de-population of the region (Prelz Oltramonti 2015: 301).

government does not deliver stable political and economic progress for the sake of better governance itself, its attractiveness for the secessionist entities probably keeps low. Without the acknowledgement of its own responsibility for the current situation and the fundamental willingness to consider Abkhazia's and South Ossetia's interests also to be important, chances are high that nothing will change in the stagnant situation with high Russian interference and low Georgian overall agency.

Turkey in the Region: Brothers or Others?

Looking at the map, it becomes obvious that Azerbaijan and Georgia are located in multiple Near Abroads. And besides Russia, Turkey springs to mind not only as another powerful neighbour but as a former ruler in the region as well. The sudden reappearance of the partly former Ottoman territories to its North and East after the dissolution of the Soviet Union came like a surprise and Turkey "suddenly found itself at the epicentre of the rapidly changing Eurasian geopolitics" (Aydin 2004: 1). Nevertheless, besides of geopolitics, there was a big sentimental element in the early stages as well. Turkey was quite euphoric about its rediscovered neighbours (Aleksanyan 2017: 310f.). Onis describes this psychological element to be important, because it helped to overcome "Turkey's traditional fear of isolation and insecurity" (Onis 2001: 67). Since this emotional start, Ankara could not only develop fruitful cooperation with Azerbaijan and Georgia but also readjusted its relation to its former arch enemy Russia. Turkey has found new partners and old allies among the newly independent states and showed an interest driven and sometimes impulsive approach in its Near Abroad in the southern Caucasus.

The Near Abroad does not come with such massive implication like in Russia's case and is no common term with regards to territories bordering Turkey. The respectively deducted duty to protect citizens abroad is absent or rather twisted inwards in the Turkish case. With an estimated population share of 10% originating from the Caucasus, diaspora groups are important participants in the Turkish domestic political discourse

(Markedonov 2018: 353). Nonetheless, the biggest difference to Russia is that the Republic Turkey never had any claims of a special sphere of influence in its immediate neighbourhood or was willing to use any hard power to enforce its interests.[15] The complex conflict configuration creates a particular "in-between-ness", which makes it hard for Turkey to play a more active role as a political actor, given the dominant conflicts between Armenia and Azerbaijan on one hand and between Russia and Georgia on the other hand (Veliyev 2015: 91, Hill & Taspinar 2006: 13).

The Turkish foreign policy in the Caucasus has undergone significant changes and pragmatic re-adjustments. The interest in the former Ottoman territories in general and in the so called "outside Turks" in particular has been purposely muted since the foundation of the Republic of Turkey in 1923 (Aydin 2004: 2). Ankara's foreign policy was guided by a passive, inward orientated, rather defensive attitude and a clear pro-Western orientation (Onis 2001: 66). Ankara did not take an active approach, but a "wait and see" attitude (Çelikpala 2005: 170). Cornell goes as far as to say that before the dissolution of the Soviet Union, Turkey basically had forgotten about its Turkic cousins outside the country and that besides of some academic experts or diaspora groups, knowledge about other Turks became very limited in society over time (Cornell 2003: 278f.). One changing factor to this passive attitude was the neo-liberal economic agenda of Prime Minister/President Turgut Özal in the 1980ies. Focusing on expanding Turkey's opportunities for trade and business development, Özal fostered a more active policy in the Caucasus and beyond (Onis 2001: 66). Turkey focused quickly on the opportunities its historic heritage, trade, geographic proximity and its attachment to the West and the US would bring. For its part, Ankara saw a more proactive foreign policy as a way to counterbalance its perceived loss of strategic importance as a bulwark against the Soviet Union (Çelikpala 2005: 174). Besides of those internal motivations, the rather assertive new course was

---

15 Turkey's former military activities in Cyprus, against the PKK in Iraq or its recent involvement in Syria are exceptions in this respect.

fostered by external influences as well. The United States encouraged its ally Turkey to perform a more active role as a regional leader in the Caucasus, Central Asia and the Balkans (Cornell 2003: 279).

The Westernizers in Russia in the 1990ies considered the southern Caucasus as a burden and aspired to liberate themselves from the imperial past (Rywkin 2016: 230, Isachenko 2012: 135, Jemil' & Lija 2012: 10f.). Turkey on the contrary, encouraged by the West, saw the opportunity to become more influential and to serve as a secular, modern and democratic model country (Adam 2013: 238). It was hoped that Turkey could speak to the countries in the South Caucasus more effectively than any Western partner ever could (Gianjumian 2014: 106). Turkey was the only country within reach with direct and long lasting ties to the West. Integration into EU and NATO should be enabled by Turkey, which was seen as an essential NATO member and on the path to successful EU accession. Goksel describes the idea that gas and oil would flow from the East to the West and good governance in return from Europe to the South Caucasus via Europeanizing Turkey. Thus, Turkey was seen to take the role of a "proactive integration corridor" (Goksel 2011b: 6). Over time it became clear that this ambitious goal could not get materialized. As a result, none of the countries in question has a specific EU accession perspective and today Georgia, not Turkey is in the lead with regards to integration due to its visa free travel and a Deep and Comprehensive Free Trade Area (DCFTA) with the EU.

In hindsight, Turkey's initial push into the region might be interpreted as understandably enthusiastic, but simultaneously over-optimistic. Turkey failed to convince as a model state due to its own flawed democracy situation and continuous economic domestic turmoil (Yesilkaya 2006: 4f.). It became obvious that Ankara had neither technologically nor financially the means to enable socio-economic progress in the former Soviet republics (Aleksanyan 2017: 309). Relations developed by all means positively in many fields and show steady overall progress (Cecire 2013: 115). But Turkey could not grow into the role of a regional leader as well and subsequently muted its engagement in its Near Abroad.

On paper, the South Caucasus re-emerged as a region of interest for Turkey with the advent of AKP's Ahmed Davutoglu in foreign policy and his understanding of "Strategic Depth", "Zero Problems with Neighbours" and a more active foreign policy orientation towards the former Ottoman territories (Oskanian 2011: 24). The early stages of the AKP foreign policy were characterized by its attempts to foster Europeanization and EU integration as well as conflict resolution in chronic conflicts such as Armenia or Cyprus (Aras 2017: 4). With the departure of Davutoglu from the political scene in 2016, another shift in Turkey's foreign policy can be observed. Prioritising the survival of the ruling AKP, Dalacoura described Erdogan's presidential foreign policy of as a "more 'transactional', unplanned, ad hoc type of foreign policy, based on expediency" (Dalacoura 2017: 2).

In comparison to Moscow, Ankara's agenda in Azerbaijan and Georgia is less complex. Turkey has significant economic interests which express themselves through a certain pragmatism in the region (Gaber 2011: 145). To a lesser extent than Russia, Turkey was as well concerned with the spillover of conflicts from the South Caucasus. These worries were on one hand related to a mobilization of its domestic Caucasian diaspora groups as well as the fear of potential consequences for its own secessionist questions (Çelikpala 2005: 171). The recognition of Abkhazia and South Ossetia were seen from that perspective as dangerous developments with regards to Turkey's Kurdish populated areas in its own Southeast (Baskan et al. 2012: 64). As a consequence, Turkey never changed course with regards to the support of the territorial integrity of Georgia and Azerbaijan, although this position comes at relatively high costs. Particularly Ankara's unconditional support for Azerbaijan in the Karabakh conflict creates disadvantages for Turkey, too. Although the solidarity helps to keep Azerbaijani-Turkish relations on a fraternal level, at the same time, it limits Turkey's scope of action in the region significantly, especially with regards to Armenia.

Azerbaijani-Turkish Relations: Put Offside with Football Diplomacy

Turkey is of exceptional importance for Azerbaijan. After the Turkish rediscovery of its forgotten cousins, Azerbaijan reacted most euphorically to reconnect to the Turkic brother, despite the initial clear power imbalance (Balci 2014: 46). Heydar Aliyev spoke about "One Nation, Two States". Those early relations and rhetoric were emotionally overloaded and moved over time gradually towards a more pragmatic partnership, with the focus on mutual benefits.[16] What sets Azerbaijan's role in the South Caucasus apart is its importance in a nationalist context. One particular motive behind Ankara's efforts was to connect with Baku as the closest partner in the pan-Turkist project[17] (Sadri 2003: 186).

After the bloody struggle for independence, the mood in Azerbaijan was that there are no allies, but Turkey (Mehdiyeva 2011: 95f.). Up to now, opinion polls regularly demonstrate that Azerbaijan and Turkey are considered to be mutually best friends (Kadir Has University 2017, The Caucasus Research Resource Center 2013). Turkey's cultural presence is very dominant in Azerbaijan and it aims to deepen these ties and to foster exchange through universities, high schools or Turkish media and businesses. One important aspect is the promotion of Turkish language education in order to replace Russian as the language of the political and economic elite (Dikkaya & Strakes 2017: 90). Turks form the second biggest minority group after Russians, but unlike the latter in growing numbers (Musabekov 2012: 41). Increasingly, the overemphasize of similarities and dominance from the Turkish side was in some respects irritating for Azerbaijan, because after its independence it was not looking for the next "Big Brother", but for

---

16 A similar *"cooling down"* of emotions took place in the Russian-Azerbaijani relations. The start was overloaded with negativity and emotional accusations. Pragmatism started to take over only after some time.
17 Pan-Turkism fosters the unity of Turkic people. According to Oskanian, pan Turkism is *"the idea that ethnic Turkic peoples throughout the Eurasian landmass would have to unite politically"* (Oskanian 2011: 26).

a relation on eye level with respect for its national characteristics and heritage (Cornell 2011: 361, Babajew 2007: 61, Aydin 2004: 7).

While family continuity in the presidential office of Azerbaijan led to a stable situation, the picture in Turkey is rather volatile. Although the AKP is the ruling power since 2002, its course is more dynamic. At the beginning of Erdogan's term, he was primarily focused on domestic economic growth and entering the EU. Despite the fact, that his first state visit took him to Baku, the nationalist project of Turkic unity had lost the priority (Ismailzade 2005: 7). Some other parts of society had never been particularly enthusiastic about "One Nation, Two States". The pro-Western elites in Turkey had been traditionally rather pro-EU than pro-Baku and Islamic conservatives used to marginalize Muslims from the former Soviet territory because they doubted the authenticity of their "Sovietized" religion. Additionally, Muslims from Azerbaijan follow the Shia and not the Sunni orientation (Cornell 2011: 362). Over time, the focus shifted from blood and history to market and trade. Accordingly, as Ismailzade puts it after an euphoric start, "The 'Honeymoon' in Turkish-Azeri relations was over" (Ismailzade 2005: 7).

Azerbaijan had seen significant annual economic growth in the past, but with Ilham Aliyev coming to power in 2003 the GDP-increase was massive.[18] The revenues could be pushed to completely new levels and provided Ilham Aliyev with a boosted self-esteem, which fostered a different position in Azerbaijanis' foreign policy matters and a respective growing agency. All partners, including Turkey, had to deal with an Azerbaijan, which was fully aware of its strength and importance and not willing to sell itself at lower price but to use its increased bargaining power.

One impressive example of Baku's new confidence and growing agency was its harsh reaction to rapprochement in the form of "Football Diplomacy"[19] between Turkey and Armenia in

---

18 The GDP went up for 934% from 7.28 Billion in 2003 to a maximum of 75.24 Billion USD in 2014 according to the World Bank data. Since then, the GDP fell back to 37,87 Billion USD in 2016 and reached 46,94 Billion USD in 2018.

19 In August 2008 the Turkish president Abdullah Gül visited a national football match in Yerevan and met with his Armenian counterpart sometime later. In

2008/2009. Azerbaijan was shocked by the bold step of its close ally. "Football Diplomacy" provoked prompt and decisive pressure from Baku not to change the status quo. Brothers or not, Azerbaijan could not allow Turkey to break Armenia's isolation unconditionally, which was seen to be one of Baku's strongest leverages in the Karabakh conflict. Consequently, Azerbaijan demanded from Turkey to include the solution of the conflict into the negotiations. This led to an immediate deadlock of the high profile Turkish initiative (Dikkaya & Strakes 2017: 97, Karademir 2017: 84, Musabekov 2012: 42, Goksel 2011a: 6). Turkey failed to solve the dilemma of normalizing ties with Armenia on one hand, and to keep Azerbaijan happy on the other hand (Torbakov 2010: 35). Davutoglu's paradigm of "Zero Problems with Neighbours" faced its limits in the Caucasus as a region, because local conflicting interests did not allow a coherent policy (Jackson 2010: 82). The rather impulsive and uncoordinated approach did not only harm Azerbaijan's national interests but the relations between Azerbaijan and Turkey as well (Mehdiyeva 2011: 252f.).

Baku had means to react and to exert influence on Turkey. Azerbaijan stressed that bypassing Turkey and involving Russia in exports to Europe would be an alternative option and indeed Gazprom and SOCAR did sign a contract shortly afterwards (Abilov & Isayev 2015: 130, Balci 2014: 49, Mehdiyeva 2011: 253). Since then, the discounted gas price for Turkey was put on discussion (Musabekov 2012: 42). In late 2008, the Moscow Declaration was signed as well. Excluding Turkey; Russia, Armenia and Azerbaijan agreed on sticking to international law and to aim for a political solution to the conflict. "Football Diplomacy" is an example not only for Azerbaijan's agency as such not being limited by Turkey, but even an example for Azerbaijan placing a big bargain and even limiting the agency of bigger Turkey. Balci goes as far as to say that "Turkey's foreign policy towards Armenia is decided, really, in Baku rather than in Ankara" (Balci 2014: 48).

---

order to normalize ties with Armenia, negotiations started at the highest level and were supposed to lead to an opening of the border.

Despite the turmoil about Turkey's "Football Diplomacy" at that time, relations between the countries are too stable and deep to be sustainably disturbed by current problems (Cornell 2011: 389). Nonetheless, Baku does not stand unconditionally by Ankara anymore, as it could be seen during the crisis about the shot down Russian aircraft in 2015/2016. Azerbaijan did not support Turkey's position in the conflict with Russia (Fischer 2016: 84). Although it needs to be said, that Baku helped behind the scenes to reach a rapprochement between Moscow and Ankara in 2016 (Hafizoglu 2016). Overall, Azerbaijan has shown an increasingly high level of agency in the handling of Turkey in recent years. Baku has demonstrated that it can exert substantial influence on Turkey and grew out of the role as a small brother.

Georgian-Turkish Relations: A Marriage of Inconvenience?

Being no Turkic country, Georgia received relatively little attention from Turkey after the dissolution of the Soviet Union. Despite this relatively unambitious start, there are steady mutual connections between both states, shaped by minorities and migration. Two Georgian provinces (Abkhazia and Adjara) have traditionally and persistently complex relations to Ankara and are home to Muslim minorities (Balci 2014: 49). Turkey for its part has big diaspora populations from the entire Caucasus region. It is estimated that Abkhazians living in Turkey outnumber today Abkhazians living in Abkhazia itself (Hill & Taspinar 2006: 19). Turkey stresses officially its rigid support for Georgia's territorial integrity but shows a rather flexible approach to the embargo. There are active trade connections with Abkhazia and through Abkhazia to Russia. Turkish ships heading to Abkhazian ports have been regularly detained by Georgia (Goksel 2013: 4f.). Although the secession is treated as an inner Georgian issue, the Abkhaz diaspora lobbies for a more active Turkish involvement (Gültekin Punsmann 2011: 295). While a majority of authors highlights the activism and impact of the Abkhazian community in Turkey[20], Vinatier argues that the strategic importance of the diaspora is overestimated. He emphasizes that they are quantitatively too small to have any actual effect in Turkish elections and that returning diaspora members have not much influence in Abkhazia either (Vinatier 2009: 83). Turkish activity in Abkhazia is considered to be a problem by parent Georgia. Despite contrary official rhetoric, Turkey does not enforce the isolation of Abkhazia and does not inhibit communication channels between the diaspora, Abkhazia and Turkish officials (Smolnik et al. 2015: 421). This laissez faire attitude by the Turkish government limits Georgia's agency since it cannot enforce to fully control relations to the secessionist entities.

On the other hand, it would be useful to look at the chances Turkish engagement could bring, too. Ankara managed to keep fruitful connections to Abkhazia, without seriously harming its relations with Georgia or Russia. This gives Ankara a unique stance in the conflict (International Crisis Group 2018: 24). A more active Turkish approach and more legal trade could reduce the Abkhazian dependence on Russia's aid, which is the only form of support since the recognition in 2008 resulted in even stronger international isolation (Eissler 2013: 134f.). De Waal points in the same direction. He stresses that an encouraging take towards EWR measures, such as Turkish-Abkhaz trade activity would be more productive for Georgia and the inhabitants of Abkhazia than the recent intended full stop international isolation (Waal 2018: 20).

For Turkey, Georgia's main value stems from its geography and its respective function as a transport corridor. Since the border to Armenia is closed, Georgia is the only land connection to Azerbaijan and further to Central Asia as well as to Russia. For Georgia on the other hand, "Turkey became a 'window overlooking Europe'" (Kononczuk 2008: 32). The isolation of Armenia, although a friendly neighbour of Georgia, provided therefore an exceptional opportunity for Georgia's development, because economically and geographically it would have been more efficient to use the direct

---

20 Exemplary: Smolnik et al. 2018: 568, Balci 2014: 50, Çelikpala 2005: 180, Cornell 2003: 296f.

link Azerbaijan-Armenia-Turkey for the pipelines (Sadri 2003: 188). From 1994[21] onwards, the question of alternative routes for gas and oil to Europe had been discussed actively and Turkey moved into focus as the main energy hub for the distribution to Western Europe, bypassing Russia. Respectively, the idea to build new pipelines took shape and Georgia got "promoted" to be a major transit country.

With the growing importance of Georgia for Turkey, integration between both countries deepened. The main affected policy fields are economy with the Free Trade Agreement (FTA) from 2007; and people to people contacts with visa liberalisations and passport free travel. Those liberalisations go far beyond arrangements between Turkey and Azerbaijan (Kirisci & Moffatt 2015: 74f.). According to Gültekin Punsmann, the recent full openness of the interstate border to human and trade interaction could eventually lead to an integration of the Turkish and Georgian borderland which is comparable to that of the inner-European integration with meaningless national borders (Gültekin Punsmann 2011: 288). Toktaş and Celik elaborate that this creates an asymmetrical, but mutually beneficial situation for both countries, which enables Georgians to work in Turkey and Turkey to profit from Georgian labour migration (Toktaş & Celik 2017: 400f.).

Relations between Turkey and Georgia are flourishing in various fields including economy, infrastructure and security and there is no doubt that Turkey became an essential partner for Georgia. At the same time, their cooperation probably was never a love marriage. Despite free movement of goods and people, the partners don't show a high degree of familiarity with each other. Besides of issues related to Georgia's identity, xenophobia or Turkey's complex relations to Abkhazia and Adjara, Ankara's volatile foreign policy course since the AKP came to power results in certain unease for Tbilisi.

---

21 The Contract of the Century had been concluded between different Western partners, Turkey and to lesser extents Russia in order to enable further exploitation of gas and oil in Azerbaijan.

One main aspect of the Georgian-Turkish relations had been to make use of Turkey's Western orientation and its function as an enabler to enter NATO and the EU. But due to changing dynamics and priorities in Turkish foreign politics, things turned out to be less straightforward. Today, not only Russia, but Turkey as well is an authoritarian power, actively challenging and questioning the norms of the European Union (Fischer & Seufert 2018: 271). The most important developments in this respect are increasing domestic autocracy, growing distance from the West and its institutions and stark rapprochement with Russia. Although these tendencies might complement each other, they do not run in parallel as well. To make it even more complex, there is not only a changing attitude towards NATO and EU within Turkey, but the attitude towards Georgia's accession to those alliances is dynamic as well. Additionally, there is a significant difference between political rhetoric on one hand and institutional realities on the other hand.

If we look at the NATO discourse, initially Turkey had not been in favour of a quick accession, because of its traditional unwillingness to accept any additional NATO or US presence in or around the Black Sea (Weiss & Zabanova 2016: 6). Unlike a large number of researchers, who stress Ankara's significant military aid and training efforts[22], Oskanian describes the support from Turkey for the Georgian military in order to keep up with NATO standards "lukewarm and piecemeal" (Oskanian 2011: 24). This rather unenthusiastic attitude towards Georgia's NATO entry changed when the trilateral pipeline infrastructure cooperation with Azerbaijan was extended by military aspects in 2014. Another turning point came in 2015, when the shooting of a Russian jet by Turkey provoked a severe crisis with Moscow and strengthened the wish in Ankara to limit Russian presence in the Black Sea. This became even more urgent after the annexation of Crimea (Weiss & Zabanova 2016: 2).

---

22 Exemplary: Frahm et al. 2018: 18f., Cecire 2013: 120f., Kononczuk 2008: 38, Çelikpala 2005: 191, Aydin 2004: 12.

Turkey's own commitment to NATO and its support for Georgia's accession is officially not questioned[23] but remains blurred in reality. This is often connected to Ankara's position towards Moscow and the ups and downs of this asymmetric partnership, which produces certain dilemmas for Turkey with respect to its relations to Georgia. During the war in 2008 and afterwards, Turkey refrained from taking Georgia's side in the conflict with Russia (Oskanian 2011: 24). The public discourse in Turkey was highlighting the double standards of US involvement, the miscalculations of Saakashvili and the discomfort of having brought an US-Russian conflict to the immediate neighbourhood (Goksel 2013: 6f.). Might it have been ideological or material interest, Turkey also did not join the EU sanctions against Russia in 2014 as a consequence of the annexation of Crimea. Contradictions of Ankara's policies in the region came to light and demonstrated the "limitations of Turkey's power in its immediate surroundings" (Balci 2014: 50). Loyalty towards Moscow resulted in disappointment in Tbilisi. Georgia's hope for a more proactive involvement of Turkey as a supporter of NATO extension seemed to have been in vain because Ankara did not challenge Moscow's interests in the region (Goksel 2011b: 9).

With regards to EU accession, things do not look less complicated, but more promising for Georgia. The role of Turkey for Georgia's EU entry had been to a lesser extent that of an enabler, but rather that of an argument by itself. The advantages for Georgia to border an EU country would be quite extensive: First, there would be immediate economic and political benefits despite Georgia's own membership (Hill & Taspinar 2006: 17). Second, if Turkey would be in the EU, Georgia's accession would be a geographical continuation of an enlargement area instead of a

---

23   The Turkish Ambassador to Georgia Fatma Seren Yazgan emphasized Turkey's relation to NATO at the South Caucasus Security Forum in Tbilisi in May 2019: *"Turkey is committed to NATO and fully supports Georgia's accession"*. Her Georgian counterpart Irakli Koplatadze in 2018: "*We have excellent relations with Turkey both in bilateral and multilateral formats [and] enjoy each other's support in international forums. Turkey unwaveringly supports Georgia's Euro-Atlantic and NATO aspirations as well as Georgia's sovereignty, territorial integrity and non-recognition policy of Georgia's occupied territories*" (Sevinc 2018).

status as a single geographically detached EU member (Gogolashvili 2018: 125, Kakachia et al. 2018a: 289). The deadlock in the Turkish accession talks is therefore negative for Georgia but doesn't have any actual impact on its cooperation with the EU in the framework of the Eastern Partnership Programme. Although less orientated on actual accession, with the DCFTA and visa free travel in place, Georgia enjoys today more privileges than EU candidate Turkey.

At the end of the day, relations between Ankara and Tbilisi are determined by shared geography rather than by shared ideas or values. Since there is a clear power asymmetry between Georgia and increasingly impulsive Turkey, there is not much room to manoeuvre for the smaller neighbour, who cannot offer brotherhood or energy resources like Azerbaijan. Although Georgia's agency is not directly limited by bigger Turkey, the neighbour turned out to be far less helpful than it was hoped for in the beginning. Still, the neighbours are on their way to deepen integration. But this does not take place in a NATO or EU context like aspired by Georgia. Since the Azerbaijani-Turkish-Georgian triangle is more or less the only game in town for Georgia at the moment; despite a whole range of issues with its western neighbour, Tbilisi has no means but to accept its limited agency in the asymmetric relation to Turkey. Georgia finds itself encircled by illiberal democracies, of which no one is willing to support its foreign policy aim of accession. The new status quo for Georgia results in a certain fatalistic keep-calm-and-carry-on-attitude. Or, as Ajeganov puts it "In the gathering storm, Georgia can do little else but inevitably concede to Turkish demands and prepare for uncertain times ahead" (Ajeganov 2016).

Conclusion

The guiding question in this analysis was how much foreign policy agency parent states Azerbaijan and Georgia do have as small states vis-à-vis Russia and Turkey. Despite the danger of generalisation when comparing both South Caucasian countries with respect to their level of agency, the analysis could show significant differences between both cases in all three introduced agency components (dynamic dimension, external dimension, positive/negative outcomes). For Azerbaijan and Georgia alike, their main similarity smallness has certain implications but does not lead to identical foreign policy goals, strategies or successes. Both countries follow a specific geographical, political and historical vector instead, which defines as well whether their agency is rather high or low. One striking similarity is that the influence they exert does not always show positive outcomes. Particularly in their relations to their secessionist entities, Azerbaijan and Georgia demonstrate a high level of agency, using punitive and non-punitive instruments, but their aim of territorial integrity is still out of reach. In their relation to Russia and Turkey, it could be shown that both states do not always behave like small states, but have moments, where they rather resemble big bargainers with much agency. Taking into account the outcome dimension of agency again, whether the exerted influence led to the desired result, is a completely different question.

Azerbaijan

The country has been very successful in pursuing its goal of independence over time. Baku has consistently been able to refuse integration into Western alliances and Russia-led organisations alike. After a rocky start, Russia represents today rather a role model than a threat. Accordingly, Russia does not use its foreign policy instruments within the category of "controlled instability" towards Azerbaijan. Instead, the Russian model is voluntarily copied by Baku in some of its authoritarian best practices, like the Anti-NGO law. Azerbaijan's ability to exert influence is not limited by Russia and Baku's agency remains therefore high. The same can be said about the fraternal relations to Turkey, where after an enthusiastic start the emphasis shifted from pan-Turkism to the primacy of mutual benefits. Bringing Turkey's initiative to unconditionally open the border to Armenia to an end, Azerbaijan demonstrated a high level of agency vis-à-vis the bigger brother. The influence Baku exerted served its purpose and had a positive outcome. Accordingly, Azerbaijan's agency is not only not limited by Turkey, but also Azerbaijan was able to successfully enforce its interests. Taking all agency dimensions together, Azerbaijan possesses accordingly a high level of agency, despite being a small state.

Georgia

Georgia has not been successful in pursuing its goal of integration into the Western alliances. Despite a high level of rhetoric from all sides, there are no specific plans for Georgia to be granted access neither to NATO nor EU. According to Georgia, the reason for that can be solely found in Russia's aggression. This external attribution turns a blind eye to Georgia's own actions. Saakashvili demonstrated a high level of agency with the assault on South Ossetia, despite expectable Russian interference. But this event did not have any positive outcome for Georgia. Instead, it is not just an example of atypical behaviour for small states; but also precisely a reason for the deadlock in Georgia's accession progress. Using many of its foreign policy instruments in Georgia, Russia has been able to significantly limit Georgia's agency, which accordingly remains rather low. Relations with Turkey are characterized by a low level of Georgian agency as well. Profiting from its geography, benefits from cooperation are obvious, but at the same time dissent with Turkey in various political and societal aspects prevails. This is particularly noticeable since Turkey has increased its anti-Western rhetoric, domestic autocracy and rapprochement with Russia. Since Georgia has no means to affect the situation to its favour, Tbilisi can hardly exert any influence in its relations with Turkey. Overall, Georgia's agency therefore needs to be assessed as rather low.

Both cases show that to categorically equal smallness with weakness is not always correct. We do not necessarily look at a lack of agency of small states, which prevents the realisation of goals. Instead, the inability to achieve a positive outcome with the influence exerted plays an important role as well. Despite a high level of agency, both parent states failed so far to convince

Abkhazia, South Ossetia and Karabakh to return under central control. Pursuing its agenda in relations to neighbouring Turkey and Russia, both countries show very different successes. It could be shown that agency in Azerbaijan's and Georgia's external relations is not a matter of size per se, but a function of the ability to place a bargain, which is accepted by the other players – a task, which is recently better mastered in Baku than in Tbilisi.

Bibliography

Abilov, S. & Isayev, I. (2015). Azerbaijan-Russian relations: Azerbaijan's pursuit of successful balanced foreign policy. *Orta Asya ve Kafkasya Araştırmaları* 9(19): 113–143.

Abushov, K. (2009). Policing the Near Abroad: Russian foreign policy in the South Caucasus. *Australian Journal of International Affairs* 63(2): 187–212.

Adam, L. B. (2013). Turkey's role in the South Caucasus: Can peace be achieved? *Turkish Review* 3(3): 238–243.

Ajeganov, B. (2016). Real friends? Georgia-Turkey relations in the wake of the July 15 coup attempt, *The Central Asia-Caucasus Analyst*, https://www.cacianalyst.org/publications/analytical-articles/item/13388-real-friends?-georgia-turkey-relations-in-the-wake-of-the-july-15-coup-attempt.html (accessed 21 November 2019).

Aleksanyan, L. M. (2017). Turkish-Georgian relations in the context of Turkey's regional policy at the current stage. *Problemy Postsovetskogo Prostranstvo (Post-Soviet Issues)* 4(4): 307–320.

Ambrosio, T. (2016). *Authoritarian backlash. Russian resistance to democratization in the former Soviet Union*. London, New York: Routledge.

Antonopoulos, P., Velez, R. & Cottle, D. (2017). NATO's push into the Caucasus: geopolitical flashpoints and limits for expansion. *Defense & Security Analysis* 33(4): 366–379.

Aras, B. (2017). *Turkish foreign policy after July 15*. Istanbul: Istanbul Policy Center.

Aslani, A. (2010). Azerbaijan-Russia relations: Is the foreign policy strategy of Azerbaijan changing? *Turkish Policy quarterly* 9(9): 137–145.

Aydin, M. (2004). Foucault's Pendulum: Turkey in Central Asia and the Caucasus. *Turkish Studies* 5(2): 1–22.

Babajew, A. (2007). Welchen Weg geht Aserbaidschan? Zwischen „geölter" Westintegration und autoritärer Ostorientierung. *KAS-Auslandsinformationen* 1: 50–72.

Baev, P. K. (2017). Russia: A declining counter-change force. In *The international politics of the Armenian-Azerbaijani conflict. The original "Frozen Conflict" and European security*, Cornell, S. E. (ed.). New York: Palgrave Macmillan, 71–88.

Bailes, A. J., Thayer, B. A. & Thorhallsson, B. (2016). Alliance theory and alliance 'Shelter': The complexities of small state alliance behaviour. *Third World Thematics* 1(1): 9–26.

Balci, B. (2014). Strengths and constraints of Turkish policy in the South Caucasus. *Insight Turkey* 16(2): 43–52.

Baskan, A., Tosun, T. & Ibrahimov, A. (2012). The main parameters of Turkish foreign policy and the post-2008 Central Caucasus. *The Caucasus & Globalization* 6(2): 58–65.

Beacháin, D. Ó. & Coene, F. (2014). Go West: Georgia's European identity and its role in domestic politics and foreign policy objectives. *Nationalities Papers* 42(6): 923–941.

Bláhová, P. (2019). Nagorno-Karabakh: obstacles to the resolution of the frozen conflict. *Asia Europe Journal* 17(1): 69–85.

Blakkisrud, H. & Kolstø, P. (2012). Dynamics of de facto statehood: the South Caucasian de facto states between secession and sovereignty. *Southeast European and Black Sea Studies* 12(2): 281–298.

Bonn International Center for Conversion. Global Militarization Index, *Bonn International Center for Conversion*, https://gmi.bicc.de/index.php?page=ranking-table&year=2018&sort=country_asc (accessed 21 November 2019).

Braun, B., Schindler, S. & Wille, T. (2018). Rethinking agency in International Relations: performativity, performances and actor-networks. *Journal of International Relations and Development* 33(1): 1–21.

Brown, W. (2012). A question of agency: Africa in international politics. *Third World Quarterly* 33(10): 1889–1908.

Bueger, C. & Wivel, A. (2018). How do small island states maximize influence? Creole diplomacy and the smart state foreign policy of the Seychelles. *Journal of the Indian Ocean Region* 14(2): 170–188.

Caspersen, N. (2018). Recognition, Status Quo or Reintegration: Engagement with de facto States. *Ethnopolitics* 17(4): 373–389.

Cecire, M. H. (2013). The Merchant Hegemon: Georgia's role in Turkey's Caucasus system. In *Georgian foreign policy. The quest for sustainable security*, Kakachia, K. & Cecire, M. H. (eds.). Tbilisi: Konrad Adenauer Stiftung, 111–124.

Çelikpala, M. (2005). From a failed state to a weak one? Georgia and Turkish-Georgian relations. *The Turkish Yearbook* 35: 159–199.

Chernjavskij, S. (2013). *Desjat' let istorii Azerbajdzhana 2003–2013 gody [Ten years of history of Azerbaijan from 2003-2013]*. Moskva: Izdatel'stvo "Flinta".

Cooley, A. (2012). *Great games, local rules. The new great power contest in central Asia*. New York: Oxford University Press.

Cooley, A. (2017). Whose rules, whose sphere? Russian governance and influence in post-Soviet states, *Carnegie Endowment for International Peace*, https://carnegieendowment.org/2017/06/30/whose-rules-whose-sphere-russian-governance-and-influence-in-post-soviet-states-pub-71403 (accessed 21 November 2019).

Cornell, S. E. (2003). *Small nations and great powers. A study of ethnopolitical conflict in the Caucasus*. Reprinted. Richmond: Curzon.

Cornell, S. E. (2011). *Azerbaijan since independence*. Armonk, New York: M.E. Sharpe.

Cornell, S. E. (2014). *Getting Georgia right*. Brussels: Centre for European Studies.

Cornell, S. E. (2018). The impact of Ukraine and Syria conflicts on the geopolitics of the South Caucasus. In *Geopolitics and security. A new strategy for the South Caucasus*, Kakachia, K., Meister, S. & Fricke, B. (eds.). Tbilisi: Konrad Adenauer Stiftung, 231-265.

Dalacoura, K. (2017). A new phase in Turkish foreign policy: Expediency and AKP survival, *CIDOB - Barcelona Center for International Affairs*, http://www.menaraproject.eu/portfolio-items/a-new-phase-in-turkish-foreign-policy-expediency-and-akp-survival/ (accessed 21 November 2019).

de Waal, T. (2008). South Ossetia: the avoidable tragedy, *Open Democracy Foundation*, https://www.opendemocracy.net/article/south-ossetia-the-avoidable-tragedy (accessed 21 November 2019).

de Waal, T. (2017). Enhancing the EU's Engagement with Separatist Territories, *Carnegie Europe*, https://carnegieendowment.org/files/DeWaal_EU_Engagement_with_Seperatist_Territories.pdf (accessed 21 November 2019).

de Waal, T. (2018). *Uncertain ground. Engaging with Europe's de facto states and breakaway territories*. Washington D.C.: Carnegie Europe.

de Waal, T. (2019). Why the Long Conflict Over Nagorno-Karabakh Could Heat Up Again, *World Politics Review*, https://www.worldpoliticsreview.com/articles/28275/why-the-long-conflict-over-nagorno-karabakh-could-heat-up-again (accessed 21 November 2019).

Dikkaya, M. & Strakes, J. E. (2017). A paradigm shift in Turkish-Azerbaijani relations? Result for Turkish Armenian reconciliation process between 2008 and 2010. *Review of Socio-Economic Perspectives* 2(1): 84–102.

Eissler, E. C. (2013). Can Turkey de-isolate Abkhazia? *Turkish Policy quarterly* 12(3): 125–135.

Elman, M. F. (1995). The foreign policies of small states: challenging neorealism in its own backyard. *British Journal of Political Science* 25(2): 171–217.

Emirbayer, M. & Mische, A. (1998). What is agency? *American Journal of Sociology* 103(4): 962–1023.

Fischer, S. (2016). *Nicht eingefroren! Die ungelösten Konflikte um Transnistrien, Abchasien, Südossetien und Berg-Karabach im Lichte der Krise um die Ukraine*. Berlin: Stiftung Wissenschaft und Politik.

Fischer, S. & Seufert, G. (2018). Transformation misslungen Die EU, Russland und die Türkei. *Osteuropa* 68(10/12): 271–290.

Frahm, O., Hoffmann, K. & Lehmkuhl, D. (2018). Turkey and the Eastern Partnership: Turkey's foreign policy towards its post-Soviet Black Sea neighbourhood. *EU-STRAT Working Paper* 13: 3–46.

Freire, M. R. (2010). Eurasia at the heart of Russian politics: dynamics of (in)dependence in a complex setting. In *Key players and regional dynamics in Eurasia. The return of the 'Great Game'*, Freire, M. R. & Kanet, R. E. (eds.). Houndmills, Basingstoke, Hampshire, New York: Palgrave Macmillan, 55-78.

Gaber, E. (2011). Turkey in the Caucasus and Central Asia: The post-Soviet period. *Central Asia and the Caucasus* 12(3): 138–147.

Gahrton, P. (2010). *Georgia. Pawn in the new Great Game*. London: Pluto Press.

Gegeshidze, A. & Haindrava, I. (2011). *Transformation of the Georgian-Abkhaz conflict: rethinking the paradigm*. Tbilisi: Georgian Foundation for Strategic and International Studies.

Gianjumian, V. (2014). Turkish policy in the southern Caucasus. *Central Asia and the Caucasus* 15(3): 103–111.

Gibert, M. V. & Grzelczyk, V. (2016). Non-Western small states: activists or survivors? *Third World Thematics* 1(1): 1–8.

Gigleux, V. (2016). Explaining the diversity of small states' foreign policies through role theory. *Third World Thematics* 1(1): 27–45.

Gogolashvili, K. (2018). In search of the European perspective: Georgia after the Association Agreement. In *Geopolitics and security. A new strategy for the South Caucasus*, Kakachia, K., Meister, S. & Fricke, B. (eds.). Tbilisi: Konrad Adenauer Stiftung, 101-127.

Goksel, N. (2011a). Turkey's Caucasus policies in the framework of Ankara's new foreign policy. *Caucasus Analytical Digest* 30: 5-7.

Goksel, N. (2011b). Turkish policy towards the Caucasus: A Balance Sheet of the Balancing Act. *Black Sea Discussion Paper Series*(1): 1-26.

Goksel, N. (2013). Turkey and Georgia: Zero-problems? *On Wider Europe:* 1-8.

Government of Azerbaijan (2007). National Security Concept of the Republic of Azerbaijan, *Government of Azerbaijan*, https://www.files.ethz.ch/isn/154917/Azerbaijan2007.pdf (accessed 21 November 2019).

Government of Georgia (2018). National Security Concept of Georgia, *Government of Georgia*, https://mod.gov.ge/uploads/2018/pdf/NSC-ENG.pdf (accessed 21 November 2019).

Gül, M. (2008). Russia and Azerbaijan: Relations after 1989. *Alternatives: Turkish Journal of International Relations* 7(2&3): 47-66.

Gültekin Punsmann, B. (2011). Turkey's interest and strategies in the South Caucasus. In *South Caucasus. 20 years of independence*, Friedrich-Ebert-Stiftung (ed.). Tbilisi: Friedrich-Ebert-Stiftung, 280-299.

Guluzade, M. & Bourjaily, N. (2014). Overview of the changes to NGO legislation adopted on 17 December 2013 by the parliament of the Republic of Azerbaijan, http://dev01.icnl.org/programs/eurasia/Overview%20of%20Dec%2017%20Law.pdf (accessed 21 November 2019).

Gvalia, G., Siroky, D., Lebanidze, B. & Iashvili, Z. (2013). Thinking outside the bloc. Explaining the foreign policies of small states. *Security Studies* 22(1): 98-131.

Hafizoglu, R. (2016). Davutoglu: Azerbaijan contributes to normalization of Turkey-Russia relations, *Azernews*, https://en.trend.az/world/turkey/2563306.html (accessed 21 November 2019).

Halbach, U. (1999). Moskaus Südpolitik: Russland und der Westen im Kaspischen Raum. *Berichte/BIOst* 30: 3-43.

Halbach, U. & Smolnik, F. (2014). Russlands Stellung im Südkaukasus. *SWP-Aktuell* 1: 1-8.

Handel, M. I. (1981). *Weak states in the international system*. London: Cass.

Hill, F. & Taspinar, O. (2006). Russia and Turkey in the Caucasus: Moving together to preserve the status quo? *Russie.Nei.Visions* 8: 1-19.

Hofferberth, M. (2019). Get your act(ors) together! Theorizing agency in global governance. *International Studies Review* 21(1): 127-145.

Hooper, M. (2016). Russia's bad example, *Free Russia Foundation*, https://www.4freerussia.org/russias-bad-example-read-the-report/ (accessed 21 November 2019).

Huseynov, V. (2016). The foreign policy of post-Soviet Georgia: Strategic idealism and the Russian challenge. *Caucasus International* 5(3): 117-131.

Ingebritsen, C. (2002). Norm Entrepreneurs. Scandinavia's Role in World Politics. *Cooperation and Conflict* 37(1): 11-23.

International Crisis Group (2018). *Russia and Turkey in the Black Sea and the South Caucasus*. Brussels: International Crisis Group.

Isachenko, D. (2012). *The making of informal states. Statebuilding in Northern Cyprus and Transdniestria*. London: Palgrave Macmillan.

Ismailzade, F. (2005). Turkey-Azerbaijan: The honeymoon is over. *Turkish Policy quarterly* 79(4): 1-11.

Iunusov, A. S. (2003). Migration in post-Soviet Azerbaijan. *Russian Politics and Law* 41(3): 69-83.

Jackson, A. (2010). The limits of good intentions: The Caucasus as a test case for Turkish foreign policy. *Turkish Policy quarterly* 9(4): 81-92.

Jemil', S. & Lija, J. (2012). Dve pozicii v Nagorno-Karabahskoj vojne:Rossija i Turcija (1990-1994 gg.) [Two Positions in the Nagorno-Karabakh War: Russia and Turkey (1990-1994)]. *Central'naja Azija i Kavkaz* 15(4): 7-24.

Kadir Has University (2017). Kadir Has University announces the 2017 results of the survey on Turkish foreign policy, *Kadir Has University*, http://www.khas.edu.tr/en/news/270 (accessed 21 November 2019).

Kakachia, K. (2012). Georgia's identity-driven foreign policy and the struggle for its European destiny. *Caucasus Analytical Digest* 37: 4-7.

Kakachia, K., Meister, S. & Fricke, B. (2018a). Conclusion. In *Geopolitics and security. A new strategy for the South Caucasus*, Kakachia, K., Meister, S. & Fricke, B. (eds.). Tbilisi: Konrad Adenauer Stiftung, 283-293.

Kakachia, K. & Minesashvili, S. (2015). Identity politics. Exploring Georgian foreign policy behavior. *Journal of Eurasian Studies* 6(2): 171-180.

Kakachia, K., Minesashvili, S. & Kakhishvili, L. (2018b). Change and continuity in the foreign policies of small states. Elite perceptions and Georgia's foreign policy towards Russia. *Europe-Asia Studies* 70(5): 814-831.

Karademir, H. S. (2017). Poisk metodov reshenija politicheskih voporosov na juzhnom Kavkase [Searching for methods to solve political questions in the South Caucasus]. *Krasnoyarsk Science* 6(2): 80-87.

Kassab, H. S. (2015). *Weak states in International Relations Theory*. New York: Palgrave Macmillan US.

Kelkitli, F. A. (2017). *Turkish-Russian relations. Competition and cooperation in Eurasia*. London, New York: RoutledgeTaylor & Francis Group.

Ker-Lindsay, J. (2014). Understanding state responses to secession. *Peacebuilding* 2(1): 28–44.

Ker-Lindsay, J. & Berg, E. (2018). Introduction: A Conceptual Framework for Engagement with de facto States. *Ethnopolitics* 17(4): 335–342.

Kirisci, K. & Moffatt, A. (2015). Turkey and the South Caucasus: An opportunity for soft regionalism? In *Regional security issues 2015*, Novikova, G. (ed.). Yerevan: Spektrum, 67-88.

Kononczuk, W. (2008). A Caucasian ally? Turkish-Georgian relations. In *Turkey after the start of negotiations with the European Union – foreign relations and the domestic situation*, Balcer, A. (ed.). Warsaw: CES Report, 31–40.

Levine, K. (2016). Legislating against foreign funding of human rights – A tool of repression in the former Soviet Union, *The Foreign Policy Centre*, https://fpc.org.uk/legislating-foreign-funding-human-rights-tool-repression-former-soviet-union/ (accessed 21 November 2019).

Lipman, M. (2006). Putin's "Sovereign Democracy", *Carnegie Moscow Center*, https://carnegie.ru/2006/07/15/putin-s-sovereign-democracy-pub-18540 (accessed 21 November 2019).

Long, T. (2016). Small states, great power? Gaining influence through intrinsic, derivative, and collective power. *International Studies Review* 38(5): 1–21.

Lupu, M. R. & Wivel, A. (2014). Caught in the outskirts of Europe: Georgia and Moldova. In *Small states and international security. Europe and beyond*, Archer, C., Bailes, A. J. & Wivel, A. (eds.). Hoboken: Taylor and Francis, 149-166.

Maass, M. (2009). The elusive definition of the small state. *International Politics* 46(1): 65–83.

Manutscharjan, A. (2007). Russlands Politik im Süd-Kaukasus. *KAS-Auslandsinformationen:* 28–73.

Markedonov, S. (2015). Rossija v konfliktah: est' li logika v dejstvijah Kremlja? [Russia in conflicts: is there any logic in the actions of the Kremlin?], https://www.mk.ru/politics/2015/10/15/rossiya-v-konfliktakh-est-li-logika-v-deystviyakh-kremlya.html (accessed 21 November 2019).

Markedonov, S. (2018). Kompetitive Kooperation Russland und die Türkei im Kaukasus. *Osteuropa* 68(10/12): 353–365.

Markedonov, S. & Suchkov, M. A. (2015). The Caucasus after Ukraine, *The American Interest*, https://www.the-american-interest.com/2015/01/06/the-caucasus-after-ukraine/ (accessed 21 November 2019).

Mearsheimer, J. J. (2003). *The tragedy of great power politics*. London: W. W. Norton & Company.

Mehdiyeva, N. (2011). *Power games in the Caucasus. Azerbaijan's foreign and energy policy towards the West, Russia and the Middle East*. London: I.B.Tauris.

Morfini, N. (2010). Azerbaijan as a regional leader: A stronger Turkish-Azeri policy on the southern Caucasus? *Uluslararası Hukuk ve Politika* 24: 145-148.

Musabekov, R. (2012). Azerbajdzhan mezhdu Turciej i Rossiej [Azerbaijan between Turkey and Russia]. *Rossija i Musul'manskij Mir* 235(1): 40-51.

Neumann, I. B. & de Carvalho, B. (2015). Introduction: Small states and status. In *Small states and status seeking. Norway's quest for international standing*, Neumann, I. B. & de Carvalho, B. (eds.). London, New York: Routledge, 1-21.

Nodia, G. (2017). Democracy and its deficits: The path towards becoming European-style democracies in Georgia, Moldova and Ukraine. *CEPS Working Document:* 1-27.

O'Loughlin, J., Toal, G. & Kolossov, V. (2017). Who identifies with the "Russian World"? Geopolitical attitudes in southeastern Ukraine, Crimea, Abkhazia, South Ossetia, and Transnistria. *Eurasian Geography and Economics* 57(6): 1-34.

Onis, Z. (2001). Turkey and post-Soviet states: Potential and limits of regional power influence. *Middle East Review of International Affairs* 5(2): 66-74.

Orttung, R. & Walker, C. (2015). Putin's frozen conflicts, *Foreign Policy*, https://foreignpolicy.com/2015/02/13/putins-frozen-conflicts/ (accessed 21 November 2019).

Oskanian, K. (2011). Turkey's global strategy: Turkey and the Caucasus. *LSE IDEAS:* 23-27.

Oskanian, K. (2013). *Fear, weakness and power in the post-Soviet South Caucasus. A theoretical and empirical analysis*. New York: Palgrave Macmillan.

Oskanian, K. (2014). *Balancing a tightrope: Constraints, possibilities and ideology in Georgian foreign policy, 1991-2014*. Paper presented at the 2014 UACES Conference, Cork/Ireland.

Oskanian, K. (2016). The Balance Strikes Back. Power, perceptions, and ideology in Georgian foreign policy, 1992-2014. *Foreign Policy Analysis* 2(0): 1-25.

Owen, C., Heathershaw, J. & Savin, I. (2018). How postcolonial is post-Western IR? Mimicry and mētis in the international politics of Russia and Central Asia. *Review of International Studies* 44(2): 279-300.

Pestrecov, A. R. & Babirov, I. M. (2017). Azerbajdzhano-Tureckie otnoshenija: dostizhenija i problemy [The Azerbaijani-Turkish relations: achievements and problems]. *Jelektronnyj nauchnyj zhurnal Kurskogo gosudarstvennogo universiteta* 41(1): 1–7.

Prelz Oltramonti, G. (2015). The political economy of a de facto state: the importance of local stakeholders in the case of Abkhazia. *Caucasus Survey* 3(3): 291–308.

Radnitz, S. (2019). Reinterpreting the enemy: Geopolitical beliefs and the attribution of blame in the Nagorno-Karabakh conflict. *Political Geography* 70: 64–73.

Roehrs-Weist, P. (2018). Thomas de Waal: NATO membership is not necessarily essential for Georgia, *Caucasuswatch*, http://caucasus watch.de/news/1154.html (accessed 21 November 2019).

Rogstad, A. (2017). The next Crimea? Getting Russia's Transnistria policy right. *Problems of Post-Communism* 60(1): 1–16.

Rywkin, M. (2016). Russia and the Near Abroad under Putin. *American Foreign Policy Interests* 37(4): 229–237.

Sadri, H. (2003). Elements of Azerbaijan foreign policy. *Journal of Third World Studies* 20(1): 179–192.

Sevinc, Ö. (2018). Georgian envoy praises Turkey for supporting country's territorial integrity, *Daily Sabah*, https://www.dailysabah.com/diplomacy/2018/03/01/georgian-envoy-praises-turkey-for-supporting-countrys-territorial-integrity (accessed 21 November 2019).

Shirinov, R. (2012). Azerbaijan's foreign policy: seeking a balance. *Caucasus Analytical Digest* 37: 2–4.

Siroky, D. S., Simmons, A. J. & Gvalia, G. (2017). Vodka or Bourbon? Foreign policy preferences toward Russia and the United States in Georgia. *Foreign Policy Analysis* 13: 500–518.

Smith Stegen, K. & Kusznir, J. (2015). Outcomes and strategies in the 'New Great Game': China and the Caspian states emerge as winners. *Journal of Eurasian Studies* 6(2): 91–106.

Smolnik, F., Weiss, A. & Zabanova, Y. (2015). Prekäre Balance. Die Türkei, Georgien und der De-facto-Staat Abchasien. *Osteuropa* 65(7): 407–426.

Smolnik, F., Weiss, A. & Zabanova, Y. (2018). Political space and borderland practices in Abkhazia and Adjara: Exploring the role of Ottoman legacies and contemporary Turkish influences. *Eurasian Geography and Economics* 58(5): 557–581.

Strakes, J. E. (2015). Azerbaijan and the Non-Aligned Movement: Institutionalizing the "Balanced Foreign Policy" doctrine. *IAI Working papers* 15: 1–24.

Strakes, J. E. (2016). Incapacity, endowment, and ambivalence: deciphering Azerbaijan's regional leadership strategy. In *Diplomatic strategies of nations in the Global South. The search for leadership*, Braveboy-Wagner, J. (ed.). New York: Palgrave Macmillan US, 293-318.

Ter-Matevosyan, V. (2013). Framing national security objectives: The cases of Georgia and Azerbaijan. *Southeast European and Black Sea Studies* 13(3): 325-340.

The Caucasus Research Resource Center (2013). Main friend of the country, *The Caucasus Research Resource Center*, http://caucasusbarometer.org/en/cb2013az/MAINFRN/ (accessed 21 November 2019).

Thorhallsson, B. & Bailes, A. J. (2017). Do small states need 'Alliance Shelter'? Scotland and the Nordic Nations. In *Security in a small nation: Scotland, democracy, politics*, Neal, A. W. (ed.). Cambridge: Open Book Publishers, 49-76.

Toal, G. (2008). Russia's Kosovo: A critical geopolitics of the August 2008 war over South Ossetia. *Eurasian Geography and Economics* 49(6): 670-705.

Toal, G. (2017). *Near Abroad. Putin, the West and the contest over Ukraine and the Caucasus*. Oxford: Oxford University Press.

Toal, G. & O'Loughlin, J. (2014). How people in South Ossetia, Abkhazia and Transnistria feel about annexation by Russia, http://www.washingtonpost.com/blogs/monkey-cage/wp/2014/03/20/how-people-in-south-ossetia-abkhazia-and-transnistria-feel-about-annexation-by-russia/ (accessed 21 November 2019).

Toktaş, Ş. & Celik, N. (2017). Border crossings between Georgia and Turkey. The Sarp land border gate. *Geopolitics* 22(2): 383-406.

Torbakov, I. (2010). Russia and Turkish-Armenian normalization: Competing interests in the South Caucasus. *Insight Turkey* 12(2): 31-39.

Tsygankov, A. P. (2016). *Russia's foreign policy. Change and continuity in national identity*. Fourth edition. Lanham: Rowman & Littlefield.

Valiyev, A. (2011). Azerbaijan-Russia relations after the five-day war: Friendship, enmity, or pragmatism? *Turkish Policy quarterly* 10(3): 133-143.

Valiyev, A. (2014). The Ukrainian crisis and implications for Azerbaijan. *Caucasus Analytical Digest* 67-68: 11-13.

Veliyev, C. (2015). Turkey's role in the South Caucasus: between fragmentation and integration. In *The South Caucasus. Between integration and fragmentation*, Center for Strategic Studies under the President of the Republic of Azerbaijan & European Policy Centre (eds.)., 85-94.

Vinatier, L. (2009). Between Russia and the West: Turkey as an emerging power and the case of Abkhazia. *China and Eurasia Forum Quarterly* 7(4): 73-94.

Walt, S. M. (1987). *The origins of alliances*. Ithaca: Cornell University Press.

Weiss, A. & Zabanova, Y. (2016). Georgia and Abkhazia caught between Turkey and Russia. Turkey's changing relations with Russia and the West in 2015-2016 and their impact on Georgia and Abkhazia. *SWP-Comments* 54: 1-8.

Wight, C. (2006). *Agents, structures and international relations. Politics as ontology*. Cambridge: Cambridge University Press.

Wivel, A. (2016). Living on the edge: Georgian foreign policy between the West and the rest. *Third World Thematics* 1(1): 92-109.

Wivel, A., Bailes, A. J. & Archer, C. (2014). Setting the scene: Small states and international security. In *Small states and international security. Europe and beyond*, Archer, C., Bailes, A. J. & Wivel, A. (eds.). Hoboken: Taylor and Francis, 3-25.

Wohlforth, W. C. (2010). Revisiting balance of power theory in Central Eurasia. In *Balance of power. Theory and practice in the 21st century*, Paul, T. V., Wirtz, J. J. & Fortmann, M. (eds.). Stanford: Stanford University Press, 214-238.

Yesilkaya, Ö. (2006). "The Great Game" im Kaukasus: das neue Strategiespiel zweier ungleicher Akteure. Der schwierige Spagat eines Interessenausgleichs zwischen den USA und der Türkei. *KFIBS-Analysis:* 1-13.

War and State-Making in Ukraine
Forging a Civic Identity from Below?

Gwendolyn Sasse and Alice Lackner

Introduction

In the 2019 presidential elections, the incumbent president Petro Poroshenko campaigned on the slogan 'Army. Language. Faith', thereby explicitly linking the experience of war with the status of the Ukrainian language and the newly created Ukrainian Orthodox Church. The slogan summarized the increasing securitization of identity issues and state policies in the context of war. The fact that Poroshenko was defeated by Volodymyr Zelenskyy, an openly Russian-speaking and politically inexperienced candidate campaigning on little more than the slogan of 'unity' across Ukraine, promising peace and an end to corruption, highlights the limitations of the state identity projected onto society by the Ukrainian government and parliament in recent years.

By tracing changes in public attitudes across Ukraine based on original survey data from 2017 and 2018, this chapter shows that the election result is neither a complete surprise nor irrational behavior on the part of the electorate. Instead, it has deeper roots in societal perceptions of the Ukrainian state. The cross-sectional data at the heart of the analysis presented is from the regular nationally representative KIIS survey (without Crimea and the non-government-controlled territories), supplemented by specific questions commissioned by the Centre for East European and International Studies (ZOiS).

In this chapter we focus on two major issues: people's self-reported identities, and on the attitudes regarding the future political status of the Donbas, a question that goes to the heart of peace-making but also relates to the conception of the territorial and political make-up of the Ukrainian state. The issue of autonomy or 'special status' is a highly sensitive one in Ukraine. It is closely connected to the idea of state sovereignty. The Ukrainian government has been opposed to the concept of autonomy, though the 2015 Minsk Agreement contains a provision for a 'special status' for specified territories in the non-government-controlled areas. Russia's support for the self-declared people's republics of Donetsk and Luhansk and its repeated calls for the federalization of Ukraine have further eroded the political space in Ukraine for a discussion about decentralization at the regional level. Nevertheless, ideas about autonomy and decentralization are typical elements of peace agreements and the management of conflict-potential more generally. Therefore, public opinion on these issues helps to gauge the scope for political solutions to the war in eastern Ukraine and the underpinnings of identities during war.

This paper contributes to the study of the effects of war on societies and states. Tilly's famous dictum about the close link between war-making and state-making refers to the effects of war on central state capacity and the monopoly over violence. However, wars also shape the attitudes and identities of people experiencing challenges to the territorial integrity of their state. This is our focus in this chapter.

We proceed as follows: we first provide an overview of the literature on cleavages in Ukraine and the broader comparative literature on the effects of war on identity and statehood. Ultimately, we seek an answer to the question if identities change during war and engage with the polarization hypothesis that characterizes much of the literature on war: does the experience of war bring about or reinforce a polarization of (ethnic) identities? We find that even within a single year during a war, identities can change significantly. From 2017 to 2018 a 'Ukrainian ethnic identity' has been replaced as the primary identity by a civic identity centred on the more inclusive notion of Ukrainian citizenship. This identity shift maps an element of state-building from below that goes against the polarization hypothesis in the study of war and, more specifically, against the official state rhetoric during the Poroshenko presidency (2014–19).

Similarly, Ukrainian society has become more open to different notions of autonomy, even though the majority of people still prefers the *status quo ante* without any special status for parts of the Donbas or other regions of Ukraine. Together, these changes in public opinion help to explain the outcome of the 2019 presidential elections where ethno-linguistic cleavages and the war in eastern Ukraine failed to mobilize voters for the incumbent president.

The Effects of War on Identities

In the study of war, the consequences of war have been given less attention than the causes of war. Scholars have acknowledged that potential identity shifts amidst war or in its aftermath remain insufficiently explored (Esteban and Schneider 2002; Kalyvas 2008; Sambanis 2002; Wood 2015). Ethnic, regional and other political identities can be an important part of mobilization for war, and, in turn, war puts these identities to a test. A war setting provides a window onto the dynamics of identity shifts (Onuch, Hale & Sasse 2018). The hypothesis that war reinforces divisive identities resulting in an increase in polarization along the conflict lines is widespread, but often remains unsubstantiated in the absence of data collection during war (Posner 1993; Esteban & Schneider 2000; Fearon & Laitin 2003; Gurr 2000). However, empirical research on Bosnia and Herzegovina and Croatia, for example, has shown that those directly affected by war do not become more ethnonationalist (Dyrstad 2012; Massey et al. 2003; Sekulic 2004), thereby calling the polarization thesis into question. In the case of Ukraine, recent survey data has also revealed that the experience of war does not only streamline identities, but can maintain or even reinforce mixed identities (Sasse & Lackner 2018).

Wars and state-building are intertwined processes. Tilly's phrase about "wars making states, and states making war" is a frequent reference point in this regard (Tilly 1985). Scholars before and after him have tried to spell out parts of this dynamic interrelationship (e.g. Cohen et al. 1981; Coggins 2014). Tilly's focus was on the formation of the modern European state but his thesis has been applied both as a loose description and a research hypothesis to contemporary cases in and beyond Europe. Some scholars have criticized the overstretching of Tilly's argument, while emphasizing the detrimental effects of war on states as well as the greater importance of non-state actors in contemporary wars (e.g. Leander 2004). This strand of research is related to the vast literature on 'state capture' and 'state failure'. In the public debate the term 'failed state' is at times used when discussing Ukraine, but we do not consider the term an adequate concept framing contemporary developments in Ukraine.

Building on the two key strands of Tilly's work, Tarrow tried to link the politics of contention to the study of war (Tarrow 2015). His focus was on the role of contention in the mobilization for war — though he also briefly referred to the possibility of preventing war through mobilization — and the emergence of movements and contention in the aftermath of war rather than the dynamics during war. In this chapter our emphasis is not on organized social movements, but on the conflict-defusing and state-building potential reflected in societal attitudes.

An increasing number of scholars have concentrated on post-war state-building. Scholars working on different conflicts around the globe have pointed to a critical commitment problem at the heart of conflict-related security dilemma (e.g. Coyne & Boettke 2009; Keefer 2008; Posen 1993; Walter 2002). In particular, the scope and limitations of public trust in post-war settings have attracted more scholarly attention in recent years (De Juan & Pierskalla 2016; Wong 2016). Research on the long-term effects of external and internal conflicts has found that violent conflict tends to embed low institutional and inter-group trust in society (Grosjean 2014). This finding is in line with the hypothesized hardening of identities undermining a sense of civic unity.

More recently, survey research has helped to spell out the dynamics behind the lack of public trust in the new or old authorities providing security and public goods, linking them to instability and further violence (Bakke et al., 2018; Blair 2016; Blattman 2009; Cassar et al. 2013; De Juan & Pierskalla 2016). However, another strand of research focusing on the implications of war on the prospects for democratization has also highlighted that war-related experiences do not have to inhibit and can even foster democratization (Bermeo 2003, 2007; Jarstad & Sisk 2008; Roeder & Rothchild 2005; Zürcher et al. 2013).

From the as yet inconclusive literature on the effects of war, our analysis engages with the three dominant and interrelated hypotheses discussed above: the polarization of identities during war, the mobilization for war, and the erosion of public trust or a sense of a shared polity. Our analysis departs from the bulk of the literature that is concerned with the aftermath of war, and instead explores the dynamics of state-building *during* war.

Identity and Cleavages in Ukraine

Identities are multi-layered and changeable categories (Brubaker 2009; Fearon & Laitin 2000; Hale 2004), though the moment and nature of identity shifts is difficult to pinpoint empirically. Political crises have the potential to disrupt and reassemble identities and provide scholars with a window to study these processes (Onuch, Hale & Sasse 2018).

As a result of its history, the Ukrainian state in its post-1991 boundaries is characterized by regional, ethnic, linguistic, socio-economic and political diversity. Scholars have analysed and argued over the electoral and general political salience of individual cleavages, in particular the role of language, ethnicity and region (e.g. Arel 1995, 2014; Barrington 2002; Barrington & Faranda 2009; Birch 2000; Bremmer 1994; D'Anieri 2007; Frye 2015; Holdar 1995; Lushnycky & Riabchuk 2009; Kubicek 2000; Kulyk 2011; Osipian & Osipian 2012; Pirie 1996; Shevel 2002, 2009; Zimmermann 1998). The conditions under which particular cleavages gain in importance remain underexplored, although scholars have warned against seeing Ukrainian politics solely through the prism of ethnicity and language (Kulyk 2014) or equating "region" with these cleavages (Sasse 2010, Shulman 2004).

Research on the dynamics of the Euromaidan protests has shown that language or ethnicity was not a significant factor shaping political attitudes and action (Onuch & Sasse 2016). In a similar vein, it has been argued that the political developments since 2013 have strengthened the sense of political unity and state identity in Ukraine, including a higher regard for the Ukrainian language as the symbolic marker of this state identity (Alexseev 2015; Kulyk 2016, 2018).

In our analysis, we probe the relative importance of different cleavages in times of war and test the polarization hypothesis drawn from the literature on war vs. the recent suggestion that a civic state identity and identification with the Ukrainian language have become more important as a result of the political developments since 2013.

Data and Methodology

The survey data at the heart of this chapter was collected by the Kyiv International Institute of Sociology (KIIS). KIIS regularly conducts a cross-sectional all-Ukrainian public opinion poll 'Opinions and Views of Ukrainian People'. For the KIIS surveys in May–June 2017 and May–June 2018, the Centre for Eastern European and International Studies (ZOiS) commissioned a set of specific questions asking about people's identity, native language, views related to the war in Donbas, and personal ties to Russia and the EU. KIIS applies a stratified random sample design, and interviews were held with respondents from 110 settlements in Ukraine (2017: 2,040 respondents; 2018: 2,025 respondents). The data was weighted for gender, six age groups, four macro regions and urban/rural to adjust for socio-demographic differences between the samples and the overall population.

Dependent Variables. This chapter is concerned with potential changes in public opinion in Ukraine between 2017 and 2018. Our analysis focuses on the following issues: ethnic, civic and linguistic identity, and attitudes towards the war in Donbas and the Minsk Agreement. Corresponding question items on these issues were operationalized as the dependent variables in our regression analysis.

Respondents were asked to choose the identity most important to them from a list of ten different options, such as

'Ukrainian citizen', 'ethnic Ukrainian'[1], 'ethnic Russian', 'European' etc. From this list, 'Ukrainian citizen' and 'ethnic Ukrainian' emerged as the most frequent choices. Each of these two answers was recoded as a dummy variable. With regard to the symbolic category 'native language', respondents could choose between 'Ukrainian', 'Russian', 'both' or 'other'. As before, dummy variables were generated for each answer category.

Another question inserted by ZOiS into the KIIS survey tried to gauge the respondents' views about the status for the non-government-controlled areas and the Donbas region as a whole. Respondents were presented various statements on what should be done, and they had to choose the one with which they agreed most. The categories included options ranging from 'give the occupied territories the same status as before the war' to 'give up on the occupied territories and let them be officially or unofficially administered by Russia'.[2] Four statements were used in the regression analysis: "Give the occupied territories the same status as before"; "Give the occupied territories a temporary autonomy status within Ukraine"; "Give the occupied territories a permanent autonomy status within Ukraine"; and "Give up on the occupied territories and let them be officially or unofficially administered by

---

[1] We deliberately chose the category 'ethnic Ukrainian' to juxtapose an ethnic identity with a civic identity linked to Ukrainian citizenship. Although the reference to ethnicity is a more recent addition to the Ukrainian- and Russian-language discourse about identities and may not be the wording chosen by respondents in open-ended questions, we wanted to introduce a clear distinction rather than risking conceptual confusion when using the widespread term 'nationality' (natsional'nist'), In the Soviet era, the term 'nationality' had a stronger ethnic connotation but it seems to have moved towards a more civic understanding over time (Kulyk 2016, 2018).

[2] Question: "In your view, what should the government do in response to the situation in the Donbas?" Answer categories: 1 "Give the occupied territories the same status as other region"; 2 "Give the occupied territories extended rights in comparison with other regions of Ukraine"; 3 "Give the whole of Donbas, including the occupied territories, extended rights in comparison with other regions of Ukraine"; 4 "Give the occupied territories a temporary autonomy status within Ukraine"; 5 "Give the occupied territories a permanent autonomy status within Ukraine"; 6 "Give the whole of Donbas, including the occupied territories, an autonomy status"; 7 "Give all oblasts of Ukraine an autonomy status"; 8 "Give up on the occupied territories and let them be officially or unofficially be administered by Russia".

Russia". The statements were recoded as dummy variables, with a 1 for everyone agreeing with a given statement, and a 0 for everyone who had chosen a different statement.

In order to measure attitudes towards the Minsk Agreement, respondents were asked to what extent they agreed with the following statements:

1. 'The Minsk process is slow, but there is no alternative to this attempt at conflict-resolution.'
2. 'Without the Minsk process there would not have been any ceasefire and the death toll would have been higher.'
3. 'Ukraine should stop participating in the Minsk negotiations as the framework demands more of Ukraine than of Russia.'
4. 'A new international format is needed that includes the US.'

The reactions to the Minsk-related questions drew on a five-level Likert-scale ranging from 'agree' to 'disagree', including a neutral middle category. This neutral category was recoded to missing, as it was considered to be conceptually close to the answer 'don't know'. Then, the categories 'agree' and 'somewhat agree' were coded as 1, and the categories 'disagree' and 'somewhat disagree' as 0.

Independent Variables. The main interest in our analysis are the potential changes in public opinion between our data points in 2017 and 2018. Given that we are dealing with cross-sectional rather than panel data, this change was measured by comparing the 2017 and 2018 samples with each other. Thus, the datasets from 2017 and 2018 were merged into one, and a dummy variable was generated which has the value 0 for all respondents in the 2017 sample, and the value 1 for all respondents in the 2018 sample.

Furthermore, several standard sociodemographic controls were introduced. Gender as well as whether the respondent lived in an urban or rural area were measured with the help of dummies (female=0, male=1; 0=rural, 1=urban). A 9-level income variable based on monthly estimates from 'less than 1001 UAH' to 'more than 10000 UAH' was introduced as a continuous variable, as was age (measured in years, starting from age 18).

A simplified variable indicating the educational level of the respondent was introduced, reducing an eight-level scale to a dummy variable: the levels 'vocational secondary (technical school etc.)', 'incomplete higher education (3 years and more)' and 'complete higher education' were combined to make up the value 1, while all lower educational levels were coded as 0.

The respondents' religious denomination was controlled for in three ways. First, all orthodox respondents were compared with all others with the help of a dummy variable (all others=0; orthodox=1). Second, a dummy variable was introduced in order to compare Greek Catholics with all others (all other=0; Greek Catholics=1). Third, a factor variable was introduced to compare the effects for followers of the Kyiv and the Moscow Patriarchate[3]. This variable is a three-level variable with the followers of the Kyiv Patriarchate being the reference category (2=Moscow Patriarchate; 3=all others). Lastly, a factor variable was introduced controlling for the macro region of the respondents; people from southern, central and eastern Ukraine were compared to the reference group 'western Ukraine'.

Analytical Strategy. Our analysis is based on cross-sectional data. Thus, it captures opinions from different sets of people at two points in time rather than from the same panel over time. We first present the descriptive statistics for the variables of interest. As the observed differences between the 2017 and 2018 samples may stem from the specific socio-demographic composition of the respective sample (e.g. gender, age, education), this chapter includes the results of regression models that control for the main socio-demographic effects and investigates the links between the two samples as well as factors accounting for the reported trends.

As all dependent variables are dummy-coded, logistic regression models were applied. Independent variables were introduced step by step in three models to investigate possible

---

[3] The research was conducted before the establishment of the Orthodox Church of Ukraine in 2019 and therefore asked for the old denominations.

overlaying effects. The regression results are reported as odds ratios.

Descriptive Statistics

Figure 1 highlights the two most prevalent answers to the survey question about the respondents' primary self-identification: 'ethnic Ukrainian' and 'Ukrainian citizen'. The trends over time point in opposite directions: the ethnic identity appears to have become less important, while the civic identity tied to the Ukrainian state becomes stronger. In 2017, 46 per cent of the respondents self-identified as 'ethnic Ukrainians'; and about 37 per cent of the 2018 sample chose this answer category. Conversely, 'Ukrainian citizenship' was chosen by about 38 per cent of respondents in the 2017 sample and by 49 per cent in the 2018 sample.

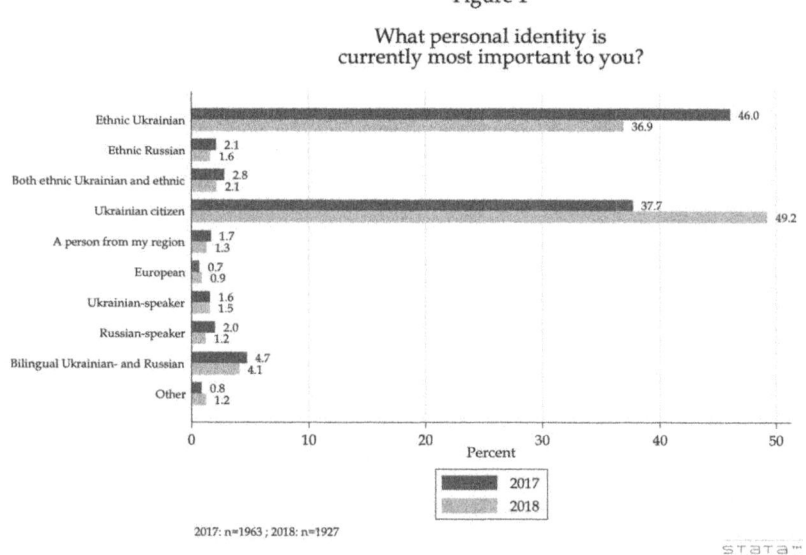

Figure 1

What personal identity is currently most important to you?

Language identities can be different from both citizenship and ethnic identities. The ZOiS survey question asked about the more symbolic category 'native language' rather than language practice. It allowed for the choice between 'Ukrainian', 'Russian', 'both Ukrainian and Russian' and 'other'. Figure 2 displays the results for

2017 and 2018. The majority of the respondents (about 68 per cent in 2017 and 59 per cent in 2018) said that they considered Ukrainian to be their native language. The choices 'Russian' and 'both Ukrainian and Russian' were less prevalent but increased from 13 to 20 per cent and from 19 to 21 per cent respectively between samples.

Figure 2

What language do you consider to be the native one for you currently?

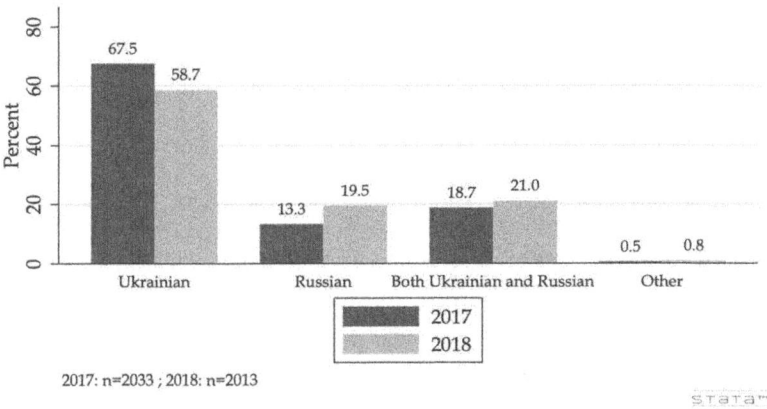

2017: n=2033 ; 2018: n=2013

With respect to the status of the non-government-controlled territories in the Donbas, the ZOiS question in the KIIS survey asked respondents to choose one of nine institutional templates. Figure 3 displays the descriptives for those templates and demonstrates that the majority of respondents in 2017 and 2018 said that they would like the non-government-controlled areas to have the same status as before the war, i.e. as parts of the Donetsk and Luhansk oblasts without any special status (2017: 60 per cent; 2018: 53 per cent). All the other answer categories were met with similarly low approval rates in both years, with less than 10 per cent of respondents choosing any one category.

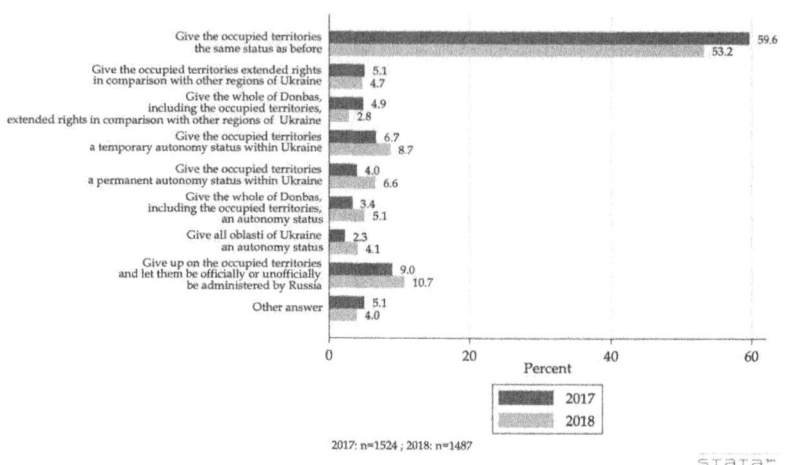

Figure 3

In your view, what should the government do in response to the situation in the Donbas?

In a second step, we wanted to know the relation between people who preferred an autonomy status (of whatever kind) for the Donbas region or parts thereof, versus those who rejected any kind of autonomy. Figure 4 shows that in 2017, altogether 16 per cent of the respondents supported some sort of an autonomy status; in 2018 support stood at about 25 per cent.

Figure 4

Support for any kind of autonomy

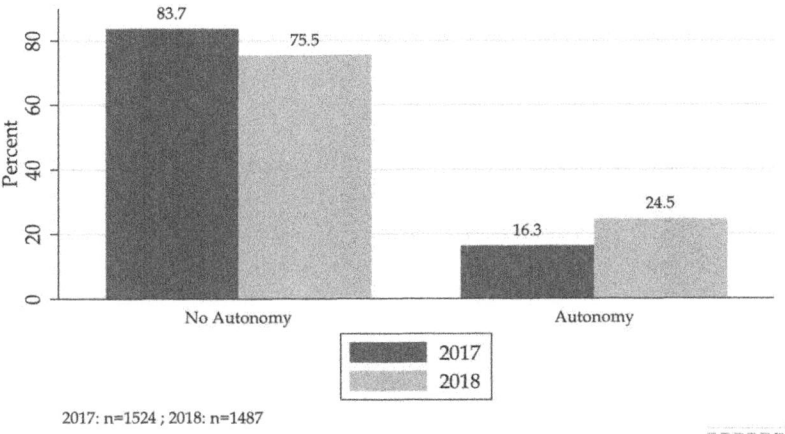

2017: n=1524 ; 2018: n=1487

The ZOiS survey questions related to the Minsk Agreement tried to establish the public mood regarding the negotiation process as well as potential add-ons like a more formalized US involvement. Figures 5 to 8 show the descriptive results for each of the questions.

Figure 5

Without the Minsk Process there would not have been any ceasefire and the death toll would have been higher

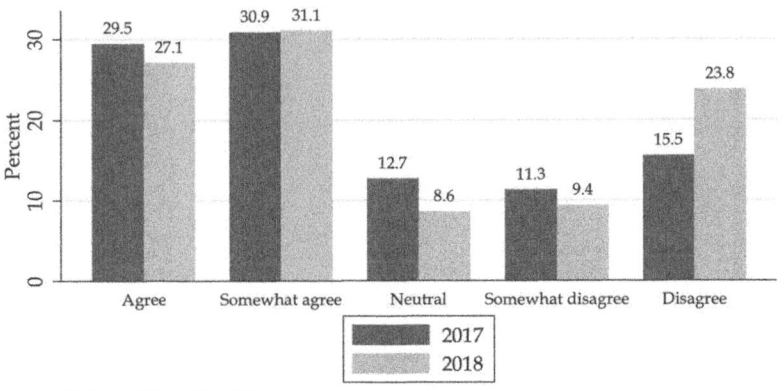

2017: n=1502 ; 2018: n=1543

Figure 6

Ukraine should stop participating
in the Minsk negotiations as the framework demands
more of Ukraine than of Russia

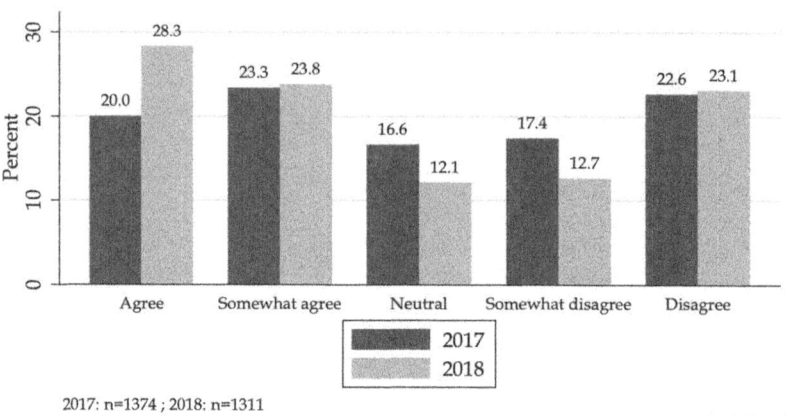

2017: n=1374 ; 2018: n=1311

Figure 7

The Minsk process is slow
but there is no alternative to this attempt at conflict-resolution

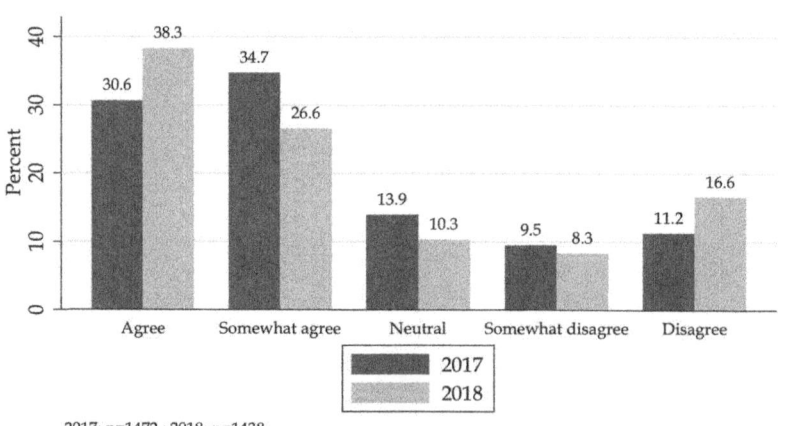

2017: n=1472 ; 2018: n=1438

Figure 8

A new international format for negotiation
is needed that includes the US

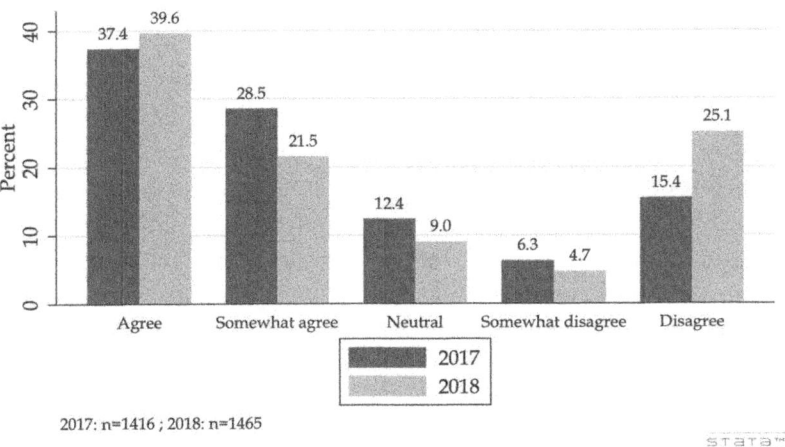

2017: n=1416 ; 2018: n=1465

Figures 5 to 8 show that the propensity to remain neutral on all Minsk-related questions was lower in 2018, and there was a tendency for the respondents in 2018 to choose the end points of the scale ('agree' or 'disagree') instead of the softer categories 'somewhat agree' or 'somewhat disagree'. The descriptive results for all four statements confirm that the Ukrainian population is divided in its views on the Minsk Agreement and potential add-ons. This is most apparent in the case of the third question ('Ukraine should stop participating in the Minsk negotiations as the framework demands more of Ukraine than of Russia'), where answers are almost equally spread across the five different answer categories. About 60 per cent in both years agree or somewhat agree with the statement 'Without the Minsk Process there would not have been any ceasefire and the death toll would have been higher'. The discrepancy suggests that the formulation of the questions affects the self-positioning vis-à-vis the Minsk process. Disappointment with the underperformance of the format is apparent, as is an overall consensus that without the Minsk Agreement the situation would have been worse.

Findings

Our analysis requires us to test the statistical significance of the observed descriptive differences between the years 2017 and 2018, including various sociodemographic control variables. Table 1 displays the significant results for the logistic regression models on the primary self-reported identity and native language, reported in odds ratios.[4] The descriptive results had indicated both a decrease in the importance of a Ukrainian ethnic identity, and an increase in the importance of a Ukrainian civic identity. Our regression analysis confirms this result: there is a significantly lower chance that respondents would choose 'ethnic Ukrainian' in 2018 as their primary identity compared to 2017 (reduced by 40 per cent), and a significantly higher chance for respondents to self-identify as 'Ukrainian citizens' (increased by close to 80 per cent), irrespective of the somewhat different socio-demographic profile of the two samples.

---

4   Recall that our data had to be weighted (using SVY logistic regression in Stata). This is why no pseudo R-squared figures are reported here: pseudo R^2 is computed using log likelihoods, and log likelihoods assume that cases are all independent of each other, which is not the case in clustered data.

Table 1.   Identity and Language

	Ukrainian citizen	Ethnic Ukrainian	Ukrainian language	Russian language	Both languages
2018 Wave	1.765** (0.360)	0.594** (0.106)	0.491*** (0.0643)	1.898*** (0.324)	
Male	0.781* (0.0724)	1.343*** (0.112)	1.252* (0.120)		
Income	1.111* (0.0446)			1.165** (0.0605)	
Age					0.987** (0.00395)
Urban			0.417** (0.124)		2.294** (0.674)
Higher education			0.673** (0.0911)		1.457** (0.202)
Orthodox					
Greek Catholic			15.68*** (6.273)	0.0357*** (0.0219)	0.153*** (0.0694)
Moscow Patriarchate (vs Kyiv)			0.482*** (0.0942)	3.190*** (0.709)	
Other Religion (vs Kyiv)				2.662* (1.122)	
Central (vs West)	2.001* (0.548)		0.250** (0.0999)	3.084* (1.602)	5.175*** (1.788)
South (vs West)			0.0693*** (0.0192)	8.592*** (3.581)	10.48*** (3.452)
East (vs West)			0.0275*** (0.0145)	15.07*** (7.934)	13.49*** (4.442)
Observations	2743	2743	2838	2838	2838

Exponentiated coefficients; Standard errors in parentheses
NOTE: Logistic Regression, dependent variable is dummy-coded
* $p < 0.05$, ** $p < 0.01$, *** $p < 0.001$

In both samples, socio-demographic factors had an effect on the self-reported primary identities. Among the control variables, gender, income and region had significant effects on identity choice across both years. Overall, men were 22 per cent less likely to choose 'Ukrainian citizen' as their main identity. Being part of a higher income group translated into a higher chance (by about 10 per cent) to self-identify as a 'Ukrainian citizen'. Furthermore, people in Central Ukraine were twice as likely to choose Ukrainian citizenship as their main identity, compared to people in Western Ukraine. As for the category 'ethnic Ukrainian', the only socio-demographic variable with a significant impact across both samples was gender: men were over 30 per cent more likely than women to say that they primarily think of themselves as 'ethnic Ukrainians'.

With respect to language, the Ukrainian language is by far the most important 'native language' in both years. However, the descriptive results had suggested that the identification with the Russian language had grown, while identification with the Ukrainian language had weakened somewhat from 2017 to 2018. This trend holds when controlling for socio-demographic differences between the two samples. The chances to say that Russian is one's 'native language' increased by 90 per cent from 2017 to 2018, while the chances for Ukrainian to be described as the 'native language' decreased by about 50 per cent. Chances for choosing both languages (i.e. a bilingual notion of 'native language') did not change significantly from one year to the next, although this mixed category remains an important counterweight to the choice between the two languages.

Several socio-demographic factors shaped the native language choices across both years. Men were 25 per cent more likely to say that Ukrainian is their native language than women; the chances for the urban population were almost 60 per cent lower, and for people with higher education the odds were about 30 per cent lower. Living in Western Ukraine significantly increased the likelihood of identifying with the Ukrainian language compared to people living in Central, Southern or Eastern Ukraine. For people describing themselves as Ukrainian Greek Catholics (concentrated in Western Ukraine), the odds were more than fifteen times as high than for people of other confessions. Among followers of the Orthodox Church of the Moscow Patriarchate the odds to consider Ukrainian one's native language were about 50 per cent lower compared to people following the Orthodox Church of the Kyiv Patriarchate.

A higher income level increased the chances of describing 'Russian' as one's native language by about 17 per cent across both samples. People living in Central, Southern or Eastern Ukraine were significantly more likely to identify with Russian as their native language than respondents in the western regions (for example, residents in Eastern Ukraine had a fifteen times higher chance compared to those in Western Ukraine). In comparison to followers of the Orthodox Church of the Kyiv Patriarchate, followers of the Moscow patriarchate were more than three times as likely to indicate that Russian was their native language.

While no significant difference could be found for the bilingual category across the two years, several socio-demographic factors had an effect in both samples. A higher age slightly reduced the chances (by 1 per cent) to say that both languages are one's native language. Conversely, living in an urban area more than doubled these chances, and being a follower of the Ukrainian Greek Catholic Church increased the chances of reporting native bilingualism by 46 per cent. Respondents from Central, Southern and Eastern Ukraine were five, ten and thirteen times more likely than respondents in Western Ukraine to say that both Ukrainian and Russian were their native languages.

We also examined people's change in opinion with respect to the status question in the Donbas. Four statements concerning the Donbas were singled out and tested in our regression analysis: "Give the occupied territories the same status as before"; "Give the occupied territories a temporary autonomy status within Ukraine"; "Give the occupied territories a permanent autonomy status within Ukraine"; and "Give up on the occupied territories and let them be officially or unofficially be administered by Russia". Furthermore, a variable had been generated testing any kind of autonomy preference versus the rejection of any kind of autonomy.

Table 2. Status of DNR/LNR

	Same status as before	Temporary autonomy status	Permanent autonomy status	Give up the occupied territories	Any kind of autonomy status
2018 Wave	0.681* (0.122)		1.820** (0.388)		1.966** (0.444)
Male					
Income					
Age				0.987* (0.00618)	
Urban					
Higher education					
Orthodox					
Greek Catholic	1.931** (0.404)		0.0990* (0.102)		0.404* (0.138)
Moscow Patriarchate (vs Kyiv)	0.603* (0.140)				1.680* (0.334)
Other Religion (vs Kyiv)					
Central (vs West)			0.398* (0.163)		
South (vs West)				0.332*** (0.103)	2.004* (0.547)
East (vs West)			3.406* (1.632)		2.712** (0.903)
Observations	2200	2200	2200	2200	2200

Exponentiated coefficients; Standard errors in parentheses
NOTE: Logistic Regression, dependent variable is dummy-coded
* $p < 0.05$, ** $p < 0.01$, *** $p < 0.001$

The descriptive results suggested that in 2018 fewer people thought that the non-government-controlled areas should have the same status as before the war. Our regression analysis (Table 2) confirms a statistically significant decrease by about 30 per cent from 2017 to 2018 in the support for a return to the status quo ante. Across both samples, the chances to opt for the 'same status as before' was about 90 per cent higher among Ukrainian Greek Catholics than for respondents of other religions denominations, and followers of the Orthodox Church of the Moscow Patriarchate were 40 per cent less likely to opt for this option compared to followers of the Orthodox Church of the Kyiv Patriarchate.

According to the descriptive results in Figure 3, in 2017 only 4 per cent of the respondents thought that the non-government-controlled areas should receive a permanent autonomy status, a figure that increased to about 7 per cent by 2018. Even though the overall percentages are low, the statistical analysis shows that significantly more people chose this option: the odds for choosing this answer in 2018 were increased by about 80 per cent. Region once again had a clear effect: respondents based in Eastern Ukraine were over three times as likely (compared to people in Western Ukraine) to agree with a permanent autonomy option, while respondents in Central Ukraine were 60 per cent less likely to favour this option, making them more critical of autonomy than the respondents based in Western Ukraine.

No statistically significant difference could be found between 2017 and 2018 with regard to the preferences for a temporary autonomy status or giving up on the non-government-controlled territories. Yet, across both samples older respondents had a slightly reduced chance (by 1 per cent for each year of age) to opt for giving up on the non-government-controlled territories, and people in the South were about 70 per cent less likely than people in the West to choose this option.

Figure 4 had shown that in 2017, altogether 16 per cent of the respondents supported some sort of an autonomy status, while in 2018 support stood at about 25 per cent. The regression analysis confirms a significant increase by 2018: the odds of agreeing with the principle of autonomy, however defined, increased by over 90 per cent. The chances of respondents from the southern and eastern regions to agree with one of the suggested types of autonomy were twice and almost three times as high compared to the western regions. Moreover, across both years, Greek Catholics were particularly sceptical of autonomy (60 per cent less likely to be in favour compared to all other religions), and followers of the Orthodox Church of the Moscow Patriarchate were about 70 per cent more likely than followers of the Orthodox Church of the Kyiv Patriarchate to support the idea.

The descriptive results had suggested rather diverse views of Ukraine's population on each question item related to the Minsk Agreement.[5]

---

5   For the regression analysis the categories 'agree' and 'somewhat agree' were collapsed, as well as the categories 'disagree' and 'somewhat disagree'. The neutral middle category was coded to a missing. Thus, a comparison takes place here between 'agreeing/somewhat agreeing' and 'disagreeing/somewhat disagreeing'.

Table 3. Minsk Agreement

	The Minsk process is slow, but there is no alternative to this attempt at conflict-resolution	Without the Minsk process there would not have been any ceasefire and the death toll would have been higher	Ukraine should stop participating in the Minsk negotiations as the framework demands more of Ukraine than of Russia	A new international format is needed that includes the US
2018 Wave				0.560* (0.145)
Male	0.677** (0.0875)			
Income				
Age				
Urban				
Higher Education			0.716* (0.112)	
Orthodox				5.085** (2.746)
Greek Catholic			2.358** (0.697)	2.244* (0.827)
Moscow Patriarchate (vs Kyiv)				0.485** (0.114)
Other Religion (vs Kyiv)				
Central (vs West)				
South (vs West)	2.421*** (0.561)			0.329*** (0.0778)
East (vs West)	2.317*** (0.487)		0.299*** (0.0938)	0.170*** (0.0841)
Observations	1900	1980	1705	1881

Exponentiated coefficients; Standard errors in parentheses
NOTE: Logistic Regression, dependent variable is dummy-coded
* $p < 0.05$, ** $p < 0.01$, *** $p < 0.001$

The regression analysis (Table 3) reveals that in only one case there was a significant change from 2017 to 2018: in 2018, significantly fewer people agreed with the statement that Ukraine should stop participating in the Minsk negotiations (chances to agree were reduced by over 40 per cent compared to 2017). Several sociodemographic factors had a significant effect on both samples. People living in the southern or eastern regions were significantly less likely (by close to 70 and over 80 per cent respectively) than those in Western Ukraine to agree with the statement. Furthermore, Greek Catholics were more than twice as likely to agree than those identifying with other religious denominations. Followers of the Orthodox Church of the Moscow Patriarchate were half as likely to agree with the statement than followers of the Orthodox Church of the Kyiv Patriarchate.

In both years, respondents in southern and eastern Ukraine were more than twice as likely to agree with the statement 'The Minsk process is slow but there is no alternative to this attempt at conflict-resolution', compared to people in western Ukraine. Men were significantly less likely to agree. There was no sociodemographic factor that had a significant effect on agreeing or disagreeing with the statement 'Without the Minsk Process there would not have been any ceasefire and the death toll would have been higher'.

Despite persisting regional and identity-based differences, the overall realization that there is no alternative to the Minsk Process has become more prevalent over time.

Conclusion

This chapter has traced recent trends and changes in public opinion across Ukraine on selected identity and war-related issues. We have shown that in only one year, attitudes in Ukraine have shifted quite significantly. While most respondents consider either 'Ukrainian citizen' or 'ethnic Ukrainian' their main identity, the notion of Ukrainian citizenship as the most prominent identity has increased in importance from 2017 to 2018 and overtook self-identification as an 'ethnic Ukrainian'. The time period 2017–2018 thus emerges as a critical period during which a broader identity shift from a more ethnic to a more inclusive civic Ukrainian identity occurred. Further research is needed, but our survey seems to have captured a rare moment of identity change. Thus, the research points to an important effect of war on state-building. It highlights the need to study state-building *during* war rather than only in the aftermath of war. Moreover, the finding that a civic self-identification with the Ukrainian state has intensified amidst war goes against the hypothesized ethnification, polarization, and mobilization for war — themes that dominate the scholarship in this field.

With regard to language identities, the surveys have confirmed that Ukrainian is the language most Ukrainians consider to be their native one. Yet, the propensity to say that Ukrainian is one's native language has decreased somewhat from 2017 to 2018 regardless of age, educational background, religion, and other sociodemographic factors. Instead, by 2018 Ukrainians have developed a somewhat higher propensity to single out Russian as their native language. The direction of this change within the space of only one year is noteworthy. It seems that there was a perceived need on the part of the population to highlight the presence of the Russian language in Ukraine. This could be interpreted as a response to the official discourse and legislation at the time that aimed to strengthen the role of the Ukrainian language in schools and in public life. The bilingual native language category, which was clearly an important reference for a sizeable number of respondents in both years, further underlines this point, though this language identity did not undergo a significant change across the two years.

As for the highly contentious issue of autonomy, a majority of Ukrainians thinks that the non-government-controlled territories should have the same status as before the war, i.e. belong to Donetsk and Luhansk oblasts without any special status. While a clear majority of Ukrainians is still opposed to an autonomy status for the non-government-controlled areas, we have also shown that the level of support for autonomy as a principle has increased from 2017 to 2018.

Over the two years, Ukrainians continue to display a diversity of views on the Minsk Agreement and potential revisions of the negotiation format. Only one of the more categorical statements in the survey showed a statistically significant change: by 2018 fewer people thought that Ukraine should stop participating in the Minsk negotiations.

In sum, our analysis of public opinion over the course of one critical year in Ukrainian politics demonstrates that views and identities can change within a remarkably short period of time, in particular in a context of war. It is important to pay close attention to these trends, as they contain clues as to how closely the public at large is aligned with state policy and official rhetoric, about the role of inclusive or mixed identities in view of more exclusive state policies, and about the space for difficult institutional choices. As the survey results have shown, public opinion has been more nuanced than the official state rhetoric or policy on 'Ukrainianness' towards the end of the Poroshenko presidency.

The result of the Ukrainian presidential elections in the spring of 2019, which saw the inexperienced comedian Zelenskyy win a landslide against the incumbent Poroshenko, confirms the analysis presented in this chapter. Zelenskyy is a Russian-speaker from the south-east of the country who galvanized opposition to Poroshenko and projected a message of unity for all Ukrainians regardless of their ethnolinguistic or regional socialization. While the south-east was his strongest support base, he was popular across the country. Zelenskyy's emphasis on the diversity of identities in Ukraine was either openly endorsed by the electorate or at least not seen as objectionable. Whether a protest vote or an expression of hope, his message of unity channeled the population's unease about unnecessarily stark internal divisions that had been opened up by the outgoing Ukrainian leadership as part of its political strategy of state-making through war. The ballot box proved to be the corrective to this trend, at least for the time being. In a situation of war, identities can be expected to remain volatile and responsive to changes in policy or rhetoric. Thus, Ukraine continues to be an important case to track the interaction between state-building from above and from below and the identity shifts this interaction can entail.

Bibliography

Alexseev, M. (2015). War and Sociopolitical Identities in Ukraine, *Ponars Eurasia, Policy Memo 392*, http://www.ponarseurasia.org/memo/war-and-sociopolitical-identities-ukraine (accessed 12 October 2019).

Arel, D. (1995). Language Politics in Independent Ukraine: Towards One or Two State Languages? *Nationalities Papers* 23(3): 597–622.

Arel, D. (2002). Interpreting 'Nationality' and 'Language' in the 2001 Ukrainian Census. *Post-Soviet Affairs* 18(3): 213–249.

Bakke, K.M. et al. (2018). Dynamics of state-building after war: External-internal relations in Eurasian de facto states. *Political Geography* 63: 159–173.

Barrington, L. W. (2002). Examining Rival Theories of Demographic Influences on Political Support: The Power of Regional, Ethnic, and Linguistic Divisions in Ukraine. *European Journal of Political Research* 41(4): 455–491.

Barrington, L., Feranda, R. (2009). Re-Examining Region, Ethnicity, and Language in Ukraine. *Post-Soviet Affairs* 25(3): 232–256.

Bermeo, N. (2003). Democratization After War: What the Democratization Literature Says—and Fails to Say—About Building Democracy in Post-Conflict Settings, Global Governance, 9, 2: 159–177.

Bermeo, N. (2007). War and Democratization: Lessons from the Portugese Experience. *Democratization* 14(3): 388–406.

Birch, S. (2000). Interpreting the Regional Effect in Ukrainian Politics. *Europe-Asia Studies* 52(6): 1017–1041.

Blair, R.A. (2016). Legitimacy after violence: Evidence from two lab-in-the-field experiments in Liberia. *Working Paper, Brown University*, http://ssrn.com/abstract¼2326671 (accessed 12 October 2019).

Blattman, C. (2009). From violence to voting: War and political participation in Uganda. *American Political Science Review* 103(2): 231–247.

Bremmer, I. (1994). The Politics of Ethnicity: Russians in the New Ukraine. *Europe-Asia Studies* 46(2): 261–283.

Brubaker, R. (2009). Ethnicity, Race, and Nationalism. *Annual Review of Sociology* 35: 21–42.

Coggins, B. (2014). *Power politics and state formation in the twentieth century: The dynamics of recognition*. New York: Cambridge University Press.

Cohen, Y., Brown, B.R., Organski, A.F.K. (1981). The Paradoxical Nature of State Making: The Violent Creation of Order. *The American Political Science Review* 75(4): 901–910.

Coyne, C.J., Boettke, P.J. (2009). The problem of credible commitment in reconstruction. *Journal of Institutional Economics* 5(1): 1–23.

D'Anieri, P. (2007). Ethnic Tensions and State Strategies: Understanding the Survival of the Ukrainian State. *Journal of Communist Studies and Transition Politics* 23(1): 4–29.

De Jun, A. Pierskalla, J.H. (2016). Civil war violence and political trust: Micro-level evidence from Nepal. *Conflict Management and Peace Science* 33(1): 67–88.

Dyrstad, K. (2012). After Ethnic Civil War: Ethno-Nationalism in the Western Balkans. *Journal of Peace Research* 49(6): 817–831.

Esteban, J., Schneider, G. (2008). Polarization and Conflict: Theoretical and Empirical Issues. *Journal of Peace Research* 45(2): 131–141.

Fabbe, K., Hazlett, C., Sınmazdemir, T. (2019). A persuasive peace: Syrian refugees' attitudes towards compromise and civil war termination. *Journal of Peace Research* 56(1): 103–117.

Fearon, J. D., Laitin, D. D. (2000). Violence and the Social Construction of Ethnic Identity. *International Organization* 54(4): 845–877.

Frye, T. (2015). What Do Voters in Ukraine Want? A Survey Experiment on Candidate Ethnicity, Language, and Policy Orientation. *Problems of Post-Communism* 62(5): 247–257.

Grosjean, P. (2014). Conflict and Social and Political Preferences: Evidence from World War II and Civil Conflict in 35 European Countries. *Comparative Economic Studies* 56(3): 424–451.

Gurr, T. (2000) *Peoples versus States. Minorities at Risk in the New Century.* Washington, DC: United States Institute of Peace Press.

Hale, H. E. (2004). Explaining Ethnicity. *Comparative Political Studies* 37(4): 458–485.

Hale, H. E. (2010). Ukraine: The Uses of Divided Power. *Journal of Democracy* 21(3): 84–98.

Holdar, S. (1995). Torn between East and West: The Regional Factor in Ukrainian Politics. *Post-Soviet Geography* 36(2): 112–132.

Jarstad, A.K., Sisk, T.D. (eds.) (2008). *From War to Democracy: Dilemmas of Peacebuilding.* Cambridge: Cambridge University Press.

Kalyvas, S. N. (2008). Ethnic Defection in Civil War. *Comparative Political Studies* 41(8): 1034–1068.

Keefer, P. (2008). Insurgency and credible commitment in autocracies and democracies. *World Bank Economic Review* 22(1): 33–61.

Kubicek, P. (2000). Regional Polarisation in Ukraine: Public Opinion, Voting, and Legislative Behaviour. *Europe-Asia Studies* 52(2): 273–294.

Kulyk, V. (2011). Language Identity, Linguistic Diversity and Political Cleavages: Evidence from Ukraine. *Nations and Nationalism* 17(3): 627–648.

Kulyk, V. (2016). National Identity in Ukraine: Impact of Euromaidan and the War. *Europe-Asia Studies* 68(4): 588–608.

Kulyk, V. (2018). Shedding Russianness, recasting Ukrainianness: the post-Euromaidan dynamics of ethnonational identifications in Ukraine. *Post-Soviet Affairs* 34(2–3): 119–138.

Leander, A. (2004). Wars and the Un-Making of States: Taking Tilly Seriously in the Contemporary World. In *Copenhagen Peace Research: Conceptual Innovations and Contemporary Security Analysis*, Stefano Guzzini and Dietrich Jung (eds.). London and New York: Routledge, 69–80.

Massey, G., Hodson, R., Sekulic, D. (2003). Nationalism, Liberalism, and Liberal Nationalism in Post-War Croatia. *Nations and Nationalism* 9(1): 55–82.

O'Loughlin, J. (2001). The Regional Factor in Contemporary Ukrainian Politics: Scale, Place, Space, or Bogus Effect? *Post-Soviet Geography and Economics* 42(1): 1–33.

Onuch, O., Hale, H., Sasse, G. (2018). Studying identity in Ukraine. *Post-Soviet Affairs* 34(2–3): 79–83.

Onuch, O. Sasse, G. (2016). The Maidan in Movement: Diversity and the Cycles of Protest. *Europe-Asia-Studies* 68(3): 556–587.

Osipian, A. L., Osipian A. L. (2012). Regional Diversity and Divided Memories in Ukraine: Contested Past as Electoral Resource, 2004–2010. *East European Politics & Societies* 26(3): 616–642.

Pirie, P. S. (1996). National Identity and Politics in Southern and Eastern Ukraine. *Europe-Asia Studies* 48(7): 1079–1104.

Posen, B. (1993). Nationalism, the Mass Army, and Military Power. *International Security* 18(2): 80–124.

Roeder, P. G. Rothchild, D. S. (2005). *Sustainable Peace: Power and Democracy after Civil Wars*. Ithaca: Cornell University Press.

Sambanis, N. (2002). A Review of Recent Advances and Future Directions in the Quantitative Literature on Civil War. *Defence and Peace Economics* 13(3): 215–243.

Sasse, G. (2010). Ukraine: The Role of Regionalism. *Journal of Democracy* 21(3): 99–106.

Sasse, G., Lackner, A. (2018). War and Identity: the case of the Donbas in Ukraine. *Post-Soviet Affairs* 34(2–3): 139–157.

Sekulic, D. (2004). Civic and Ethnic Identity: The Case of Croatia. *Ethnic and Racial Studies* 27(3): 215–243.

Shevel, O. (2009). The Politics of Citizenship Policy in New States. *Comparative Politics* 41(3): 273–291.

Shulman, S. (2004). The Contours of Civic and Ethnic National Identification in Ukraine. *Europe-Asia Studies* 56(1): 35–56.

Smith, A.D. (1994). *The Ethnic Origins of Nations*. Oxford: Blackwell.

Tarrow, S. (2015). *War, States, and Contention*. Ithaca: Cornell University Press.

Tilly, C. (1985). War-Making and State-Making as Organized Crime. In *Bringing the State Back*, P. Evans, D. Rueschemeyer and T. Skocpol (eds.). Cambridge: Cambridge University Press, 169–91.

Walter, B. (2002). *Committing to peace: The successful settlement of civil wars*. Princeton: Princeton University Press.

Wong, P. (2016). How can political trust be built after civil wars? Evidence from post-conflict Sierra Leone. *Journal of Peace Research* 53(6): 772–785.

Wood, E. J. (2015). Social Mobilization and Violence in Civil War and Their Social Legacies. In *The Oxford Handbook of Social Movements*, Donatella della Porta and Mario Diani (eds.). Oxford: Oxford University Press, 452–467.

Zürcher, C. et al. (2013). *Costly democracy: Peacebuilding and democratization after war*. Stanford: Stanford University Press.

Internal Legitimacy and Governance in the Absence of Recognition
The Cases of the Donetsk and Luhansk "People's Republics"

Nataliia Kasianenko

In the spring of 2014, amid political instability that engulfed Ukraine, pro-Russian rebel leaders in the east of Ukraine (the Donbas) took control of the local government buildings. They opposed the upcoming presidential elections in Ukraine and called for the independence of the "Donetsk People's Republic" (DPR) and the "Luhansk People's Republic" (LPR).[1] Surveys out of eastern Ukraine suggest that 71% of residents in Donetsk and 61% of residents in Luhansk believed the Euromaidan anti-government protests in 2014 were orchestrated by the West (KIIS 2014). The regime change initiated after the ouster of President Viktor Yanukovych created a power vacuum in the Donbas. New regional leaders rose up on the wave of mass opposition to the new political leadership in Kyiv (KIIS 2014). In May 2014, as the separatists clashed with the Ukrainian military, the rebel leadership conducted referendums on the status of the DPR and LPR respectively. While the Ukrainian government and the larger international community condemned these referendums as undemocratic and illegal, their results showed overwhelming public support for independence and spearheaded the efforts of the rebel leadership to consolidate the two polities politically and economically (Zadorozhny & Korotkiy 2015).

The war in the Donbas continues since 2014, the death toll now exceeds 13,000 people (UN 2019). The international peace agreements Minsk I (2014) and Minsk II (2015) helped contain the

---

[1] In this paper, I use several references for the occupied regions of the Donbas, including 'polities', 'de facto states', 'unrecognized states', and 'people's republics'.

conflict but did not bring the war between the Ukrainian military and the separatists to an end. As the war persists, the region of the Donbas remains divided into the territory of Donetsk and Luhansk oblasts controlled by the Ukrainian government and the territories controlled by the self-proclaimed governments of the DPR and the LPR. These unrecognized states are increasingly isolated from the rest of Ukraine. The Ukrainian government engaged in the economic blockade of the DPR and LPR in 2017, while the Russian government has been actively involved in supporting them from the start. The leadership of the DPR/LPR is slowly aligning its political and economic institutions with those of the Russian Federation with the ultimate goal of full integration with Russia in the future. The Russian government is cautious about recognizing the sovereignty of the two polities and only assists them with governance and security with no promises extended regarding future integration (Sasse & Lackner 2018). Although the validity of the 2014 referendums has been questioned by both Ukraine and the West, public opinion surveys and interviews out of the Donbas show that the population of the DPR/LPR feels abandoned by the Ukrainian government (Giuliano 2018) and largely supports the idea of independence from Ukraine (Kudelia 2014). The residents of the Donbas trust the leadership of the two de facto states and remain optimistic about the future integration with Russia (Kudelia 2014). As the DPR and the LPR remain dependent on Russia for security and economic support, the question of legitimacy remains important. This paper focuses on the efforts of the two regimes in obtaining legitimacy in the absence of external recognition through the use of referendums and the provision of basic public goods and services for DPR/LPR residents. I specifically explore the areas of security, economic governance, and social welfare in the two de facto states.

Degrees of Legitimacy

Academic literature traditionally treats unrecognized states and territories as entities that lack both sovereignty and legitimacy. Yet, in recent years, scholars started to highlight the fact that legitimacy defined as popular consent to the authority of the regime (Weber 1978) is not a binary concept (Caspersen 2012). It is important to distinguish between different degrees of legitimacy and statehood (Clapham 1998; Caspersen 2012). Specifically, Caspersen (2015) examines external and internal legitimacy arguing that non-recognized states may still have internal legitimacy if the population accepts the regime and the regime successfully delivers key public goods. Scholars have long tied legitimacy to the provision of security and basic welfare (Lipset 1960; Berg 2012). Internal legitimacy can be obtained through effective governance and can be facilitated by the external sources of funding and support. At the same time, even incomplete displays of democratic governance in the form of organized elections and referendums may serve to further legitimize the ruling regime in the eyes of the local population. Additionally, if an unrecognized state is dealing with an ongoing conflict or international isolation, political elites may use this situation to develop a narrative of victimhood, which can help unite the majority of the public behind the elites (Caspersen 2015).

Scholars also noted the importance of external support for unrecognized states showing that there are hardly any state entities that are completely isolated from the international system (Berg & Toomla 2009; Ker-Lindsay 2012). Thus, relying on some form of outside assistance may not necessarily translate into statehood, yet it helps achieve internal legitimacy. Attaining this degree of legitimacy is both difficult and important for the survival of unrecognized states.

Using two cases of unrecognized states in the Donbas, I will highlight the efforts of the self-proclaimed leaders of the DPR and the LPR to obtain internal legitimacy through the use of direct democracy mechanisms (referendums) and governance with the assistance of the external patron (Russia). The analysis of legitimacy is methodologically challenging in unrecognized states engaged in conflict. Data collection in the DPR and the LPR is also complicated by the fact that media channels in the two polities are state-controlled, and the two regimes are not releasing official statistics related to their budgets and finances. Yet, the main purpose of this chapter is to describe key strategies of achieving internal legitimacy in these unrecognized states.

The Use of Referendums

The calls for a referendum on the status of the Donbas were first made in 2004 during the Orange revolution that discredited the President-elect Viktor Yanukovych, a Donbas local. The residents of the Donetsk region disagreed with the victory of the pro-Western candidate Viktor Yushchenko as Ukraine's president and made calls for the autonomy of the Donbas. The idea of the autonomy was reinforced by the notion that "the Donbas feeds Ukraine" (Haran & Yakovlev 2017). Subsequent (and this time successful) calls for a new referendum came in 2014, following the Euromaidan revolution that ousted Yanukovych from power. After the Euromaidan and the annexation of Crimea, the wave of patriotism swept all over Ukraine with the exception of the Donbas. In fact, a large number of survey respondents (around 25%) in the Donetsk and Luhansk regions in 2014 have clearly expressed the desire to separate from Ukraine and join Russia (Vedernikova, Mostova & Rakhmanin 2014).

The referendums on the independent status of Donetsk and Luhansk took place in May of 2014. The rebel leaders have set up hundreds of polling stations with assistance from the Russian government (Vandysheva 2018). The question posed at the referendums directly addressed the political status of the two polities. It was worded in an ambivalent way, "Do you support the Act of state "samostoyatel'nost" of the Donetsk (Luhansk) People's Republic?" The term "samostoyatel'nost" may be interpreted as either complete or partial independence (Dubova & Bigg 2014). Moreover, many people in the Donbas believed that "samostoyatel'nost" meant integration into the Russian state. The responses involved two options of either "yes" or "no" (Matveeva 2016).

In both de facto states, the organizers claimed that the results of the referendum would be accepted regardless of the voter turnout since some voters might be unwilling to participate in the referendum due to security concerns (RIA News 2014a). The declared turnout for both referendums was nonetheless impressive. In the Donetsk region with over 3 million eligible voters, the referendum turnout was almost 75%. The official results showed that nearly 90% of voters supported the independent status of "the Donetsk People's Republic" (DNR 2016). The Luhansk region has about 1.6 million eligible voters. The turnout in the Luhansk oblast was 81% (Vesti 2014). The Russian media confirmed high turnout rates on the referendum day and reportedly interviewed the Donbas residents at the polling stations who expressed support for independence from Ukraine (RIA News 2014b).

The international community has condemned the referendums as illegal and undemocratic. No international observers (beyond the representatives from Russia) were present to monitor the voting process. Additionally, the referendums were organized and run by the separatists themselves. The organizers cited security concerns and had armed soldiers present at some of the polling stations (Giuliano 2015; Chizhova 2014). Western and Ukrainian critics noted the similarities between the Donbas referendums and the referendum in Crimea, organized a few months earlier with the heavy presence of the "little green men", the uniformed Russian soldiers. Other irregularities included the printing of referendum bulletins on regular printers without any additional anti-fraud security measures. The organizers also reportedly allowed voters individuals to cast multiple votes and brought people from Ukraine-controlled regions to vote in the referendum (Zadorozhny & Korotkiy 2015).

While there is little doubt that the turnout numbers were significantly inflated, there is documented evidence from local media and social media suggesting that many residents of the DPR/LPR participated in the voting. Local observers in the Donbas noted lines of people waiting to vote on the referendum day at most polling stations (LiveJournal 2015). Reports, surveys, and interviews from the rebel-controlled Donbas indicate that most residents supported the idea of either independence for Donetsk and Luhansk or the integration of the Donbas into Russia (Giuliano 2015). Some voters believed the Donbas referendums to be similar to the Crimean referendum, in which people were voting to join Russia as a subject of the federation (Denyer & Nemstova 2014).

While the Ukrainian government and the West primarily blame Russia for the rise of separatism in eastern Ukraine, the residents of the Donbas have clearly expressed their resistance to the Euromaidan protests and their anxiety over the pro-Western policy course of the new Ukrainian government (Giuliano 2015). Public opinion surveys showed that over a quarter of the population in Donetsk and Luhansk expressed support for independence from Ukraine in April of 2014. Another 12–17% of respondents claimed to be unsure about the prospect of independence for the Donbas (KIIS 2014). Documented evidence suggests that the military units that emerged in Donetsk and Luhansk in 2014 were initially made up of local Donbas residents, not the Russian military (Kudelia 2014; Chivers & Sneider 2014). At the same time, the influence of the external patron, Russia, cannot be ignored. The Russian government without a doubt played a role in initiating and supporting the separatist conflict in the east of Ukraine. Still, self-proclaimed leaders of the two polities do not seem to be passive executors of the decisions made in Russia. Reportedly, in 2014, President Putin encouraged the separatist leaders to postpone the independence referendums without success (Traynor et al. 2014). Russia's refusal to formally annex the DPR and the LPR was a major disappointment for the rebel leaders and many residents of the Donbas region (Sakwa 2015). Nevertheless, the two polities continue to seek external recognition and maintain their position of independence from Ukraine.

The results of the referendums gave new legitimacy to the rebel leaders in the region. The day after the referendums took place, the DPR and LPR officially declared independence from Ukraine. Within a week after the referendums, the two polities adopted new constitutions (Zadorozhny & Korotkiy 2015). Despite the absence of international recognition, the leadership of the two de facto states used the referendums as a foundation for gaining internal legitimacy in the DPR and LPR. The leaders of the two polities refute the argument that the DPR and LPR are completely dependent on the Russian government. In 2015, the president of the

DPR, Aleksandr Zakharchenko claimed, "Those who say this, do not see the independent will of the Donbas, do not see the ability to make decisions in Donetsk. They think that the destiny of Donbas is decided somewhere outside its borders—in Moscow, Washington, Berlin, Paris … During the referendum we expressed our will" (DNR 2016c). The declaration of independence from Ukraine also helped reinforce the main ideological narrative in the two de facto states. This narrative of victimhood pictures the peaceful people of the Donbas who used legal procedures to express their desire for self-rule pitted against their main enemy, the Ukrainian government that uses military force and brings destruction to the region (Matveeva 2016). Yet, internal legitimacy cannot survive on ideology alone. Effective governance and policy-making are critical to maintaining this degree of legitimacy.

External Support and Governance in the DPR/LPR

From the early days of protests in April of 2014, the rebel leaders in the Donbas made a formal commitment to democratic governance and claimed to represent the will of the people. The notion of "people's republics" was developed by the rebel leaders early on in 2014. The two entities were part of the single political project of Novorossiya (New Russia), which was historically used as a term for the southeastern regions of modern-day Ukraine. The idea of Novorossiya was not supported by the Minsk agreements and the project was soon abandoned by the rebel leaders in the Donbas (Matveeva 2016). Over time and despite the absence of international recognition, the self-proclaimed "people's republics" have set up major government institutions, including legislative and judicial bodies, as well as law enforcement agencies (Matveeva 2016; UN OHCHR 2015). Speaking in 2016, Zakharchenko highlighted two main tasks of the "Donetsk People's Republic". The first task was to focus on local governance by communicating with the residents of Donbas and establishing close ties between the political leaders and the population of the DPR. The second task involved ideological work of promoting major values of the DPR such as "freedom, justice, conscience, equality" (DNR 2017).

In 2015, in another attempt at enhancing internal legitimacy through governance with the help of the external patron, the LPR government started to issue passports of the "Luhansk People's Republic" to its residents. The passports of the LPR not only allowed entry into Russia but also and made it possible for the citizens of the de facto state to apply to Russian universities. In 2016, the government of the DPR followed suit and started issuing its own passports (Dergachev, Holmogorova & Dzyadko 2017).

In an attempt to increase the base of its supporters in the whole region, the government of the DPR started opening special centers for administrative and social assistance to the residents of Ukraine-controlled Donbas. These centers offered humanitarian help to individuals who needed medical and financial assistance or wanted to reconnect with their family or friends in the DPR/LPR (HPDPR 2017). The humanitarian program also involved securing thousands of spots for university students in the universities of the DPR. According to Zakharchenko,

> "These people are now under the heel of the enemy, they are on the territory controlled by Ukraine, but these are our sisters and brothers...We are one people! Donbas is one country" (DNR 2018b).

These calls for unity and consolidation may have been welcomed by the people of the Ukraine-controlled Donbas who were targeted by the Ukrainian media as Moscow loyalists and traitors.

Significant gaps remain when it comes to governance in the occupied Donbas. The first gap involves the status of the two polities. The leadership and the residents of the DPR/LPR seem to be unsure whether the goal of independence from Ukraine is state sovereignty and international recognition or whether it is the future integration into the Russian Federation. Specifically, the leaders of the DPR claim to be waiting for the repetition of the "Crimean scenario" in the Donbas (DNR 2017). In the spring of 2017, Zakharchenko announced that the people of Donbas would be celebrating the victory of reintegration with Russia in the near future (DNR 2018a). LPR's leader, Leonid Pasechnik similarly argued,

> "Our goal is the construction of strong and independent Republic capable of ensuring a decent life for its citizens, the preservation of the people and their security in a single political, cultural, economic and civilizational space with the Russian Federation" (NAH 2018).

In any of these two scenarios (sovereignty or integration), attaining internal legitimacy is necessary for the survival of the de facto states.

The centralization of political power in the DPR/LPR has been another major challenge since 2014 when multiple local rebel leaders exercised control over different areas of the Donbas representing horizontal government structures in the two polities.

> "The self-declared 'people's mayors' of different Donbas towns were local political opportunists who used the implosion of authority to claim power rather than members of a clandestine organization coordinated from a single center" (Kudelia 2014: 6).

The rebels in the DPR/LPR also pursued different strategies of separatism. In the DPR, the local leaders announced independence from Ukraine and then organized a referendum a month later. In the LPR, the rebels have announced independence only after the May 2014 referendum (Kudelia 2014). The Russian government has therefore made efforts to centralize local political power by helping organize elections in the DPR and LPR in the fall of 2014 (Robinson 2016; Matveeva 2016). These elections have "turned into confidence votes for Zakharchenko (79%) and Igor Plotnitsky (63%) identified by Kremlin as the most suitable candidates" for the leadership of the "people's republics" (Matveeva 2016: 38). The representatives to the legislative bodies (People's Councils) were chosen from major civic associations in the region. Both councils have elected members from two civic associations with 100 deputies representing the DPR and 50 deputies in the People's Council of the LPR (DNR 2016a). While these elections might not have been completely free and fair, they certainly helped with the centralization of power in the region and served to further legitimize the leadership of the two de facto states (Matveeva 2016). The Minsk II agreement in 2015 highlighted the need for a future agreement between the government of Ukraine and the political leaders in Donbas to set up the procedures for local elections in the region. Yet, the government of Ukraine has been unwilling to negotiate with the rebels that are labeled as terrorists, not popular representatives (Katchanovski 2016; Robinson 2016).

I will now turn to the discussion of specific aspects of governance in the DPR/LPR, including security, economics, and social welfare. The analysis is based on the diverse body of sources, including the official reports published by the governments of the two de facto states, academic sources, the local Donbas media, as well as social media out of the region.

Security

Defense has been a priority for the local leaders in the DPR/LPR since April of 2014 when the protesters took over the local administration buildings in Donetsk and Luhansk. After declaring independence from Ukraine, the rebels set up regional military units (people's armies) to maintain control and security within the borders of the de facto states (Sakwa 2015). The people's army was created on the basis of voluntary paramilitary units. At the time, local military battalions coexisted with the Chechen, Serbian and Hungarian military units that operated in the Donbas (Beroyeva 2016). The newly minted army of the DPR was small, yet over the years the local government had the ability to recruit thousands more for the military service (DNR 2018b). To maintain order and peace in the major cities, the government of the DPR also created local patrol units. These units established control over the military personnel and seized weapons from individuals who did not have the necessary permits (Grigoryuk 2015). As a result, violence in the DPR and LPR has declined significantly and stability has returned to the major cities outside of the conflict zone (Matveeva 2016).

The two de facto states have also introduced the curfew system from 11 PM to 5 AM. The curfew was initially justified because of the security concerns in the region. However, as the rates of violence have declined over the years, many residents feel frustrated with the enforcement of the curfew and the penalties that curfew violations involve. In the DPR, the first curfew violation involves an arrest until next morning. The repeated offense entails a 15-day arrest. As a result of the curfew system, hundreds of people are arrested every night in the DPR. The enforcement of curfew is less strict in the LPR with violators being subject to a $10–30 fine (DN 2018). Due to the curfew system, taxis, ambulances, and pharmacies are largely unavailable at night, which complicates the lives of the residents of the DPR/LPR (DN 2017). Overall, the authorities were able to restore peace in the major cities yet problems with security remain. Ultimately, the leadership of the DPR/LPR cannot guarantee the safety of the Donbas residents without a strict curfew system in place.

Economy

The military conflict in the Donbas contributed to the economic downturn in the region. Local businesses were either moving out of the Donbas or completely ceasing their operations. Economic production was further disrupted by the economic blockade the Ukrainian government has imposed on the DPR/LPR in 2014 (Matveeva 2016). By 2015, all bank branches in the occupied Donbas were shut down. The residents of the two polities were unable to collect pensions or access their bank accounts. Local stores and businesses did not accept electronic payments and instead relied on cash. Currency shortages led to a reliance on payments in the U.S. dollars, the euros, along with the Russian rubles and the Ukrainian hryvnias (Silchenko 2015).

The new regimes initiated sweeping changes to bring the DPR/LPR out of the economic crisis. Central banks were created in 2015 (Beroyeva 2016). A year later, the residents of the Donbas could make online payments through the newly created web banking system (DNR 2017). The separatist leaders quickly took control over the coal mines of the DPR/LPR and announced growing levels of coal production in the "people's republics" (DNR 2016c). In 2016, both de facto states adopted the law on nationalization, giving the regimes formal authority to impose temporary government control over the businesses (Beroyeva 2016). Yet, the authorities do not have full control over the economic activity in the DPR/LPR. The territories of the two de facto states do not have a large base for taxation since a portion of big industries located within the DPR/LPR still pay taxes to the government of Ukraine (Skorik 2017a). According to Matveeva,

> "Industrial connections with the mainland are not wholly disrupted, and there are actors on both sides who are interested in their preservation" (Matveeva 2016: 42).

Despite Ukraine's trade blockade, the two polities continue to receive contraband goods from the Ukrainian territory. The contraband out of Ukraine is risky and requires bribing both the Ukrainian and the "people's republics'" customs authorities. As a result, the volume of trade is rather low leading to the shortage of consumer goods in the DPR/LPR. The two de facto states largely rely on trade with Russia. Trade mostly flows through South Ossetia, the only territorial entity that has officially recognized the sovereignty of the DPR/LPR. Business contracts are reportedly signed between the exporters in the occupied Donbas and the importers in South Ossetia, then South Ossetia transfers the imports to Russia. The same mechanism works for money transfers out of Russia and into the DPR/LPR (Beroyeva 2016).

The leaders of the DPR/LPR do not publicize information about the official state budgets arguing that this lack of transparency is necessary in times of war. According to some estimates from the DPR, around 50% of the budget is spent on pensions and other social welfare payments, and around 25% of the budget is spent on salaries of state officials and government employees (Skorik 2017a). Budgetary lines were set up for the reconstruction of roads, bridges, and homes in the Donbas (Skorik 2017a). Specifically, the DPR's construction program has focused on building hundreds of new homes to replace the apartments damaged during the conflict (DNR 2016e).

Despite the absence of any documented evidence, there are grounds to doubt that the DPR/LPR are economically independent. In highlighting the status of the DPR, Zakharchenko argued,

> "We are an economically self-sufficient state with our own history and culture, with our own development path" (Zakharchenko 2018).

However, Russia offers significant financial support to the two de facto states. Government officials in the DPR estimate that "70% of the republic's budget expenditure is covered by Moscow" (Matveeva 2016: 42). Other estimates suggest that Russia covers closer to 82% of the local budgetary expenses in the DPR/LPR (Skorik 2017a). Every year, the Russian government sends billions of euros in humanitarian aid to cover salaries and social welfare payments in the Donbas (Matveeva 2016: Skorik 2017a). Over 30 million euros a month are sent towards the pension payments alone. Additionally, Moscow sends military assistance to the Donbas in the form of ammunition, oil and natural gas. Some estimates suggest that over 0.6% of the Russian annual budget is spent on financial assistance to the DPR/LPR (Donbass News 2017). At the same time, the Russian government is putting pressure on the local leadership in the two republics to become financially independent. Reportedly, the assistance from Moscow has declined over the years, as the Russian government prioritized economic development in the Crimea over the formally independent Donbas (Skorik 2017a). In general, the two de facto states are struggling to maintain economic independence from Ukraine and likely rely on the Russian government to cover the majority of their social expenditures.

Social Welfare Programs

Both the DPR and the LPR formally advance the idea that the state should work for the benefit of the people, suggesting that the focus on social programs should guide the political and economic development of the "people's republics" (Zakharchenko 2018). Yet, in reality, the salaries and pensions in the DPR/LPR are quite low. In 2017, the average monthly salary in Donetsk was between 150 and 200 U.S. dollars (Skorik 2017b). In the LPR, the local government stated even lower average salaries in 2018, around 110 U.S. dollars for doctors and 75 U.S. dollars for teachers (LIC 2018). When it comes to pensions, the 2016 minimum pension was set at

39 U.S. dollars in the DPR (DNR, 2018). The regimes regularly announce minimum wage and pension increases in all of the major government sectors (DNR 2018). Still, average salaries and pensions lag behind those in Russia (Silchenko 2016). Most residents of the DPR/LPR have to rely on either humanitarian aid or additional pension payments from Ukraine.

As a result of the ongoing conflict, the Ukrainian government officially stopped sending pension payments to the residents of the DPR/LPR. The pensions are available only to those residents who cross the border into the Ukrainian territory and register with the government authorities in Ukraine. This registration requires regular renewals and frequent travel to the Ukrainian territory, which could be quite dangerous for the residents of the Donbas. Once registered, the pensioners obtain debit cards, which cannot be used inside the DPR/LPR to cash out the pensions. Thus, some people rely on local entrepreneurs who travel to Ukraine-controlled territories to cash out pensions in exchange for a fee (Silchenko 2015). The difficulty of receiving pensions from Ukraine has enraged and alienated many residents of the self-proclaimed "people's republics". When interviewed in 2016, one pensioner in the DPR argued, "I have worked for this country for 40 years and it is now sending me bombs instead of pensions" (Beroyeva 2016).

The ability of the unrecognized regimes to obtain internal legitimacy through provision of social benefits is complicated since the residents of the two polities continue relying on humanitarian aid from private foundations, international non-governmental organizations, and the Russian government. Reportedly, regular humanitarian aid from Russia helps deliver food packages to large families, state schools, hospitals, and orphanages (DNR 2017).

Conclusion: Prospects for Reintegrating the Donbas?

The 2014 referendums in the Donbas led to the creation of the DPR and LPR and helped enhance the internal legitimacy of the self-proclaimed leaders in the two polities. Yet, these direct democracy campaigns did not immediately result in improved governance for the residents of the Donbas. The de facto states struggle when it comes to self-governance, independence and the ability to provide basic public goods and services. What does it mean for the Ukrainian government? Does the government in Kyiv have an ability to gain the support of the Donbas residents and successfully reintegrate the region?

Since the start of the war in the Donbas the Ukrainian government labeled the conflict as the "anti-terrorist operation" and largely disregarded political and economic concerns of the local residents. As a result, Ukraine's military actions were severely undermined by the lack of local support in the Donbas.

> "Surrounded by locals, the soldiers surrendered their vehicles or retreated back to their bases" (Kudelia 2014: 3).

This lack of political legitimacy undermines the prospects for reintegration of the Donbas. Although the new leaders of the DPR/LPR are struggling when it comes to governance, the government in Kyiv is unable to step in and provide help to the residents of the occupied territories. The Ukrainian government lost access to the occupied territories of the DPR/LPR. Still, some pro-Ukrainian residents of the occupied regions were disappointed with the fact that the Ukrainian leadership was isolating the Donbas economically and politically.

> "Medical staff, teachers, social care workers and prison staff have not been paid by Kiev since July 2014, although many continued with their duties" (Matveeva 2016: 41).

In addition, the Ukrainian government has lost legitimacy in the region as a result of the information campaign to discredit Ukraine's political leadership. Local media campaigns advanced anti-Ukraine slogans such as "Will not forget, will not forgive!" to emphasize the use of violence by the Ukrainian military and the resulting civilian casualties in the Donbas. Public opinion surveys from the region and the return of the internally displaced individuals to the Donbas suggest that the reintegration with Ukraine would be a challenging task (Matveeva 2016). Even if Russia decides to abandon the DPR and LPR and ceases all humanitarian assistance to the de facto states, it is unlikely that the

Ukrainian government will regain its influence in the region. Thus, the ideological or "soft" power approach in the occupied regions is paramount for Ukraine to obtain legitimacy in the Donbas. Successful reintegration will not be possible without the popular support for the idea that "the Donbas is Ukraine" both in the DPR/LPR and in the rest of Ukraine (Haran & Yakovlev 2017). Considering the difficulty of the task, power-sharing or autonomy presents the most optimistic political outcome for Ukraine in the current stalemate in the east.

Bibliography

Berg, E. (2012). Parent states versus secessionist entities; measuring political legitimacy in Cyprus, Moldova and Bosnia and Herzegovina. *Europe-Asia Studies* 64(7): 1271–1296.

Berg, E., & Toomla, R. (2009). Forms of normalisation in the quest for de facto statehood. *The International Spectator* 44(4): 27–45.

Beroyeva, N. (2016, August 23). Zhivoy Donetsk, Ukraina [Live Donetsk, Ukraine], *LiveJournal*, https://varlamov.ru/1907750.html (accessed 1 October 2019).

Caspersen, N. (2015). Degrees of legitimacy: Ensuring internal and external support in the absence of recognition. *Geoforum* 66: 184–192.

Caspersen, N. (2012). *Unrecognized states: The struggle for sovereignty in the modern international system*. Cambridge: Polity.

Chivers, C. J., Sneider, N. (2014). Behind the masks in Ukraine, many faces of rebellion. *The New York Times* May 3, 2014: 3.

Chizhova, L. (2014). Donbas do i posle referenduma [Donbas before and after the referendum], *Radio Svoboda*, May 21, 2014, https://www.svoboda.org/a/25393023.html (accessed 1 October 2019).

Clapham, C. (1998). Degrees of statehood. *Review of International Studies* 24(2): 143–157.

Denyer, S., Nemstova, A. (2014). Eastern Ukrainians vote for self-rule in referendum opposed by West. *The Washington Post* May 11, 2014: 1.

Dergachev, V., Holmogorova, V., & Dzyadko, T. (2017,). Rassledovaniye RBK: Kak v Rossii priznali pasporta DNR i LNR [Investigation of RBK: How the passports of DPR and LPR were recognized in Russia], *RBK*, February 2, 2017, https://www.rbc.ru/politics/02/02/2017/587cf9159a7947e5f86ee045 (accessed 1 October 2019).

DN. (2018). V DNR rasskazali kogda otmenyat komendantskiy chas [The DPR announced when the curfew would be canceled], *DN*, May 8, 2018. Retrieved from https://www.dnews.dn.ua/news/675479 (accessed 1 October 2019).

DN. (2017). Hotya by kak v LNR: Zhiteli prosyat oslabit komendantskiy chas v DNR [At least like in the LPR: Residents are asking to lighten the curfew in the DPR], *DN*, September 17, 2017, https://dnews.dn.ua/news/646106 (accessed 1 October 2019).

DNR. (2018a). Hronologiya stanovleniya Donetskoy Narodnoy Respubliki [The chronology of the establishment of the Donetsk People's Republic], *Official Website of the DPR*, March 3, 2018, http://letopis.DNR-online.ru/2018/03/03/xronologiya-stanovleniya-doneckoj-narodnoj-respubliki-sobytiya-marta-2017-goda-my-pobediteli-i-eto-nasha-sudba-aleksandr-zaxarchenko/ (accessed 1 October 2019).

DNR. (2018b). Hronologiya stanovleniya Donetskoy Narodnoy Respubliki [The chronology of the establishment of the Donetsk People's Republic], *Official Website of the DPR*, April 12, 2018, http://letopis.dnr-online.ru/2018/04/12/xronologiya-stanovleniya-doneckoj-narodnoj-respubliki-sobytiya-aprelya-2017-goda-my-odin-narod-donbass-eto-odna-strana-glava-dnr-aleksandr-zaxarchenko/ (accessed 1 October 2019).

DNR. (2017). Hronologiya stanovleniya Donetskoy Narodnoy Respubliki [The chronology of the establishment of the Donetsk People's Republic], *Official Website of the DPR*, March 6, 2017, http://letopis.DNR-online.ru/2017/03/06/xronologiya-stanovleniya-doneckoj-narodnoj-respubliki-sobytiya-marta-2016-goda-vtoraya-vesna-vsyo-toj-zhe-vojny/ (accessed 1 October 2019).

DNR. (2016a). Hronologiya stanovleniya Donetskoy Narodnoy Respubliki [The chronology of the establishment of the Donetsk People's Republic], *Official Website of the DPR*, February 20, 2016, http://letopis.dnr-online.ru/2016/02/20/xronologiya-stanovleniya-doneckoj-narodnoj-respubliki-sobytiya-oktyabrya-2014-goda-respublika-perexodit-na-doneckoe-vremya/ (accessed 1 October 2019).

DNR. (2016c). Hronologiya stanovleniya Donetskoy Narodnoy Respubliki [The chronology of the establishment of the Donetsk People's Republic], *Official Website of the DPR*, November 4, 2016, http://letopis.dnr-online.ru/2016/11/04/xronologiya-stanovleniya-doneckoj-narodnoj-respubliki-sobytiya-noyabrya-2015-goda-noyabr-novye-rubezhi-i-novye-dostizheniya-nezavisimoj-respubliki/ (accessed 1 October 2019).

DNR. (2016b). Hronologiya stanovleniya Donetskoy Narodnoy Respubliki [The chronology of the establishment of the Donetsk People's Republic], *Official Website of the DPR*, April 5, 2016, http://letopis.dnr-online.ru/2016/04/05/xronologiya-stanovleniya-doneckoj-narodnoj-respubliki-sobytiya-aprelya-2015-goda-respublika-stroitsya/ (accessed 1 October 2019).

DNR. (2016e). Hronologiya stanovleniya Donetskoy Narodnoy Respubliki [The chronology of the establishment of the Donetsk People's Republic], *Official Website of the DPR*, December 2, 2016, http://letopis.DNR-online.ru/2016/12/02/xronologiya-stanovleniya-doneckoj-narodnoj-respubliki-sobytiya-dekabrya-2015-goda-nezavisimaya-respublika-vstrechaet-svoj-vtoroj-novyj-god/ (accessed 1 October 2019).

DNR. (2016). Hronologiya stanovleniya Donetskoy Narodnoy Respubliki [The chronology of the establishment of the Donetsk People's Republic], *Official Website of the DPR*, February 10, 2016, http://letopis.dnr-online.ru/2016/02/10/xronologiya-stanovleniya-doneckoj-narodnoj-respubliki-sobytiya-iyunya-2014-goda-dnr-obretaet-konstituciyu/ (accessed 1 October 2019).

DNR. (2018). Hronologiya stanovleniya Donetskoy Narodnoy Respubliki [The chronology of the establishment of the Donetsk People's Republic], *Official Website of the DPR*, January 19, 2018, http://letopis.dnr-online.ru/2018/01/19/xronologiya-stanovleniya-doneckoj-narodnoj-respubliki-sobytiya-yanvarya-2017-goda-k-sozhaleniyu-vojna-eshhe-ne-zakonchilas-i-nam-predstoit-dokazyvat-chto-my-imeem-pravo-sami-opredelyat/ (accessed 1 October 2019).

DNR. (2017a). Hronologiya stanovleniya Donetskoy Narodnoy Respubliki [The chronology of the establishment of the Donetsk People's Republic], *Official Website of the DPR*, January 10, 2017, http://letopis.DNR-online.ru/2017/01/10/xronologiya-stanovleniya-doneckoj-narodnoj-respubliki-sobytiya-yanvarya-2016-goda-v-respublike-chtyat-pogibshix-okruzhayut-zabotoj-zhivushhix/ (accessed 1 October 2019).

Donbass News. (2017). Sekretniy budzhet "DNR" mozhet ostatsya bez rossiyskih vlivaniy? [The secret budget of the "DPR" may be left without the Russian assistance?], *Donbass News*, October 6, 2017, http://novosti.dn.ua/article/6867-sekretnyy-byudzhet-DPR-mozhet-ostatsya-bez-rossyyskykh-vlyvanyy (accessed 1 October 2019).

Dubova, V., Bigg, C. (2014). Pro-Russians in Eastern Ukraine gear up for self-rule referendums. *Radio Free Europe Radio Liberty*, May 9, 2014, https://www.rferl.org/a/pro-russians-eastern-ukraine-prepare-self-rule-referendum/25379398.html (accessed 1 October 2019).

Giuliano, E. (2015). The social bases of support for self-determination in East Ukraine. *Ethnopolitics* 14(5): 513–522.

Giuliano, E. (2018). Who supported separatism in Donbas? Ethnicity and popular opinion at the start of the Ukraine crisis. *Post-Soviet Affairs* 34(2–3): 158–178.

Grigoryuk, D. (2015). Voennaya policiya DNR [Military policy of the DPR]. *Novorossiya*, July 8, 2015, https://novorosinform.org/401348 (accessed 1 October 2019).

Haran, O., & Yakovlyev, M. (2017). *Constructing a political nation: Changes in the attitudes of Ukrainians during the war in the Donbas*. Kyiv: Stylos Publishing.

Katchanovski, I. (2016). The separatist war in Donbas: A violent break-up of Ukraine? *European Politics and Society* 17(4): 473–489.

HPDPR. (2017). V centrah socialnoy pomoshi i administrativnyh uslug zhiteliu vremenno podkontrolnoi Kievu teritorii Donbasa prodolzhayut poluchat pomosh [In the centers of social assistance and administrative services the residents of temporarily Kyiv-controlled territory of the Donbas continue to receive assistance], *Humanitarian Program on Donbas People Reunification*, February 17, 2017, http://gum-centr.su/news/v-centrah-socialnoi-pomosi-i-administrativnyh-uslug-ziteli-vremenno-podkontrolnoi-kievu (accessed 1 October 2019).

Ker-Lindsay, J. (2012). *The foreign policy of counter secession*. Oxford: Oxford University Press.

KIIS. (2014). The views and opinions of the residents of South-Eastern regions of Ukraine, *Kyiv International Institute of Sociology*, April 2014, http://www.kiis.com.ua/?lang=eng&cat=news&id=258 (accessed 1 October 2019).

Kudelia, S. (2014). Domestic Sources of the Donbas Insurgency. *PONARS Eurasia Policy Memo* No. 351, September 2014, http://www.ponarseurasia.org/memo/domestic-sources-donbas-insurgency (accessed 1 October 2019).

LIC. (2018). Povysheniye pensii na 10% kosnetsya vseh pensionerov Respubliki [The rise in pensions by 10% will apply to all of the pensioners of the Republic], *Luhansk Information Center*, June 12, 2018, http://lug-info.com/news/one/povyshenie-pensii-na-10-kosnetsya-vsekh-pensionerov-respubliki-minsotspolitiki-lnr-35991 (accessed 1 October 2019).

Lipset, S.M. (1960). *Political man: The social bases of politics*. Garden City: Doubleday.

LiveJournal. (2015). Godovshina referenduma v DNR I LNR [The anniversary of the referendum in the DPR and LPR], *LiveJournal*, May 11, 2015, https://friend.livejournal.com/1892028.html (accessed 1 October 2019).

Matveeva, A. (2016). No Moscow stooges: identity polarization and guerrilla movements in Donbass. *Southeast European and Black Sea Studies* 16(1): 25–50.

NAH. (2018). LDNR pokazhut na chto sposobny [The LDPR will show what they're capable of], *Novostnoye Agenstvo Har'kov*, May 13, 2018, https://nahnews.org/1003735-IDPR-pokazhut-na-chto-sposobny-pasechnik-nazval-glavnoe-uslovie-dlya-nalazhivaniya-otnoshenii-s-ukrainoi (accessed 1 October 2019).

RIA News. (2014a). Na yugo-vostoke Ukrainy idet golosovaniye na referendum. [Referendum voting is taking place in the south-east of Ukraine], *RIA News*, May 11, 2014, https://ria.ru/world/20140511/1007319429.html (accessed 1 October 2019).

RIA News. (2014b). Referendum v Slavyanske i Kramatorske proshel aktivno, otmetil chlen SPCh [The referendum in Slavyansk and Kramatorsk was active, noted the member of the HRC], *RIA News*, May 11, 2014, https://ria.ru/world/20140511/1007394602.html (accessed 1 October 2019).

Robinson, P. (2016). Russia's role in the war in Donbass, and the threat to European security. *European Politics and Society* 17(4): 506–521.

Sakwa, R. (2015). *Frontline Ukraine: Crisis in the borderlands*. London, UK: I.B. Tauris.

Sasse, G., Lackner, A. (2018). War and identity: the case of the Donbas in Ukraine. *Post-Soviet Affairs* 34(2–3): 139–157.

Silchenko, V. (2015). Donetsk, chast 1 [Donetsk, part 1], *LiveJournal*, February 18, 2015, https://varlamov.ru/1279197.html (accessed 1 October 2019).

Skorik, M. (2017a). Kak dela delayutsya. Na chem derzhatsya ekonomika i finansy DNR i LNR [How business is made. What supports the economy and the finances of DPR and LPR], *SpektrPress*, February 8, 2017, http://spektr.press/kak-dela-delayutsya-na-chem-derzhatsya-ekonomika-i-finansy-DNR-i-LNR/ (accessed 1 October 2019).

Skorik, M. (2017b). Chto pochem na Donbase. Po kakim schetam rasplachivayutsya zhiteli DNR i LNR. [How much are things in the Donbas. What accounts the residents of DNR and LNR use], *SpektrPress*, January 17, 2017, https://spektr.press/chto-pochem-na-donbasse-po-kakim-schetam-rasplachivayutsya-zhiteli-dnr-i-lnr/ (accessed 1 October 2019).

Traynor, I., Walker, S., Salem, H., Lewis, P. (2014). Putin says Eastern Ukraine referendum on autonomy should be postponed, The Guardian, May 8, 2014, http://www.theguardian.com/world/2014/may/07/ukraine-crisis-putin-referendum-autonomy-postponed (accessed 1 October 2019).

UN OHCHR. (2015). *11th report on the human rights situation in Ukraine*. Geneva: United Nations Office of High Commissioner on Human Rights (UN OHCHR).

UN Meetings Coverage. (2019). Senior officials urge steps to make Eastern Ukraine ceasefire irreversible, telling Security Council Minsk Accords remain largely unimplemented, UN Official Website, February 12, 2019, https://www.un.org/press/en/2019/sc13698.doc.htm (accessed 1 October 2019).

Vandysheva, O. (2018). Referendum sostoyalsia [Referendum took place]. Expert Online, *Expert.Ru*, November 20, 2018, http://expert.ru/2014/05/11/referendum-v-donbasse-sostoyalsya/ (accessed 1 October 2019).

Vedernikova, I., Mostova, Y., Rakhmanin, S. (2014). Southeast: A branch of our tree. Dzerkalo Tyzhnia, April 18, 2014: 1–2.

Vesti. (2014). Za nezavisimost LNR progolosovali pochti 100% izbirateley [Almost 100% of voters supported the independence of the LPR], Vesti.UA, May 12, 2014, https://vesti-ukr.com/donbass/51220-za-nezavisimost-lnr-progolosovali-pochti-100-izbiratelej (accessed 1 October 2019).

Weber, M. (1978). *Economy and society: An outline of interpretive sociology*. Berkeley: University of California Press.

Zadorozhny, O., Korotkyi, T. (2015). Legal assessment of the Russian Federation's policy in the context of the establishment and activities of terrorist organizations «Donetsk People's Republic» («DPR») and «Lugansk People's Republic» («LPR») in Eastern Ukraine. *European Political and Law Discourse* 2(1): 8–18.

Zakharchenko, A. (2018). Aleksandr Zakharchenko: "Strategiya razvitiya Respubliki budet razrabatyvatsya narodom" [Aleksandr Zakharchenko: "The strategy of the republic's development will be designed by the people"], *The Official Website of Alexander Zakharchenko*, March 1, 2018, https://av-zakharchenko.su/inner-article/Stati/Aleksandr-Zaharchenko-Strategiya-razvitiya-Respubliki2/ (accessed 1 October 2019).

Post-Soviet Separatism in Historical Perspective

Jan Claas Behrends

Nation or Empire? The Questions of 1917 and the Questions of Today

Separatism has many faces. This essay argues that in order to understand post-Soviet separatism we need to address both the conflicts of the 20th century, i.e. the instable geopolitical order in modern Eastern Europe as well as the role of force, i.e. both international and civil wars and their actors, to support separatist claims and imperial politics. A combined assessment of these two factors will help us to explain the peculiarities that distinguish post-Soviet conflict from other European cases of separatism and from the post-colonial world. We will see that the geopolitical disputes of the region may serve as a key to understand post-Soviet separatism[1] and understand that the tension between the concepts of nation and empire has shaped the region for the last century. It continues to be a matter of war and peace. The establishment of sovereign nation-states in Eastern Europe in 1918 and again in 1989/91 has been contested by imperial powers that did not accept the loss of prestige, territory and influence in the area. Successful state-building following imperial collapse was often tied to the use of military force and war (Connelly 2019).

Russia's conquests since the times of Ivan IV, Peter I and Catherine II had made it the largest land empire and it had introduced the country as a player in European geopolitics (Hosking 1997; Kappeler 1992; for the ideology of Russian Empire: Plokhy 2017). To this day, this history of successful expansion and domination influences the way Russian élites define themselves and their country's foreign policy. Despite internal weaknesses and

---

1   On separatism see e.g. Paković & Radan 2001; Cabestan & Paković 2013; George 2009; Hughes & Sasse 2002.

the persistent notion of cultural and social backwardness, Russian imperial and military prowess loomed large throughout the 18th and 19th century. Russian elites attempted to build a strong state in order to modernize their country and keep it competitive in a rapidly changing international arena (Kotkin 2014: 11–138). This strategy, however, led primarily to the formation and petrification of autocracy. Instead of modern institutions Russian statehood was characterized by personal power at the top and in various fiefdoms. With the rise of Germany to the West and Japan in the East from the 1860s onwards as well as the advent of nationalism within its borders, Russia's past imperial conquests became increasingly contested as the empire entered the 20th century.

The results of World War I marked the end of imperial domination in Eastern Europe. Russia, Germany, Habsburg and the Ottoman Empire—all dominating powers of the region—lost the war and their empire. Their collapse in 1917/18 shattered the pre-1914 geopolitical order. While there had long been national movements in Eastern Europe, the support of US-president Woodrow Wilson for a new national order was crucial. Wilson first imagined and then pushed for peoples to receive "their" nation-states (Wolff 2020). The vacuum left behind by once mighty dynasties eventually led to the (re)establishment of nation-states in Eastern Europe. However, this was a long and bloody process: in contrast to the West, the Great War in the East did not end in 1918 (Holquist 2002; Borodziej & Górny 2018; Gerwarth 2016; Engelstein 2018: 235–360; Böhler 2018).

Initially, imperial collapse created a *Gewaltraum,* or sphere of violence where different actors competed for power and territory. Various conflicts lingered on for years and became even more violent and unpredictable until, in the end, new borders were determined not by political settlement as in the Paris treaties but in a series of inter-state and civil wars. The wars of 1917–1922 resulted in a partial reconstruction of Russian imperial statehood—from 1924 onwards in the form of the USSR—and in the establishment of (semi-)sovereign nation-states on its periphery and between Germany and Russia. With the exception of the Austrian case and Western Poland, where the Allies intervened, this new order was determined on the battlefield – this was true in Finland, the Baltic region, as well as the Polish-Russian borderlands, Ukraine and the Caucasus (Zamoisky 2014; Borzecki 2008). Initially successfully independent states such as Georgia (1918–1921) and (to a lesser degree) Ukraine were defeated by the Red Army during the Soviet Reconquista of the former imperial lands (Schnell 2012; Mawdsley 2005; Meinander 2011: 125–142). Thus, in 1917–1922, the establishment of nation-states in the region depended on their performance in war. There was no negotiated separation from the collapsed empire; the alternatives were either successful or failed armed struggle for independence. Like in the 19th century (in Western Europe and the Americas) separation from empire and nation-building was only possible through war. Only those states that built and commanded strong armies persisted; the Bolsheviks or Piłsudki's Poland serve as a prime examples of successful state building while e.g. Ukraine largely failed to establish a central authority and armed forces that could defend the country. The wars fought did not merely define the new states but also shaped the new elites. Both the circle of civil war-hardened men around Stalin as well as the former members of the *Legiony Polskie* remained influential; their political style and their fondness for force had to be reckoned with. This led to a more violent political culture than e.g. in Czechoslovakia where the collapse of empire had been peaceful and civil war could be avoided (for an extended version of this argument see Langewiesche 2019; for an Eastern European perspective Snyder 2003).

Crucially, the results of this armed struggle in the East and the inter-war order established in Paris were not accepted by the former imperial powers Russia and Germany. Both Weimar Germany and Soviet Russia were revisionist powers in their own right (Laqueur 1990: 25–157). Berlin and Moscow believed that the situation of 1918, when both Russia and Germany were defeated, could not be the basis for any legitimate and lasting order in Europe. They opposed the Wilsonian project. In the view of their elites, newly established nation-states of Eastern Europe such as Poland, Finland or the Baltic States had limited legitimacy and sovereignty and were often seen as a temporary phenomenon (in

Germany they were marked as "Randstaaten", i.e. "states on the margin" or "Saisonstaaten", i.e. "seasonal states"). Both the USSR and Germany did not accept their post-war borders as permanent. They strove to undermine and ultimately destroy an order which they perceived was forced on them in an instance of weakness. Crucially for our subject, there were many players—representatives of ethnic minorities as well as states—in inter-war Europe that disputed the post-war borders and were looking for opportunities to change them—peacefully or by force. The question of minorities and their rights loomed large and became a vehicle for inter-state conflict as well as separatist desires (Scheuermann 2000). Thus, the post-World War I era was a time of geopolitical instability. During the 1920s, the Wilsonian notion that Eastern Europe could be organized in a similar way as the West of the continent remained contested. The foundation for imperial rollback was laid even before Stalin or Hitler came to power.

The imperial roll-back of 1939, however, was extremely violent because it was driven by totalitarian powers. It proved to be genocidal from the onset in September 1939 (Moorhouse 2014; Kotkin 2017: 642–701; Moorhouse 2019; Weber 2019). At the same time, both the Nazis and the Soviets had shown throughout the 1930s that they could fan separatism in order to pursue their imperial goals. The case of the Sudetenland-Germans, the establishment of separatist Communist parties within Poland as well as the Soviet pan-Slavism of September 1939 directed against the Polish Republic were examples of the use of *völkisch* separatism against sovereign states (Behrends 2016). Thus, separatism in 20th century Eastern Europe could be a movement to gain a nation-state—such as the Ukrainian nationalists in inter-war Poland. But it could also be used by great powers in order to justify their revisionist ambition against smaller states. Clearly, the great power sponsors of ethnic separatism had an overwhelming military capacity as well as diplomatic means to back up their claims and sponsor separatist movements or parties.

In geopolitical terms the results of the Second World War meant the end of the Wilsonian vision and the return to an imperial order in Eastern Europe. Moscow's victory gave it a position it had not enjoyed since the year 1813. The pact between Hitler and Stalin in 1939, the Allied conferences in Yalta and Potsdam in 1945 as well as Helsinki in 1975 cemented the notion of Eastern Europe as an imperial space. While Stalin did not choose to nominally integrate the entire region into the USSR—he annexed what he had gained in his agreement with Germany in 1939 but not the formally independent nation-states (re)created in Yalta. In 1945, even Stalin could not return to the geopolitical order of 1914 or to the post-revolutionary phantasy of a multinational communist super-state. Rather, the USSR allowed the re-establishment of nation-states, governed by communist parties (sometimes in disguise) that would from now on serve as the outer ring of the Soviet empire (Naimark & Gibianskii 1997; for Poland: Kersten 1991). During the years of 1944–48 it became clear that the "people's republics" enjoyed only limited sovereignty; they could, e.g., not join the Marshal Plan even if they strove to like the Czechoslovakia before 1948. Their foreign policy was subject to approval by the Kremlin long before this was officially spelled out in the "Brezhnev-doctrine" of 1968. The uprisings in Berlin (1953) and in Budapest (1956) had clarified that the death of Stalin did not spell out the end of Soviet empire in Eastern Europe.

Again, in the East the World War did not end in May 1945 but was translated into various regional low-scale insurgencies against Soviet domination. In the Baltics, in Poland and in parts of Ukraine it took the Soviets many years before the partisan movements were eventually defeated (Weiner 2001). During the Warsaw Uprising the Poles fought in vain against an imperial order dominated by Stalin's USSR (Borodziej 2006). While the United States initially promoted the idea of "captive nations" in Eastern Europe, the imperial order gained international legitimacy and was finally recognized during détente and through the treaty of Helsinki (Stöver 2002; Westad 2017 for a global perspective). Those fighting for national independence from the Soviet Union were confined to the fringes of European politics. By and large, Western leaders began to value the stability provided by the Cold War in Europe. By the 1980s, even the German public widely accepted the Iron Curtain that divided their country. The Federal Republic enjoyed a privileged partnership with the Soviet leaders through *Ostpolitik* which was begun by Willy Brandt and continued by chancellors Schmidt and Kohl (Ruchniewicz 2012). While *Ostpolitik* initially claimed to stand for 'change through rapprochement', it actually legitimized and stabilized the imperial post-war order in Europe. For the sake of détente and business relations Bonn accepted the Brezhnev-doctrine of Eastern Europe as a Soviet sphere of influence. Until 1988, the geopolitical order in Eastern Europe seemed stable; so stable that Chancellor Kohl hosted East Germany's Erich Honecker as a guest of honor in Bonn in 1987. The key to stability was the combination of imperial domination and absence of war.

The period from 1914 to 1945 was one of geopolitical instability, war, civil war and genocide in Eastern Europe. In contrast, after the initial Sovietization was accomplished, partisans were defeated and the party-state established, the years 1944/45 to 1989/91 were marked by geopolitical stability. The overwhelming power of the Soviet military did not allow countries to break the chains of empire—where this was attempted in 1953, 1956 or in 1968 force was used to suppress national uprisings. Still, nation-building continued under Soviet domination and even within the USSR (Liber 2016). In many ways, the results of the war as well as the communist persecution of traditional elites created more homogenous societies. Communist propaganda widely revived tropes created in the inter-war period or the 19th century (for Poland Zaremba 2001). By the middle of the 1970s, the Soviet domination of Eastern Europe seemed to stay for the foreseeable future. The geopolitical order of the Cold War had the advantages of being seemingly stable, predictable and peaceful. It was also simple in that only one player—the USSR—was able to control the entire region. But any reform of the communist system might clearly revive the national aspirations throughout the region. Nationalism and the quest for self-determination were just contained as long as the restrictions of late socialism applied.

Violence and Civility: Perestroika, End of Empire and the Return of Separatism

While any challenge to the geopolitical order in Eastern Europe that arose before 1985 was suppressed using massive military force – for the last time in Poland during 'martial law' of 1981 when the regime put hundreds of tanks on the streets – things changed considerably, albeit not completely, with the tenure of Mikhail Gorbachev as Soviet leader (Taubman 2017; Behrends 2018). We know now that his advisors were early on toying with the idea to let East Central Europe part ways in order to modernize and save the USSR. Empire was increasingly seen as more of a burden than an asset. In order to understand this process, it should be pointed out that the means of imperial domination within East Central Europe and in the Soviet Union differed. Outside the USSR, the stability of the Communist system was ensured by the presence of the Soviet Army (acting on orders of the Soviet leadership) which could be used to put down any attempts to escape Moscow's domination. Inside the USSR, however, it was primarily the CPSU itself that served as an iron bond to keep the empire together. While the Army as well as the KGB were also important pillars of Leninist statehood (Party, Army, and secret police), they were technically under the supervision of the party. The rapprochement with the West pursued by Mikhail Gorbachev and his foreign policy team would soon limit his potential to use armed force in Eastern Europe – if he wanted to continue the policy of disarmament and keep his status as a partner of the West. Clearly, Moscow's partnership with Washington and Bonn began to outweigh the benefits of the USSR's post war empire (Westad 2017: 527–578; Taubman 2017: 393–500). This is certainly the geopolitical reason for its mostly peaceful demise during the year 1989. The emergence of a culture of civil dissidence in East Central Europe since the 1960s contributed to the peaceful end of communist rule – despite the fact that the party-states remained armed to their teeth until the final days of their existence. Change within the Soviet Empire, however, could only begin when the centre relinquished control and hesitated to use military force.

The situation in the inner core of the Soviet empire—the USSR itself—was somewhat different from East Central Europe. Ideologically, the problem of ethnic diversity was explained away using the discourse of "friendship of the peoples". In reality, however, the federal structures were important. The individual Soviet republics offered an alternative point of reference and—within the confines of Soviet ideology—could promote national culture and identity. Therefore, they may be interpreted as arenas of nation-building under communist rule. The republics did not only integrate different ethnic groups into the larger Union state, they also served as engines of national integration within their own borders. After the massacres of Stalinism, (communist) national elites made a comeback under his successors. To a certain degree, national culture as well as the fostering of identities in Soviet republics were tolerated and even supported under Khrushchev and Brezhnev. This trend may be observed from the Baltic States to Ukraine to the Caucasus. At the same time, Russian nationalism and the idea of Russian empire made a comeback—both in dissident circles and within the structures of the party-state (Brudny 1998; Mitrokhin 2003; Plokhy 2017: 277–299). This increasing nationalization of public life during late socialism may be interpreted as one of the possible breaking points of the Union. Nonetheless, it took the policies of Mikhail Gorbachev to turn national cultures into actual separatism and the end of the USSR into a plausible scenario.

At the beginning of his tenure, Mikhail Gorbachev and his team strove to reform the USSR in order to regain competitiveness in the Cold War (Behrends 2012; Taubman 2017: 205–251). The new Soviet leadership took several steps to enable first economic, then political reform. After having tried the quintessential Soviet approach through mobilization (*"uskorenie"*) and prohibition of alcohol, Gorbachev began to experiment with more openness (*"glasnost'"*) and with an overhaul of the system itself (*"perestroika"*). Allowing public debate proved to be a crucial step in many ways: it enabled people not merely to voice their grievances but also to begin a discussion about Soviet history. The Bolsheviks crimes against specific nations and ethnic groups—from the Cossacks to Ukrainians, Kazakhs, Tartars, the Baltic peoples and the Jews, to name just a few — could for the first time be publicly remembered (Davies 1991; for a history of Soviet genocide: Naimark 2010). The discussion about terror and repression against various ethnic groups triggered the collapse of the official discourse of the 'friendship of the people'. In the preceding years, this discourse about the past became especially formative in regions that had been annexed in 1939 and 1940 such as Western Ukraine and the Baltic Republics. Here, the memory of Soviet, initial repression and deportations as well as the post-1945 civil war resurfaced. They were no longer a taboo. Thus, Gorbachev's rule allowed the rediscovery of national identities across the USSR but first and foremost in its borderlands that had preserved them more vividly. They were also the first to demand "sovereignty" from Moscow — although initially this did not necessarily mean complete independence, i.e. separation, from the USSR (Kramer 2011). Rather, the initial goal in the Baltic states was to strengthen local institutions and establish something akin to "home rule" within the confines of a reformed Soviet Union. After the peaceful revolutions in the fall of 1989, the Baltic States and Western Ukraine were clearly influenced by the example of Poland, the GDR and the ČSSR (for details: Kramer 2003; Kramer 2004; Kramer 2005). If the outer empire could peacefully secede, why was the same scenario not plausible within the USSR? Would Moscow use force within the USSR when it abstained from doing so in Central Europe?

During the late 1980s, the Soviet leadership reacted in two distinctly different ways to the disintegration of the Soviet empire. Despite the strong presence of the Soviet Armed Forces in East Central Europe and the GDR and the examples of 1953, 1956 and 1968, Gorbachev clearly ruled out the use of military force in this region — even during the dramatic days between October and New Year of 1989 when communist power in the region disintegrated rapidly. Soviet troops stayed in their barracks and supported neither the ruling parties nor the opposition. They remained neutral. With the exception of Romania, where a violent coup took place, a peaceful transition characterized the fall of communism in

Europe. This was, however, not the case within the borders of the USSR (for case studies: Sabrow 2012).

The disintegration of the Soviet Union began long before it was dissolved by the leaders of Russia, Belarus and Ukraine in December 1991 (Taubman 2017: 500–538; for an overview Kotkin 2001; Plokhy 2014). Violent conflict between different nations and ethnic groups erupted from 1988 onwards and eventually led to civil war, violent clashes between the Army and civilians, pogroms and expulsions as well as partial state collapse in the North Caucasus, parts of Central Asia and in Lithuania. Thus, although the collapse of the Soviet military complex was largely peaceful — in Stephen Kotkin's famous words Armageddon was averted — there were significant pockets of violence that persisted through the Soviet collapse and sometimes — as in Karabakh, Georgia or Transnistria — escalated into regular military conflicts between local forces that often involved the center and persist until today (Sussex 2012; van Herpen 2015).

In order to understand these (post-)Soviet wars it is paramount to address the war in Afghanistan and to understand how it was fought (Galeotti 1995; Kalinovsky 2011; Behrends 2015a; Penter 2017). The invasion of Afghanistan at the end of 1979 ended a long period of peace for the USSR that had lasted since 1945. Since the beginning of the campaign at the Hindu Kush, however, the USSR and Russia, its main successor state, have been continuously involved in counter-insurgency operations, low scale wars, or so-called "peace keeping" missions mostly on the Soviet Union and Russia's southern periphery like in Tajikistan or Karabakh. Therefore, when it comes to the use of military force, the year 1979 marks a watershed because it eventually led to the rise of a milieu of veterans of these wars, experts in the use of violence, who became increasingly influential. These post-World War II Soviet military men first gained prominence in the campaign to elect the "congress of people's deputies" in early 1989. They formed a large and aggressive group within the congress itself and staunchly defended the interests of the Soviet Army and its conduct during the war in Afghanistan against such critics as Andrei Sakharov and other liberal dissidents. They could be seen as the spearhead of what Yuri Afanasyevs dubbed the infamous "passive obedient majority" and would soon become instrumental in their rejection of liberal reform as well as in their promotion of the use of force in political conflicts (Horvarth 2005: 81-138). The emerging post-Soviet political class in Russia as well as the KGB understood early on, that they would constitute an important political factor in post-communist Russia. Boris Yeltsin himself, the supposed leader of a democratic Russia, nominated Afghanistan war hero Aleksander Rutskoy as his running mate in his bid for the Russian presidency (Colton 2008: 177-236). He clearly anticipated that he needed the support and loyalty of the military in order to establish a power base for himself. He could do without the party, but not without the army.

Liberalization, the end of party-rule and the demise of the USSR are remembered today as the legacies of the Gorbachev-era. The lack of change in other areas—especially the military and the secret services—is often overlooked. In the medium term it proved to be just as important as the reforms of the political system and the economy. While the Army and the *siloviki* had to withdraw from Eastern Europe, their institutional power at home remained unbroken (Albats 1994; Soldatov 2010). During his seven-year-reign, the last general secretary never bothered to reform these important pillars of the Leninist dictatorship. He occasionally purged their leaders, but he did not develop a vision what role they could play in a more open society. Thus, when the empire fell the party disintegrated but the other main pillars of repression—the army and the secret police—remained. They were instruments that could be used in the post-imperial struggles that lay ahead. Like in 1917/18, the remnants of the imperial army would be the fanning the flames of future conflict. As in 1917, in 1991 there was an abundance of weapons and armed men in the region. The collapse of empire in peace-time precluded a catastrophe like in 1917-1922. Still, the ingredients for war and strife were certainly there. And as in the years after 1917, new groups of militarized and violent men emerged and left their mark on politics and on society at large. While the emergence of violent conflict after the Cold War was slower and more restrained than after World War I, we can nevertheless observe similarities: the partial breakdown of statehood, roaming armed groups, local separatism and warlordism as well as continued nation-building. Again, the collapse created both opportunities for new order and for the type of breakdown that led to the emergence of a *Gewaltraum*.

Imperial Disintegration and Post-Imperial Conflict: 1991 and the End of the USSR

Mikhail Gorbachev's attempt to "civilize from above" led to ambivalent results. The end of stagnation and the return of history led to increasing tensions between different ethnic groups. It also undermined the foundations of the Soviet empire — both abroad and closer to home. In 1989, the communist nation-states of Eastern Europe broke free peacefully. This was only allowed to happen because, as outlined above, Moscow had abandoned the Brezhnev doctrine. Nevertheless, at the same time, during 1989, 1990 and even in 1991, Gorbachev's leadership — increasingly in coalition with the enemies of reform within the Soviet *nomenklatura* — attempted to preserve the Soviet Union by oppressing national movements and separatist sentiments. During the year 1990, this resulted in a stalemate between Moscow and local politics in the Baltic States — the presence of Soviet troops and the persistent threat to use force kept them in the USSR. Neither side was ready to mount an assault. With troops on the streets and barricades, Vilnius, Riga or Tallinn looked more than ever like cities under Soviet occupation.

For other reasons, throughout the North Caucasus and in parts of Central Asia the situation remained volatile and prone to military violence. Locally, this was a result of the breakdown of state order and of ethnic strife. Where the institutions of the party-state collapsed, local strongmen would become the new power brokers. In retrospect, it remains unclear how long the decay of central authority in the USSR that started in 1990 could have continued. The putsch of August 1991 certainly ushered in a new phase of imperial collapse: it buried the project of a new union treaty that those *siloviki* allied with Gorbachev had launched in the first place (Lozo 2014). The defeat of the putschists allowed republics like Ukraine or Belarus but also the Russian leadership under Yeltsin more room for manoeuvre. The Baltic states seized the opportunity to leave the Soviet Union straight away and regain sovereignty first won in 1918 (Plokhy 2014: 73–170). They followed the example of East-Central Europe and left the empire almost without bloodshed. After the putsch Gorbachev himself quickly turned into a head-of-state acting under supervision of the Russian president who was increasingly in charge. Boris Yeltsin, however, needed allies in order to destroy the centre of Soviet power. Crucially, the Russian president was willing to sacrifice Moscow's control of other republics in his struggle against Gorbachev. In the fall of 1991, power meant more to him than empire (and he could not have both). This situation opened up the path to Belavezha where the end of the USSR was sealed by Belarus, Russia, and, as Serhii Plokhy has argued, most crucially by Ukraine (Plokhy 2014: 275–294). Ukraine's intention to leave the union was legitimized by the referendum that had taken place there in December. Public support in all parts of Ukraine for leaving the Union made the project feasible. While the accords of Belavezha successfully undermined Gorbachev's power, they created new uncertainties. The SNG, although most of the remaining Soviet republics joined, was more or less stillborn. There simply could be no Soviet empire of sovereign nations.

At first glance, it looked like the USSR had dissolved into 15 independent nation-states. For a short while, Russian president Boris Yeltsin even contemplated leading Russia onto the path to a nation-state (Colton 2008: 263–320). In the end, however, the traditionalists in Moscow prevented this option and steered Russia back onto its traditional imperial course. Thus, the USSR dissolved into 14 nation-states—initially mostly lacking many of the basic institutions needed to function as a sovereign nation—and one post-imperial actor, i.e. the Russian Federation. The various ongoing military conflicts between and within these new states were not addressed in the accords that ended seven decades of Soviet power. In 1992, there were territorial strives in Moldova, between Armenia and Azerbaijan, within Georgia, there was civil war in Tajikistan and, at best, fragile state power throughout most of Central Asia. In the relationship between Russia and Ukraine it seemed early on, that the Crimean question as well as the fate of the Black Sea Fleet might become points of contention (Sasse 2007; Zofka 2015: 281–397). It was equally unclear whether the imperial disintegration that had begun in 1989 in East Central Europe might not continue in 1992. Inside the Russian state, several regions — including Chechnya and Tatarstan — strove for sovereignty (Kondrashov 1999; Galeotti 2014: 22–29). Given the logic of the times, this could eventually lead them to independence from the Russian Federation. One could, indeed, again pose the question of 1917: where are the legitimate borders of Russia? The 1990s would have to provide an answer to that crucial question. Certainly, separatism had now become an issue comparable to the years after the First World War.

The Paradoxes of Post-Soviet Separatism

The immediate challenge in the post-Soviet space of the early 1990s was to prevent further state collapse and consolidate the borders inherited from the USSR. New states and especially Russia as the largest multi-ethnic successor had to deal with the remnants of the "affirmative action empire", i.e. with the leftovers of Soviet federalism (Martin 2001; Graziosi 2017). What rights and privileges would be allocated after the Soviet collapse to autonomous republics and regions? Clearly, some republics like Chechnya were willing to fight for their separation from Moscow while others like Tatarstan strove for the attributes of sovereign statehood but tried to resolve the situation through a negotiated settlement. Again, much depended on the local actors. The first stand-off in Chechnya occurred already during the final months of the Soviet Union. Russia was represented by vice-president Alexander Rutskoy, veteran commander of the Soviet Air Force, while Chechnya was headed by Dzhokhar Dudaev, yet another veteran of the Afghanistan war. At this point, a military conflict between the two sides was avoided because bloodshed was not in the interest of Boris Yeltsin (Plokhy 2014, 243-249). Still, this incident of 1991 reveals a decisive development: straight from the battlefield, the *afgantsy* had risen to positions of political power (Ackermann & Galbas 2015). Not only in Russia (but especially there), the veterans of the war at the Hindu Kush became an important factor in post-communist politics. Afghanistan veterans represented the core of a new milieu of military experts. During post-imperial conflicts, the *afgantsy* would often promote the use of force to dissolve dispute. Hence, we may argue that lessons in the use of violence learned at the Hindu Kush came to influence the way post-Soviet politics evolved (Behrends 2015b).

The history of the 1990s showed that separatism played out differently in East Central Europe, the Balkans and the post-Soviet space. The ČSSR's "velvet revolution" of 1989 was succeeded by the "velvet divorce" between the Czech Republic and Slovakia in 1992 (Krapfl 2013; Žantovský 2014: 477–501). A peaceful end of dictatorship, one may argue, set the precedent for a negotiated end of the binational state. While Czechoslovakia—like all communist party-states—had a strong military, its Army had not seen action during the Cold War. There simply were no Czech *afgantsy* to push for the use of force. This might have made a crucial difference in 1992. In contrast to the Czech example, the Serbian government proved unwilling to allow the peaceful separation of Yugoslavia. The Yugoslav case showed how quickly separatist ambition could lead to the break-up of a multinational state that had long seemed stable under communist rule (Gagnon 2004). Political elites in Belgrade as well as in the Yugoslav republics created a dangerous situation because they were willing to support their claims by the use of military force. The highly militarized Yugoslav society of the Cold War certainly contributed to this explosive situation. Almost all men had received extensive military training. Although mobilization for civil war proved at times difficult (Lučić 2015), the dynamic unleashed by nationalism and the mobilization of armed men on all sides of the conflict fostered the outbreak of full-scale war. In the end, a settlement could only be reached through outside military intervention both in Bosnia and in the Kosovo conflict. The Yugoslav case illustrates how local separatism could escalate into military conflict that would eventually lead to the intervention of

NATO and the United States in the Balkans. Thus, separatist war was ended by the use of overwhelming military force from the outside. Finding a lasting diplomatic solution for the region has proved to be difficult and has still not been achieved. Borders within the former Yugoslavia remain contested and the return to military conflict is prevented merely by the presence of foreign peacekeepers. While nation-building in Croatia and Slovenia eventually succeeded, the post-war situation in the rest of former Yugoslavia remains highly volatile. It seems clear that these successive waves of separatism succeeded because they were supported, or at least not opposed, by the West.

In the post-Soviet space, the situation proved to be even more complicated than in the Balkans. There were separatist movements within Moldova and Georgia that were willing to use force to support their claims (on Georgia Marten 2012: 64–101). Already in 1992, the republic of Transnistria was created but never internationally recognized. As in Yugoslavia, outsiders—in this case Russia—intervened and played a decisive role through its support for the separatist causes. Regular Russian forces or Russian "peacekeepers" changed the military situation on the ground (Zoska 2015: 139-280). Therefore, the failure or success of these separatist struggles were tied both to the willingness of local actors to use force and to the intervention of the remaining imperial power—Moscow. From the early 1990s, the Kremlin provided cover and legitimacy to local warlords in Transnistria, Abkhazia and Ossetia. It thereby actively undermined the sovereignty and integrity of other post-Soviet states that began to lose control over their territory. These conflicts helped to establish the Russian Federation as a power that would intervene with its military beyond its own borders.

The case of Crimea in the early 1990s shows that negotiated settlements were possible—even in the post-Soviet space (Sasse 2007: 175–200; Zofka 2015: 362–397). A still nuclear-armed Ukraine had, of course, a much stronger bargaining position than Moldova or Georgia, countries that were on the brink of state failure and had no strong military of their own. While a substantial separatist movement as well as Russian military bases existed in Crimea and contested Kyiv's full sovereignty over the peninsula until the illegal annexation of 2014, all sides to the conflict remained committed to avoid military mobilization and the use of force. While Russian nationalists and established politicians like Moscow's long-term mayor Yuri Luzhkov used strong rhetoric, visited the peninsula and supported separatist groups, these actions could be contained because they refrained from violence. During the early 1990s, the institutions of the Ukrainian state in Crimea continued to function. They did not come under armed attack. These factors made a negotiated settlement possible that served to keep the peace until Russian military action of early spring 2014. Without substantial help from Moscow, the activities of the Crimean separatist decreased throughout the 1990s. The local separatists remained at the fringe of local politics. Without outside intervention, and perhaps more crucially, without the will to use force Crimean separatism was a political failure.

Only use of military force allowed statelets on separatist territory to be established and local warlords to come to power. Often, they were violent men who had gained experience either in Afghanistan or in the rapidly spreading insurgencies across the former USSR. In contrast to the states formed after the dissolution of the Union in 1991, separatists of the early 1990s largely failed to establish legitimate statehood or gain formal recognition under international law. Rather, their territory was informally ruled by coalitions of local strongmen, often including local criminals. Overall, they remained weak statelets. Similar things could be said about many of the officially recognized post-Soviet states – they also featured weak institutions and lacked rule-of-law. It might therefore be more accurate to state that places like Abkhazia or Transnistria experienced the post-Soviet condition in a most radical way. They served as examples how post-Soviet elites could rule unrestrained by institutions, law or international obligations (for examples of post-Soviet misrule: Dawisha 2014; Minakov 2018: 17–102). Similar to statelets in civil-war Ukraine after 1917, they are often ruled by warlords in highly personalized ways.

Intra-Russian separatism is yet another case to prove the argument that the use of military force is crucial to understanding the nature and the development of these conflicts. Without the use of force, institutions loyal to Moscow persisted. Again, the development of separatist conflicts within Russia was not predetermined. Rather, it very much depended on the national and local actors and their concrete decisions. Tatarstan and Chechnya may serve as the most prominent examples. In order to understand the development inside Russia, however, it is necessary to understand how the Yeltsin administration legitimized the internal use of military force. After all, the 1991 putsch against Gorbachev failed — amongst other reasons — because the conspirators could not agree on the use of force against their opponents in Moscow or against the revolting population. This gave the impression that they were not determined to see their endeavour through. Civil resistance against the coup became possible, plausible and eventually led to the failure of the plot (Lozo 2014: 159–315). Only two years later, however, the situation had changed considerably. Throughout the summer of 1993, the power struggle between the president and the Supreme Soviet escalated in Russia. Both players were left-overs from the perestroika years when Gorbachev started undermining party-rule by creating alternative centres of power — a parliament as well as the presidency. The emergence of several centres of power during times of transition was not unusual for Russia. While the presidency clearly stood in the Russian tradition of strongman-rule and autocracy, a democratically elected congress of deputies represented another experiment in parliamentarisation. The falling-out over the course of economic reform in Russia provided the background for the dispute. Still, there could have been an attempt to settle the conflict through negotiations or a national round table in the spirit of 1989. This was, however, not attempted. Rather, both sides were determined to prevail using force. In the end, president Yeltsin used his authority as commander-in-chief to let tanks shell and soldiers storm the heavily fortified and defended building on the Moskva river. The fighting in Moscow's centre and around the Ostankino television station, which rebels intended to occupy, exemplified how political questions in post-Soviet Russia could be decided by the use of force. By allowing both the presidency and a parliament to coexist,

Gorbachev had created a situation akin to 1917 with its "dual power". From 1993 onwards, there was only one single power: the president.

In many ways, the violence of October 1993 was crucial in determining the political culture of post-Soviet Russia. It marked the end of the civilizing process from above initiated by Gorbachev in 1985 (Behrends 2015c). Russia's elites aborted the path to more civility. The destruction of parliament as well as the hasty establishment of a new "super-presidential" constitution marked the return to autocracy in Russia. Once again, there would only be one centre of power: the president and his administration. The new parliament ("Duma") and the judiciary did not recover from this blow; they lost weight in the new political system and would eventually be subordinated to the executive. Furthermore, the Russian Army became a political factor in its own right. While in Soviet times, the Army had been under strict control of the Communist Party, the Russian Army of the 1990s became a political factor and a tool to be used by autocratic leaders throughout the post-Soviet realm (Barylski 1998). Soviet style militarization of society continued in Russia (Eichler 2012). Its leadership had made Yeltsin's October victory possible and could now demand pay-back from the president. The army continued to punch over its weight in post-communist politics.

The events of 1993 also help to understand the beginning of the Chechen War the following year: the president had given the Army a new privileged position and he had legitimized the use of military force inside Russia's own borders (Tiskov 2004; Galeotti 2014; Gilligan 2010; Le Huérou 2014). Additionally, Yeltsin hoped to raise his own popularity using a short and victorious campaign in the North Caucasus. Alas, Chechnya proved to be costly and difficult like Afghanistan. The first Russian campaign against the local separatists ended in defeat for Moscow's troops that proved ill-prepared for the determined fighters and the mountainous terrain in Chechnya. Even the use of superior air power against the capital Groznyi and the unrestrained terror against civilians did not give Moscow the upper hand in this war. The fight against the separatists also meant the introduction of terrorism in post-

Communist Russia. During the 1990s and early 2000s, Chechen fighters managed on several occasions to use terror to bring the war back to Russia. Clearly, the first war in Chechnya did not lead to the anticipated results: it was neither short nor did it popularize Yeltsin's rule or stabilize the Russian state. To the contrary, it helped plunge Russia and the president even more deeply into crisis. In the end, Moscow had to negotiate a peace with the Chechen separatist leadership in order to end an unpopular war and save Yeltsin's hold on power. The legacy of Chechnya was the further brutalization of Russian warfare as well as the criminalization of politics in the country. This campaign also re-established warlord rule (Marten 2012: 102–138) not seen since the 1920s. Still, Chechnya showed the separation from the Russian Federation came at a high cost: Moscow showed it was willing to use its military might against those striving to leave. The violence also served as a signal to the rest of the North Caucasus and to Tatarstan where similar separatist movements existed.

Boris Yeltsin's hand-picked successor Vladimir Putin did not wait long to leave his imprint on the history of violence in the post-Soviet space (Hill & Gaddy 2015; Meyers 2015; Greene & Robertson 2019). Putin chose to legitimize himself in 1999 by conducting an even more brutal assault on separatist Chechnya. Ever since he took the presidency in 2000, the Russian leader has left no doubt that the use of military force — be it inside or outside the Russian borders — is always considered a legitimate option. Putin used the issue of separatism to crack down on civil rights for all Russian citizens. While in the 1990s journalists were in danger in Chechnya, there was still an opportunity for critical reporting and exposing the level of violence used. This ended under Putin: the media, especially its coverage of the Chechen, but eventually also other subjects came under strict control of the Kremlin. Media control established during the Chechen campaign became a pillar of emerging Putinism (Wilson 2005; Ostrovsky 2015: 179–326).

Structurally, the 1990s brought back some of the phenomena as well as the geopolitical struggle familiar from the inter-war period. Taken together, these developments formed the paradox of post-Soviet separatism. Since 1991, separatism could be used both as a tool of imperial roll-back, as well as a threat to a unified Russian state. We therefore need to differentiate between cases were separatist movements that were "weaponized" by Moscow in its struggle to gain influence over smaller post-Soviet states and those cases where the integrity of Russia itself was in peril—especially in the North Caucasus but potentially also in other regions. Both exist but are actually quite different phenomena. The instrumental use of separatist conflict to undermine the integrity of other sovereign nations is clearly a tactic that was also used during the inter-war period by both the USSR and Germany in their quest to undermine the order of the Paris treaties. In Russia, we can observe a hegemon that simultaneously promotes separatist warlords along its borders and is willing to use overwhelming force to extinguish separatism within its own territory. Paradoxically, the Kremlin both invents and fights separatism at the same time. These conflicts are clearly tight to the unresolved question if Eastern Europe and Eurasia should remain structured by nation-states—as initially agreed after the imperial collapse of 1989/91 in the Paris accords of 1992—or whether Russia can succeed in claiming the region as its patrimony. That would mean a return to the imperial order that was dominant before 1914 and from 1939 to 1989. We must understand that the imperial rollback is also, I would argue, very much the personal project of Putin and his entourage. Vladimir Putin understands that he has the power to escalate separatist struggles and that this power gives him leverage over his neighbours (on Russian foreign policy more broadly Stent 2019). It seems plausible that a successor might abandon sponsoring separatist wars as these campaigns prove to be costly for Russia. The bigger question is, however, whether future Russian elites will abandon their imperial outlook and are able to integrate Russia into an order of nation-states in Europe (Irisova et al. 2017). In other words: will Russia be able to leave Stalin behind and embrace Wilson?

Violent Men and Imperial Come-Back: The Politics of 2014

After the imperial collapse of 1991, Russia's military interventions took place in small nations such as Moldova or Georgia. The Kremlin stayed away from larger theatres of war. This changed recently with the invasion of Ukraine and the intervention in the Syrian civil war. In many ways, these wars are consequences of political decisions made in 1979 and 1993 – the invasion of Afghanistan and the bombing of the Russian parliament. Additionally, we may observe that Russia's current wars are more deeply imbedded in the controlled social-media and mass-media of the Kremlin – a phenomenon sometimes referred to as "hybrid war". While most conflicts of the 1990s were effectively "frozen", yet remain unsolved, the war in Ukraine took the use of separatism to a new dimension. The initial aim of 2014 was nothing less than the dismemberment of the current Ukrainian state (Wynnyckyj 2019: 213–240). Clearly, to the Kremlin of 2014 Ukraine was as much a *Saisonstaat*[2] as Poland was in the interwar era.

It is worth to remember that even during the Maidan protests in the winter of 2013/14, secession of Crimea from Ukraine was not an issue (Averre/ Wolczuk 2018). The fact that Russia did not have to invade the peninsula is also often overlooked – according to the agreements with Kyiv, its troops were already stationed there. This made it much easier for the Russian Army to manoeuvre, to take over strategic spots and to destroy the presence of the Ukrainian state. Although there was no open fighting, the occupation and annexation of Crimea was accomplished by the massive presence of soldiers and their show of force (Walker 2018: 133–184; Altai 2019: 71–182). While the initial separatist movement in Crimea had petered out during the late 1990s, the new separatism may be seen as an *inscenirovka* or a scripted secession carefully stage-managed in and by Moscow. During the spring of 2014, the Kremlin was still keen to preserve "plausible deniability" of its aggression against Ukraine, but we now know from various sources – including

---

[2] A state of limited sovereignty and legitimacy.

Vladimir Putin—about the Russian involvement in every step. The "referendum" was supposed to obscure the fact that the annexation was achieved by use of military force of another sovereign state, the Russian Federation (Czaplinski et al. 2017). Again, the referendum was a tool from the inter-war playbook. It was also used in 1939/40 by Moscow to legitimate the annexation of the Baltic States and the Polish *kresy*. The relatively easy military success in Crimea—with no armed resistance by Ukrainian forces—certainly encouraged the Russian leadership to launch the "Russian spring" campaign throughout South-Eastern Ukraine. Through Russian eyes, the collapse of Ukrainian statehood in these regions must have seemed imminent. And Moscow certainly had the soldiers and the resources at its disposal that were needed for "hybrid war."

The situation on the ground in Eastern and Southern Ukraine proved to be very different from Crimea. Yet, it is also part of the larger story that started with Afghanistan and Chechnya. Many of the men that led the Russian aggression against Ukraine—with Igor 'Strelkov' just being the most prominent example—were trained in and shaped by the conflicts of the 1990s in Yugoslavia and Chechnya.[3] They have great proficiency in the use of violence, spread of fear and the destruction of legitimate state institutions. In Crimea as well as in Donbas these violent men used their expertise in order to advance Russia's goals. They were often veterans of other post-Soviet conflicts. Clearly, what we saw in 2014 and the following years was historically tied both to the military conflicts that began with Afghanistan and produced a new militarized milieu in the post-Soviet space and to the ongoing geopolitical conflict between nation and empire in the region (Galeotti 2019; Osteuropa 2019). These conflicts are being played out using both strategies of the interwar period—when the same problem was acute—and with the resources and techniques of our age. We need further studies to better understand how different separatist statelets on the territory of the former USSR function. There are clear differences in the ways Ossetia, Abkhazia, Transnistria,

---

3   Igor Girkin, nome de guerre 'Strelkov', b. 1970, Russian security officer and mercenary.

Karabakh or the "people's republics" of Eastern Ukraine are ruled. Still, a focus on violence and organized crime seems to bring us closer to the core of these statelets.

Conclusions

History is only one tool in order to better understand separatist conflict in Eastern Europe. It might be able to provide a larger framework to analyse today's conflicts. This essay aimed to point to two strands of continuities: it examined similar conflicts after the end of World War I (1917–1922) and the development of war and military conflict in the post-Soviet space starting with the Afghan invasion of 1979. In distinct ways, both historical phenomena impact on today's situation. The establishment of nation-states by war is an ongoing process in the post-Soviet space. Citizenship and ethnicity were contentious issues in the interwar period, and they are again today. Again, the experience of war and the presence of violent men are important factors shaping the development of conflict on the ground.

Today, Russia is the most important actor in the area. Her policies define what I call the paradox of post-Soviet separatism: the simultaneity of separatist movements inside Russia and the creation and support of separatism by Russia. The need of Russia's authoritarian regime to create limited conflicts will persist but the actual dynamics unleashed by war prove hard to control. Therefore, the outcome of each of the conflicts in the post-Soviet space cannot be predicted. As long as Russian elites do not accept the loss of empire in 1991 violent conflict fuelled by revanchist thought will remain likely. Given the cult of the "Great Fatherland War" in Russia it is hard to accept for the elites that the Soviet Union won the war (and an empire) in 1945 and lost the peace much later in 1989/91. Still, the consequences of the second imperial collapse of the 20th century were not nearly as catastrophic as in 1917–22. Even after 1991 nation-building is accompanied by revolution and war. On the whole the observations of Dieter Langewiesche on the role of war and violence during nation-building in Western Europe seem to hold equally true in the East of the continent. What remains is the hope that despite the violence and political difficulties, more civil nation-building in the post-Soviet space remains possible. The 20th century history of East Central Europe points into that direction.

Bibliography:

Ackermann, F., Galbas, M. (2015). Back from Afghanistan. The Experiences of Soviet Afghan Veterans. *Journal of Soviet and Post-Soviet Politics and Societies* 1: 1–196.

Albats, Y. (1994). *The State within a State. The KGB and its Hold on Russia. Past, Present, Future.* New York: Farrar.

Altai, G. (2019). *Die Wahrheit ist der Feind. Warum Russland so anders ist.* Berlin: Rowohlt.

Averre, D., Wolczuk, K. (eds.) (2018). *The Ukraine Conflict. Security, Identity, and Politics in the Wider Europe.* New York: Routledge.

Barylski, R. (1998). *The Soldier in Russian Politics. Duty, Dictatorship and Democracy under Gorbachev and Yeltsin.* New Brunswick: Transaction.

Behrends, J.C. (2012). Oktroyierte Zivilisierung. Genese und Grenzen des sowjetischen Gewaltverzichts 1989. In *1989 und die Rolle der Gewalt*, Sabrow, M. (ed.). Göttingen: Wallstein, 401–424.

Behrends, J.C. (2015a). "Some call us heroes, others call us killers." Experiencing violent spaces: Soviet soldiers in the Afghan War. *Nationalities Papers* 43: 719–734.

Behrends, J.C. (2015b). Post-Soviet Legacies of Afghanistan. A Comparative Perspective. *Journal of Soviet and Post-Soviet Politics and Societies* 1: 169–186.

Behrends, J.C. (2015c). Ein Jahr der Gewalt. Russlands Staatskrise und der Krieg gegen die Ukraine. *Osteuropa* 65: 47–66.

Behrends, J.C. (2016). Mobilization and Empire Building. Stalin´s Slavic Idea (1939-1953). In *Konzepte des Slawischen*, Voss, C., Glanc, T. (eds.). Leipzig: BiblioMedia, 45–62.

Behrends, J.C. (2018). Michail Gorbatschow. Reformer aus Leidenschaft, Zerstörer wider Willen. In *Die letzten Generalsekretäre. Kommunistische Herrschaft im Spätsozialismus*, Schattenberg, S., Sabrow, M. (eds.). Berlin: Chr. Links, 248–270.

Böhler, J. (2018). *Civil War in Eastern Europe 1918-1921: The Reconstruction of Poland.* Oxford: Oxford University Press.

Borodziej, W. (2006). *The Warsaw Uprising of 1944.* Madison: University of Wisconsin Press.

Borodziej, W., Górny, M. (2018): *Der vergessene Weltkrieg*. 2 vols. Darmstadt: WBG Theiss.

Borzecki, J. (2008). *The Soviet-Polish Peace of 1921 and the Creation of Inter-War Europe*. New Haven: Yale University Press.

Brudny, Y. (1998). *Reinventing Russia. Russian Nationalism and the Soviet State*. Cambridge, Mass.: Harvard University Press.

Cabestan, J. P., Pavković, A. (eds) (2013). *Secessionism and Separatism in Europe and Asia. To Have a State of One's Own*. London: Palgrave.

Colton, T. (2008). *Yeltsin. A Life*. New York: Basic Books.

Connelly, J. (2019). *From Peoples to Nations. A History of Eastern Europe*. Princeton: Princeton University Press.

Czaplinski, W. et al. (eds.) (2017). *The Case of Crimea's Annexation under International Law*. Warsaw: Scholar.

Davies, R.W. (1991). *Perestroika und Geschichte. Die Wende in der sowjetischen Histriographie*. Munich: dtv.

Dawisha, K. (2014): *Putin's Kleptocracy. Who owns Russia?* New York: Simon & Schuster.

Eichler, M. (2012): *Militarizing Men. Gender, Conscription and War in Post-Soviet Russia*. Stanford, Cal.: Stanford University Press.

Engelstein, L. (2018). *Russia in Flames. War, Revolution, Civil War, 1914–1921*. Oxford: Oxford University Press.

Gagnon, V. (2004). *The Myth of Ethnic War. Serbia and Croatia in the 1990s*. Ithaca, NY: Cornell University Press.

Galeotti, M. (1995). *Afghanistan. The Soviet Union's Last War*. London: Frank Cass.

Galeotti, M. (2014). *Russia's Wars in Chechnya, 1994–2009*. Oxford: Osprey.

Galeotti, M. (2019). *Armies of Russia's War in Ukraine*. Oxford: Osprey.

George, Julie A. (2009). *The Politics of Ethnic Separatism in Russia and Georgia*. London: Palgrave.

Gerwarth, Robert (2017). *The Vanquished. Why the First World War Failed to End, 1917–1923*. New York: Penguin.

Gilligan, E. (2010). *Terror in Chechnya. Russia and the Tragedy of Civilians at War*. Princeton: Princeton University Press.

Graziosi, A. (2017). Communism, Nations and Nationalism. In *The Cambridge History of Communism, vol. 1. World Revolution and Socialism in One Country, 1917-1941*, Pons, S. et al. (eds.). Cambridge, UK: Cambridge University Press, 449–474.

Greene, S., Robertson, G. (2019). *Putin v. the People. The Perilous Politics of a Divided Russia*. New Haven: Yale University Press.

Herpen, M. van (2015). *Putin's Wars. The Rise of Russia's New Imperialism*. Lanham, ML: Rowman & Littlefield.

Hill, F., Gaddy, C. (2015). *Mr. Putin. Operative in the Kremlin*. Washington, DC: Brookings Institution.

Holquist, P. (2002). *Making War, Forging Revolution. Russia's Continuum of Crisis, 1914–1921*. Cambridge, Mass.: Harvard University Press.

Horvarth, R. (2005). *The Legacy of Soviet Dissent. Dissidents, Democratization and Radical Nationalism in Russia*. London: Routledge.

Hosking, Geoffrey (1997). *Russia. People and Empire, 1552–1917*, London: Harper Collins.

Hughes, J., Sasse, G. (2002). *Ethnicity and Territory in the Former Soviet Union: Regions in Conflict*. London: Frank Cass.

Irisova, O. et al. (eds) (2017). *A Successful Failure, Russia after Crimea*. Warsaw: Centre for Polish-Russian Dialogue.

Kappeler, Andreas (1992). *Russland als Vielvölkerreich. Entstehung, Geschichte. Zerfall*. Munich: C. H. Beck.

Kersten, K. (1991). *The Establishment of Communist Rule in Poland, 1943–1948*. Berkeley: University of California Press.

Kondrashov, S. (1999). *Nationalism and the Drive for Sovereignty in Tartarstan, 1988–1992. Origins and Development*. Basingstoke: MacMillan.

Kotkin, S. (2001). *Amargeddon Averted. The Soviet Collapse, 1970-2000*, Oxford: Oxford University Press.

Kotkin, S. (2014). *Stalin. Volume 1. Paradoxes of Power 1878–1928*. Penguin: New York.

Kotkin, S. (2017). *Stalin. Volume 2. Waiting for Hitler, 1929–1941*. Penguin: New York.

Kramer, M. (2003). The Collapse of East European Communism and its Repercussions within the Soviet Union (Part 1). *The Journal of Cold War Studies* 5: 178–256.

Kramer, M. (2004). The Collapse of East European Communism and its Repercussions within the Soviet Union (Part 2). *The Journal of Cold War Studies* 6: 3–64.

Kramer, M. (2005). The Collapse of East European Communism and its Repercussions within the Soviet Union (Part 3). *The Journal of Cold War Studies* 7: 3–96.

Kramer, M. (2011). The Demise of Soviet Power. *The Journal of Modern History* 83: 788–854.

Krapfl, J. (2013). *Revolution with a Human Face. Politics, Culture and Community in Czechoslovakia*. Ithaca, NY: Cornell University Press.

Langewiesche, D. (2019). *Der gewaltsame Lehrer. Europas Kriege in der Moderne.* Munich: C. H. Beck.

Laqueur, W. (1990): *Russia and Germany. A Century of Conflict.* New Brunswick: Transaction.

Le Huérou, A. et al. (eds.). *Chechnya at War and Beyond.* London: Routledge.

Liber, G. (2016). *Total Wars and the Making of Modern Ukraine.* Toronto: The University of Toronto Press.

Lozo, I. (2014): *Der Putsch gegen Gorbatschow und das Ende der Sowjetunion.* Cologne: Böhlau.

Lučić, R. (2015). Dead heroes and living deserters. The Yuguslav People's Army and the Public of Valjevo, Serbia, on the verge of war 1991. *Nationalities Papers* 43: 735–752.

Marten, K. (2012). *Warlords. Strong Arm Brokers in Weak States.* Ithaca, NY: Cornell University Press.

Martin, T. (2001). *The Affirmative Action Empire. Nations and Nationalism in the Soviet Union, 1923–1939.* Ithaca, NY: Cornell University Press.

Mawsley, Evan (2005). *The Russian Civil War,* London: Pegasus.

Meinander, Henrik (2011). *A History of Finland.* London: C. Hurst.

Minakov, M. (2018). *Development and Dystopia. Studies in Post-Soviet Ukraine and Eastern Europe.* Stuttgart: ibidem.

Mitrokhin, N. (2003). *Russkaia partia. Dvizhenie russkikh natsionalistov v SSSR, 1953–1985.* Moscow: NLO.

Moorhouse, R. (2014). *The Devil's Alliance. Hitler's Pact with Stalin.* New York: Basic Books.

Moorhouse, R. (2019). *First to Fight. The Polish War 1939.* London: Bodley Head.

Myers, S. (2015). *The New Tsar. The Rise and Reign of Vladimir Putin.* London: Simon & Schuster.

Naimark, N., Gibianskii, L (eds.) (1997). *The Establishment of Communist Regimes in Eastern Europe, 1944–1949.* Boulder: Westview.

Naimark, N. (2010). *Stalin's Genocides.* Princeton: Princeton University Press.

Ostrovsky, A. (2015). *The Invention of Russia. The Journey from Gorbachev's Freedom to Putin's War.* London: Atlantic.

Pavković, A., Radan, P. (eds.) (2011): *The Ashgate Companion to Secession.* Franham: Ashgate.

Penter, T., Meier, E. (eds.) (2017). *Sovietnam. Die UdSSR in Afghanistan 1979–1989.* Paderborn: Schöningh.

Plokhy, S. (2014): *The Last Empire. The Final Days of the Soviet Union.* London: Oneworld.

Plokhy, S. (2017): *Lost Kingdom. A History of Russian Nationalism from Ivan the Great to Vladimir Putin.* London: Pengiun.

Ruchniewicz, K. (2012). *Die neue Ostpolitik.* Stuttgart: Kohlhammer.

Sabrow, M. (ed.) (2012). *1989 und die Rolle der Gewalt.* Göttingen: Wallstein.

Sasse, G. (2007). *The Crimea Question: Identity, Transition, and Conflict.* Cambridge, Mass.: Harvard Ukrainian Research Institute.

Scheuermann, M. (2000). *Minderheitenschutz oder Konfliktverhütung? Die Minderheitenpolitik des Völkerbundes in den zwanziger Jahren.* Marburg: Herder.

Schlachtfeld Ukraine. Studien zur Soziologie des Krieges. *Osteuropa* 3-4: 49-210

Schnell, F. (2012): *Räume des Schreckens. Gewalt und Gruppenmilitanz in der Ukraine, 1905-1933.* Hamburg: Hamburger Edition.

Snyder, T. (2003). *The Reconstruction of Nations. Poland, Ukraine, Lithuania, Belarus, 1569-1999.* New Haven: Yale University Press.

Stent, A. (2019). *Putin's World. Russia against the West and with the Rest.* New York: Twelve.

Stöver, B. (2002). *Die Befreiung vom Kommunismus. Amerikanische Liberation Policy im Kalten Krieg, 1947-1991.* Cologne: Böhlau.

Soldatov, A., Borogan, I. (2010): *The New Nobility. The Restauration of Russia's Security State and the Enduring Legacy of the KGB.* New York: Public Affairs.

Sussex, M. (ed.). *Conflict in the Former USSR.* Cambridge, UK: Cambridge University Press.

Taubman, William (2017). *Gorbachev. His Life and Times.* London: Simon & Schuster.

Tishkov, V. (2004). *Chechnya. Life in a War-Torn Society.* Berkeley: University of California Press.

Walker, S. (2018). *The Long Hangover. Putin's New Russia and the Ghosts of the Past.* Oxford: Oxford University Press.

Weber, C. (2019). *Der Pakt. Stalin, Hitler und die Geschichte einer mörderischen Allianz.* Munich: C. H. Beck.

Weiner, A. (2002). *Making Sense of War. The Second World War and the Fate of the Bolshevik Revolution.* Princeton: Princeton University Press.

Westad, O.A. (2017). *The Cold War. A World History.* London: Allen Lane.

Wilson, A. (2005). *Virtual Politics. Faking Democracy in the Post-Soviet World.* New Haven: Yale University Press.

Wolff, L. (2020). *Woodrow Wilson and the Re-Imagining of Eastern Europe.* Stanford: University of California Press.

Wynnyckyj, M. (2019). *Ukraine's Maidan, Russia's War. A Chronicle and Analysis of the Revolution of Dignity.* Stuttgart: Ibidem.

Zamoyski, A. (2014). *Warsaw 1920. Lenin's Failed Conquest of Europe.* London: William Collins.

Žantovský, M. (2014). *Václav Havel. In der Wahrheit leben.* Berlin: Propyläen.

Zaremba, M. (2001). *Komuniszm, legitimizacja, nacjonalizm. Nacjonalistyczna legitimizacja władzy komunistycznej w Polsce.* Warsaw: Trio.

Zofka, J. (2015): *Postsowjetischer Separatismus. Die pro-russländischen Bewegungen im moldauischen Dnjestr-Tal und auf der Krim, 1989–1995.* Göttingen: Wallstein.

Our Authors

Jan C. Behrends is a historian and coordinates the research network "Legacies of Communism" at the Leibniz-Centre for Contemporary History (ZZF) in Potsdam, Germany. He has taught East European history at Humboldt Universität zu Berlin, the University of Chicago and the Viadrina. His interests include Stalinism, urban history as well as war and violence in Eastern Europe and the post-Soviet space. Outside academia he occasionally comments on post-Communist politics and German Ostpolitik.

Petra Colmorgen is currently managing an international congress and training center in Minsk, Belarus. Previously she worked as an award-winning journalist for several TV and radio stations, as well as an Executive for renowned media enterprises in Germany and Russia. More recently she has been a Consultant for the Brussels based "European Endowment for Democracy". Petra holds a bachelor's degree in economics and a master's degree in European Studies. Her academic work focuses on questions of sovereignty and agency within the post-Soviet space, with particular emphasis on Russian, Turkish and EU foreign policy.

Bruno Coppieters is professor emeritus at the Department of Political Science at the Vrije Universiteit Brussel (Free University of Brussels, VUB). His published works deal with the ethics of war and secession, and conflicts on sovereignty in the Caucasus and the Balkans. He coordinated an EU financed teaching project for the Abkhaz State University in 2012-15. He has co-edited the following books: *Contextualizing Secession: Normative Studies in Comparative Perspective*, Oxford, Oxford University Press, 2003; *Statehood and Security: Georgia After the Rose Revolution*, Cambridge/Mass., MIT Press, 2005; *Moral Constraints on War: Principles and Cases*, Lanham/Md., Lexington Books, 2020 (3d edition). Recent publications are to be found in Europe-Asia Studies, Ethnopolitics and the Journal of Balkan and Near Eastern Studies.

Daria Isachenko is a researcher at the Centre for Applied Turkey Studies (CATS) of the German Institute for International and Security Affairs (SWP) in Berlin. She holds a doctorate degree from the Humboldt University of Berlin, where she was a member of the research group "Micropolitics of Armed Groups", funded by the Volkswagen Foundation. Her previous research areas included post-conflict statebuilding and peacebuilding, foreign policy and political sociology of international relations. Among her publications is *The Making of Informal States: Statebuilding in Northern Cyprus and Transdniestria* (Palgrave Macmillan Series: Rethinking Peace and Conflict Studies, 2012).

Nataliia Kasianenko is an Assistant Professor in the Department of Political Science at California State University, Fresno. She received her Ph.D. in Political Science from the University of Nevada, Reno. Her research focuses on comparative politics and international relations, with an emphasis on nationalism, identity politics, and human rights in the countries of the former Soviet Union. Her work has been published in *Nationalities Papers, Ethnopolitics, Ideology and Politics Journal*, and *East/West: Journal of Ukrainian Studies*. Nataliia's latest projects examine how television media is used as a tool of conflict in the Donbas, and how social media data can be used to analyze political trends in Russia and Ukraine.

Alice Lackner is a research assistant at the Centre for East European and International Studies (ZOiS) Berlin, where her research is mainly focused on the impact of war and displacement in Ukraine. Together with ZOiS director Gwendolyn Sasse, she recently published articles in journals such as Europe-Asia Studies, Ideology and Politics, and Post-Soviet Affairs. Alice Lackner studied philosophy and sociology at the RWTH Aachen and finished her Master of Arts "Sociology – European Societies" at the Free University Berlin in 2018. Also pursuing an international career as an opera singer, Lackner continuously searches for creative formats to interweave artistic and scientific approaches.

Mikhail (Mykhailo) **Minakov**, senior advisor at Kennan Institute, Woodrow Wilson Center for International Scholars, is a renowned philosopher and social scholar working in the areas of political philosophy, political theory and history of modernity in the Eastern Europe and Western Eurasia. Author of six books, co-author of 4 books, and many articles in philosophy, political analysis, and policy studies, Minakov has over twenty years of experience in research and teaching in Ukraine, Germany, USA and Switzerland. As an editor-in-chief he also runs a peer-reviewed *Ideology and Politics Journal* and the blog *Kennan Focus Ukraine*.

Gwendolyn Sasse is the Director of the Centre for East European and International Studies (ZOiS) in Berlin (since 2016). She is also Professor of Comparative Politics at the University of Oxford, Professorial Fellow at Nuffield College, and a non-resident Senior Fellow at Carnegie Europe. Her research interests include post-communist transitions (esp. Ukraine and Russia), the dynamics of war, displacement, migration, and protest. Her current research focuses on the war in Eastern Ukraine, youth attitudes in Russia, the social and political remittances of migrants, and the relationship between "voice" and "exit". Her book *The Crimea Question: Identity, Transition, and Conflict* (Harvard University Press 2007; paperback 2014) won the Alexander Nove Prize of the British Association for Slavonic and East European Studies. Following on from a large Leverhulme Trust grant, she is currently writing a monograph on political remittances (Oxford University Press).

Index

Abkhazia 10, 13, 15–18, 22–23, 27–36, 43–45, 47–56, 61, 68, 76–78, 80–83, 87, 90–92, 94–97, 102–111, 119–121, 123–125, 131, 133, 141–143, 152, 156–159, 228, 235
agency 5, 11, 113–116, 119, 123, 127, 129–133, 139–142, 146–148, 150, 153, 243
annexation 20, 122, 128, 144, 145, 158, 194, 229, 234, 238
Armenia 8, 13, 44, 51, 60, 70, 74, 75, 82, 91, 96, 98, 99, 105, 113, 126, 128, 135, 137, 139, 140, 142, 147, 225
authoritarianism, authoritarian 118, 122, 123, 126, 128, 129, 144, 147, 149, 236
autonomy 66, 72, 105, 115, 161, 162, 167, 172, 179, 181, 185, 194, 206, 211
Azerbaijan 5, 8, 11, 13, 51, 60, 72, 75, 82, 96, 99, 105, 113–119, 121, 123, 125–129, 134, 135, 137–144, 146, 147, 151, 154, 156–158, 225
blockade 43, 77, 192, 201, 202
Catalonia 12, 13
Caucasus 8, 13, 14, 46, 55, 56, 69, 104–106, 109, 112, 123–125, 134–138, 140, 141, 149–158, 215, 220, 224, 231, 233, 243
ceasefire 5, 10, 15–19, 22, 25–31, 33–38, 46–50, 56, 57, 168, 184, 211
Church 161, 169, 178, 179, 181, 182, 184
civic, civil 5, 11, 12, 33, 52, 90, 109, 111, 161, 164, 166, 167, 170, 176, 184, 188–190, 199, 213, 214, 218, 219, 221, 222, 225, 227, 229, 230, 232, 237, 240
Commonwealth of Independent States (CIS) 28, 77
conflict 13, 14, 19, 22, 24, 27–30, 32, 33–35, 38, 43, 47, 49, 51, 54, 61, 71, 76, 83, 90, 95, 102, 104–107, 109–111, 118, 121, 127, 132, 135, 137, 140–142, 150–152, 154, 162–164, 168, 184, 187, 188, 190, 192, 193, 200–202, 204, 213, 216, 222–224, 226, 227, 229, 233, 235–237, 239–241, 245
conflict-resolution 168, 184
core 59–66, 69, 88, 89, 97–103, 220, 227, 236
core-periphery model 60
Crimea 61, 72, 125, 128, 144, 145, 156, 157, 161, 194, 195, 203, 228, 234, 235, 238, 239, 241, 245
de facto state 8–11, 17, 23, 24, 60, 61, 80, 89, 101, 104, 110, 150, 157, 187, 192, 194, 196, 198–206
Deep and Comprehensive Free Trade Area (DCFTA) 41, 136
de-escalation 10
democracy, democratic 12, 90, 104, 108, 110, 122, 123, 126, 128, 131, 133, 151, 156, 158, 187–190, 197, 223, 237, 241, 243
Donbas 8, 61, 76, 90, 94, 95, 97, 108, 109, 161, 163, 166, 171, 179, 191, 193–206, 209, 235, 244
Donetsk People Republic (DNR) 8
East, Eastern 7–10, 13, 51, 52, 61, 90, 106, 107, 120, 134, 136, 146, 152, 161, 166, 178, 181, 188, 206, 208, 213–221, 223–227, 233, 235–240, 242–245
elections 90, 93, 110, 142, 163, 186, 191, 193, 199
ethnicity, ethnic 9, 13, 14, 19, 60, 76, 90, 104, 108, 110–112, 124, 162, 163, 166, 167, 170, 176, 178, 184, 187–190, 216, 220, 224, 226, 238, 239
Eurasian Economic Union 41, 50, 109, 127
Europe 7, 10–13, 22, 53, 66, 104–106, 136, 140, 150, 153–155, 187–190, 206, 208, 213–215, 217–221, 225, 227, 237, 242–245
Europe, Eastern 7–10, 13, 52, 60,

107, 166, 213–219, 223, 233, 236–238, 242, 243, 245
Europe, Western 9, 10, 143, 215, 236
European Union (EU) 7, 13, 14, 21, 33, 39, 41, 43, 54, 56, 57, 103, 106, 109, 144, 155
Georgia 5, 8, 11–13, 28, 33–36, 38, 43–45, 47–54, 60, 72–76, 78–80, 86, 91, 99, 102, 105, 109, 113–125, 128–137, 141–146, 148–159, 215, 222, 225, 228, 234, 238, 243
governance 5, 13, 14, 72, 90, 103, 133, 134, 151, 153, 191–193, 197, 200, 204, 205
government-in-exile 29
Greece 38
identity 5, 11, 15–20, 25, 31, 35, 38, 43–45, 48–50, 54, 64, 75, 90, 105, 122, 132, 143, 154, 158, 161–163, 165–167, 176, 184–186, 188, 189, 210, 220, 237, 241, 245
imperialism 239
inclusion 27, 31, 37, 46
independence 22, 23, 32, 35, 67, 90, 96, 113, 118, 126, 129, 138, 147, 191, 194–196, 198–200, 205, 211, 217, 226
legitimacy 5, 8, 12, 27, 32, 34, 60, 63–66, 102, 187, 191–193, 196, 199, 204–206, 215, 217, 234
liberalism, liberal 52, 122, 130, 135, 189, 222
Luhansk People Republic (LNR) 8
maidan 189, 234, 242
media 45, 56, 64, 138, 193, 195, 198, 200, 205, 232, 234, 243, 244
Minsk Agreement 162, 166, 168, 173, 175, 182, 183, 185
Minsk negotiations, Minsk process 168, 175, 184, 186
Moldova 8, 17, 22, 36–38, 40–43, 49, 54–56, 69, 70, 72, 75, 83–87, 91, 96, 99, 102, 104, 107, 110, 155, 206, 225, 228, 234
Montevideo Convention 7, 67
Nagorno-Karabakh 8, 11, 13, 51, 61, 68, 72–76, 90, 91, 94, 98, 106, 108, 150, 154, 157
nation 8, 9, 12, 14, 72, 124, 138, 158, 209, 213–218, 220, 224, 228, 233, 235
nationalism 8, 14, 104, 187–189, 214, 218, 227, 238–241, 244
nationality 9, 45, 187
negotiations 10, 16, 17, 22, 27–29, 31–36, 38, 41, 44, 46, 47, 140, 155, 230
non-recognition 10, 15, 16, 17, 18, 19, 20, 21, 22, 23, 25, 26, 27, 29, 31, 32, 33, 35, 36, 40, 44, 45, 47, 48, 49, 50, 51, 65, 69, 97, 145
non-recognized state (NRS) 8, 113, 193
North Cyprus 5, 10, 15–18, 22, 23, 38–40, 48, 51
othering 132
peace 7, 13, 28–30, 35, 37, 48, 51–53, 55–57, 77, 83, 104, 107–109, 149, 151, 161, 188–191, 200, 213, 222, 223, 229, 232, 236, 238, 244
peacekeeping 28, 30, 35, 37, 38, 48, 49, 51, 53, 57, 83
periphery 7, 60–66, 69, 71, 76, 82, 88, 93, 97–103, 105, 111, 214, 222
post-Soviet 5, 7–10, 12–14, 59–61, 66, 68–73, 80, 82, 89, 92, 96, 97, 99–102, 107, 109, 110, 118, 123, 125, 149, 152, 154, 156, 187–189, 209, 213, 223, 226–229, 231–233, 235–s238, 240, 241, 243, 244
rebel 191, 194–197, 199
recognition 5, 8, 10, 12, 15–26, 28–35, 40, 45–55, 60, 61, 67, 72, 80, 97, 98, 102, 105, 108, 117, 121, 126, 137, 142, 150, 191, 196, 198, 229
referendum 7, 72, 194, 195, 197, 199, 206, 208, 210, 225, 235
reintegration 45, 52, 61, 76, 98, 117, 150, 198, 205
revolution 51, 122, 194, 236, 238, 241–243
Russia 5, 8, 11, 22, 27, 28, 31–38, 41, 44, 47–51, 54–56, 60, 61, 73–76, 78–85, 91, 93–95, 97–99, 102, 106, 113, 118–134, 136, 137, 140–150, 153–159, 162, 166–168, 179, 192–198, 202–206, 210, 213–215, 222, 225, 228, 230, 233–245
Scotland 7, 12, 13, 158
secession 7, 10, 12, 13, 18–23, 46, 49,

51, 53, 55, 61, 65, 69, 101, 106, 108, 141, 150, 155, 209, 234, 240, 243
secessionism 5, 7, 9, 10, 11, 12, 61, 110, 238
security 7, 8, 10, 22, 28, 30-33, 35-38, 41, 43, 47, 54, 57, 61, 66, 69, 70, 75, 77, 80, 86, 90, 93, 96, 102, 106, 109, 111, 116, 118, 121, 130, 143, 145, 149-155, 158, 164, 189, 192, 195, 199, 200, 210, 235, 237, 241, 243, 244
semicore 59, 63-66, 88, 97-103
semiperiphery, semiperipheral 59, 63, 64, 100, 103
separatism 5, 7, 10, 12, 106, 196, 209, 213, 216, 219, 224, 226, 229, 232-234, 236, 238
South Ossetia 8, 11, 13, 31-35, 44, 51, 55, 56, 61, 68, 73, 76, 82, 90-92, 95-97, 99, 102, 106, 113, 119-121, 123-125, 130-133, 137, 148, 151, 156, 158, 202
sovereignty 7, 11, 12, 53, 65, 72, 80, 97, 111, 119, 122, 126, 128, 145, 150, 162, 192, 198, 202, 206, 215, 217, 221, 225, 228, 234, 243
state 5, 7-9, 11, 13, 14, 16-21, 23-27, 29, 33, 36, 45-48, 50, 53, 54, 56, 59, 62, 63, 65-69, 77, 80-82, 86, 89, 91, 94, 95, 97-99, 102-104, 106, 111, 114, 117-120, 128, 131, 136, 139, 150, 151, 155, 161-163, 165, 170, 185-188, 190, 193, 198, 202- 204, 214, 216, 218, 220, 222, 224-229, 234, 237, 241, 243, 244
state, parental 8, 10, 11, 65, 66, 69, 71, 73, 75, 82, 86, 88-90, 100-102
state, sponsor 8, 10, 60, 65, 71, 76, 82, 89-91, 93, 94, 100, 102
state-building 7, 10, 61, 71, 89, 95, 107, 162-165, 185-187, 213
statehood 7, 21, 23-26, 34, 50, 53, 56, 105, 193, 214, 219, 226, 229, 235, 243
state-making 5, 10, 11, 67, 161, 162, 186

territory, territorial 7, 8, 13, 19, 21-27, 29, 31, 34-36, 38, 42-50, 60, 65-68, 73, 77, 83, 89, 96, 101, 102, 104, 108, 110, 117, 120, 124, 126, 130-132, 137, 139, 141, 145, 147, 157, 161, 192, 198, 202, 204, 209, 213, 214, 225, 228, 233, 235, 239
Transnistria 5, 8, 11, 13, 15-18, 22, 36-38, 40-43, 47-52, 54-57, 61, 68, 72-74, 83, 86, 90, 93-96, 99, 104, 106, 107, 109-111, 156-158, 222, 228, 235
Turkey 5, 11, 25, 38, 49, 55, 63, 78, 82, 99, 106, 113, 116, 118, 124-126, 134-150, 152-159, 244
Ukraine 5, 8, 11-13, 37, 40, 51, 60, 69, 73, 82-84, 86, 95, 98, 102, 104, 106, 107, 109-111, 128, 130, 151, 155, 158, 161-169, 175, 178, 179, 181-192, 194-200, 202-206, 208-211, 215, 220-222, 225, 228, 234, 237, 238, 240-242, 244, 245
United Nations (UN) 25, 28, 30, 38, 53, 57, 211
USSR 8, 11, 60, 62, 63, 72, 76, 107, 214, 216-220, 222-226, 229, 233, 235, 241
war 5, 8, 10, 11, 13, 27, 29, 31, 32, 34-36, 41, 46, 51, 61, 66, 76, 80, 97, 101, 105, 108, 111, 113, 116, 124, 128, 130, 145, 154, 158, 161-167, 171, 184-191, 202, 205, 209, 213-220, 222, 226, 229, 231, 234-245
warlordism 78, 224
war-making 11, 66, 162
West, Western 7, 9, 10, 13, 32, 35, 54, 61, 66, 70, 75, 84, 99, 102, 104, 107, 109, 113, 116, 118, 121-126, 130-133, 135, 136, 139, 143, 147, 150, 152, 156, 158, 178, 179, 181, 184, 188, 191, 194-196, 206, 214, 216, 219, 221, 228, 236, 241, 244
world-system 10, 59-63, 66, 69, 71, 88, 97, 101, 102, 107
Yugoslavia 8, 106, 227, 228, 235

SOVIET AND POST-SOVIET POLITICS AND SOCIETY
Edited by Dr. Andreas Umland | ISSN 1614-3515

1   Андреас Умланд (ред.) | Воплощение Европейской конвенции по правам человека в России. Философские, юридические и эмпирические исследования | ISBN 3-89821-387-0

2   Christian Wipperfürth | Russland – ein vertrauenswürdiger Partner? Grundlagen, Hintergründe und Praxis gegenwärtiger russischer Außenpolitik | Mit einem Vorwort von Heinz Timmermann | ISBN 3-89821-401-X

3   Manja Hussner | Die Übernahme internationalen Rechts in die russische und deutsche Rechtsordnung. Eine vergleichende Analyse zur Völkerrechtsfreundlichkeit der Verfassungen der Russländischen Föderation und der Bundesrepublik Deutschland | Mit einem Vorwort von Rainer Arnold | ISBN 3-89821-438-9

4   Matthew Tejada | Bulgaria's Democratic Consolidation and the Kozloduy Nuclear Power Plant (KNPP). The Unattainability of Closure | With a foreword by Richard J. Crampton | ISBN 3-89821-439-7

5   Марк Григорьевич Меерович | Квадратные метры, определяющие сознание. Государственная жилищная политика в СССР. 1921 – 1941 гг | ISBN 3-89821-474-5

6   Andrei P. Tsygankov, Pavel A.Tsygankov (Eds.) | New Directions in Russian International Studies | ISBN 3-89821-422-2

7   Марк Григорьевич Меерович | Как власть народ к труду приучала. Жилище в СССР – средство управления людьми. 1917 – 1941 гг. | С предисловием Елены Осокиной | ISBN 3-89821-495-8

8   David J. Galbreath | Nation-Building and Minority Politics in Post-Socialist States. Interests, Influence and Identities in Estonia and Latvia | With a foreword by David J. Smith | ISBN 3-89821-467-2

9   Алексей Юрьевич Безугольный | Народы Кавказа в Вооруженных силах СССР в годы Великой Отечественной войны 1941-1945 гг. | С предисловием Николая Бугая | ISBN 3-89821-475-3

10 Вячеслав Лихачев и Владимир Прибыловский (ред.) | Русское Национальное Единство, 1990-2000. В 2-х томах | ISBN 3-89821-523-7

11 Николай Бугай (ред.) | Народы стран Балтии в условиях сталинизма (1940-е – 1950-е годы). Документированная история | ISBN 3-89821-525-3

12 Ingmar Bredies (Hrsg.) | Zur Anatomie der Orange Revolution in der Ukraine. Wechsel des Elitenregimes oder Triumph des Parlamentarismus? | ISBN 3-89821-524-5

13 Anastasia V. Mitrofanova | The Politicization of Russian Orthodoxy. Actors and Ideas | With a foreword by William C. Gay | ISBN 3-89821-481-8

14 Nathan D. Larson | Alexander Solzhenitsyn and the Russo-Jewish Question | ISBN 3-89821-483-4

15 Guido Houben | Kulturpolitik und Ethnizität. Staatliche Kunstförderung im Russland der neunziger Jahre | Mit einem Vorwort von Gert Weisskirchen | ISBN 3-89821-542-3

16 Leonid Luks | Der russische „Sonderweg"? Aufsätze zur neuesten Geschichte Russlands im europäischen Kontext | ISBN 3-89821-496-6

17 Евгений Мороз | История «Мёртвой воды» – от страшной сказки к большой политике. Политическое неоязычество в постсоветской России | ISBN 3-89821-551-2

18 Александр Верховский и Галина Кожевникова (ред.) | Этническая и религиозная интолерантность в российских СМИ. Результаты мониторинга 2001-2004 гг. | ISBN 3-89821-569-5

19 Christian Ganzer | Sowjetisches Erbe und ukrainische Nation. Das Museum der Geschichte des Zaporoger Kosakentums auf der Insel Chortycja | Mit einem Vorwort von Frank Golczewski | ISBN 3-89821-504-0

20 Эльза-Баир Гучинова | Помнить нельзя забыть. Антропология депортационной травмы калмыков | С предисловием Кэролайн Хамфри | ISBN 3-89821-506-7

21 Юлия Лидерман | Мотивы «проверки» и «испытания» в постсоветской культуре. Советское прошлое в российском кинематографе 1990-х годов | С предисловием Евгения Марголита | ISBN 3-89821-511-3

22 Tanya Lokshina, Ray Thomas, Mary Mayer (Eds.) | The Imposition of a Fake Political Settlement in the Northern Caucasus. The 2003 Chechen Presidential Election | ISBN 3-89821-436-2

23 Timothy McCajor Hall, Rosie Read (Eds.) | Changes in the Heart of Europe. Recent Ethnographies of Czechs, Slovaks, Roma, and Sorbs | With an afterword by Zdeněk Salzmann | ISBN 3-89821-606-3

24 *Christian Autengruber* | Die politischen Parteien in Bulgarien und Rumänien. Eine vergleichende Analyse seit Beginn der 90er Jahre | Mit einem Vorwort von Dorothée de Nève | ISBN 3-89821-476-1

25 *Annette Freyberg-Inan with Radu Cristescu* | The Ghosts in Our Classrooms, or: John Dewey Meets Ceauşescu. The Promise and the Failures of Civic Education in Romania | ISBN 3-89821-416-8

26 *John B. Dunlop* | The 2002 Dubrovka and 2004 Beslan Hostage Crises. A Critique of Russian Counter-Terrorism | With a foreword by Donald N. Jensen | ISBN 3-89821-608-X

27 *Peter Koller* | Das touristische Potenzial von Kam''janec'–Podil's'kyj. Eine fremdenverkehrsgeographische Untersuchung der Zukunftsperspektiven und Maßnahmenplanung zur Destinationsentwicklung des „ukrainischen Rothenburg" | Mit einem Vorwort von Kristiane Klemm | ISBN 3-89821-640-3

28 *Françoise Daucé, Elisabeth Sieca-Kozlowski (Eds.)* | Dedovshchina in the Post-Soviet Military. Hazing of Russian Army Conscripts in a Comparative Perspective | With a foreword by Dale Herspring | ISBN 3-89821-616-0

29 *Florian Strasser* | Zivilgesellschaftliche Einflüsse auf die Orange Revolution. Die gewaltlose Massenbewegung und die ukrainische Wahlkrise 2004 | Mit einem Vorwort von Egbert Jahn | ISBN 3-89821-648-9

30 *Rebecca S. Katz* | The Georgian Regime Crisis of 2003-2004. A Case Study in Post-Soviet Media Representation of Politics, Crime and Corruption | ISBN 3-89821-413-3

31 *Vladimir Kantor* | Willkür oder Freiheit. Beiträge zur russischen Geschichtsphilosophie | Ediert von Dagmar Herrmann sowie mit einem Vorwort versehen von Leonid Luks | ISBN 3-89821-589-X

32 *Laura A. Victoir* | The Russian Land Estate Today. A Case Study of Cultural Politics in Post-Soviet Russia | With a foreword by Priscilla Roosevelt | ISBN 3-89821-426-5

33 *Ivan Katchanovski* | Cleft Countries. Regional Political Divisions and Cultures in Post-Soviet Ukraine and Moldova| With a foreword by Francis Fukuyama | ISBN 3-89821-558-X

34 *Florian Mühlfried* | Postsowjetische Feiern. Das Georgische Bankett im Wandel | Mit einem Vorwort von Kevin Tuite | ISBN 3-89821-601-2

35 *Roger Griffin, Werner Loh, Andreas Umland (Eds.)* | Fascism Past and Present, West and East. An International Debate on Concepts and Cases in the Comparative Study of the Extreme Right | With an afterword by Walter Laqueur | ISBN 3-89821-674-8

36 *Sebastian Schlegel* | Der „Weiße Archipel". Sowjetische Atomstädte 1945-1991 | Mit einem Geleitwort von Thomas Bohn | ISBN 3-89821-679-9

37 *Vyacheslav Likhachev* | Political Anti-Semitism in Post-Soviet Russia. Actors and Ideas in 1991-2003 | Edited and translated from Russian by Eugene Veklerov | ISBN 3-89821-529-6

38 *Josette Baer (Ed.)* | Preparing Liberty in Central Europe. Political Texts from the Spring of Nations 1848 to the Spring of Prague 1968 | With a foreword by Zdeněk V. David | ISBN 3-89821-546-6

39 *Михаил Лукьянов* | Российский консерватизм и реформа, 1907-1914 | С предисловием Марка Д. Стейнберга | ISBN 3-89821-503-2

40 *Nicola Melloni* | Market Without Economy. The 1998 Russian Financial Crisis | With a foreword by Eiji Furukawa | ISBN 3-89821-407-9

41 *Dmitrij Chmelnizki* | Die Architektur Stalins | Bd. 1: Studien zu Ideologie und Stil | Bd. 2: Bilddokumentation | Mit einem Vorwort von Bruno Flierl | ISBN 3-89821-515-6

42 *Katja Yafimava* | Post-Soviet Russian-Belarussian Relationships. The Role of Gas Transit Pipelines | With a foreword by Jonathan P. Stern | ISBN 3-89821-655-1

43 *Boris Chavkin* | Verflechtungen der deutschen und russischen Zeitgeschichte. Aufsätze und Archivfunde zu den Beziehungen Deutschlands und der Sowjetunion von 1917 bis 1991 | Ediert von Markus Edlinger sowie mit einem Vorwort versehen von Leonid Luks | ISBN 3-89821-756-5

44 *Anastasija Grynenko in Zusammenarbeit mit Claudia Dathe* | Die Terminologie des Gerichtswesens der Ukraine und Deutschlands im Vergleich. Eine übersetzungswissenschaftliche Analyse juristischer Fachbegriffe im Deutschen, Ukrainischen und Russischen | Mit einem Vorwort von Ulrich Hartmann | ISBN 3-89821-691-8

45 *Anton Burkov* | The Impact of the European Convention on Human Rights on Russian Law. Legislation and Application in 1996-2006 | With a foreword by Françoise Hampson | ISBN 978-3-89821-639-6

46 *Stina Torjesen, Indra Overland (Eds.)* | International Election Observers in Post-Soviet Azerbaijan. Geopolitical Pawns or Agents of Change? | ISBN 978-3-89821-743-9

47 *Taras Kuzio* | Ukraine – Crimea – Russia. Triangle of Conflict | ISBN 978-3-89821-761-3

48 *Claudia Šabić* | „Ich erinnere mich nicht, aber L'viv!" Zur Funktion kultureller Faktoren für die Institutionalisierung und Entwicklung einer ukrainischen Region | Mit einem Vorwort von Melanie Tatur | ISBN 978-3-89821-752-1

49 *Marlies Bilz* | Tatarstan in der Transformation. Nationaler Diskurs und Politische Praxis 1988-1994 | Mit einem Vorwort von Frank Golczewski | ISBN 978-3-89821-722-4

50 *Марлен Ларюэль (ред.)* | Современные интерпретации русского национализма | ISBN 978-3-89821-795-8

51 *Sonja Schüler* | Die ethnische Dimension der Armut. Roma im postsozialistischen Rumänien | Mit einem Vorwort von Anton Sterbling | ISBN 978-3-89821-776-7

52 *Галина Кожевникова* | Радикальный национализм в России и противодействие ему. Сборник докладов Центра «Сова» за 2004-2007 гг. | С предисловием Александра Верховского | ISBN 978-3-89821-721-7

53 *Галина Кожевникова и Владимир Прибыловский* | Российская власть в биографиях I. Высшие должностные лица РФ в 2004 г. | ISBN 978-3-89821-796-5

54 *Галина Кожевникова и Владимир Прибыловский* | Российская власть в биографиях II. Члены Правительства РФ в 2004 г. | ISBN 978-3-89821-797-2

55 *Галина Кожевникова и Владимир Прибыловский* | Российская власть в биографиях III. Руководители федеральных служб и агентств РФ в 2004 г.| ISBN 978-3-89821-798-9

56 *Ileana Petroniu* | Privatisierung in Transformationsökonomien. Determinanten der Restrukturierungs-Bereitschaft am Beispiel Polens, Rumäniens und der Ukraine | Mit einem Vorwort von Rainer W. Schäfer | ISBN 978-3-89821-790-3

57 *Christian Wipperfürth* | Russland und seine GUS-Nachbarn. Hintergründe, aktuelle Entwicklungen und Konflikte in einer ressourcenreichen Region| ISBN 978-3-89821-801-6

58 *Togzhan Kassenova* | From Antagonism to Partnership. The Uneasy Path of the U.S.-Russian Cooperative Threat Reduction | With a foreword by Christoph Bluth | ISBN 978-3-89821-707-1

59 *Alexander Höllwerth* | Das sakrale eurasische Imperium des Aleksandr Dugin. Eine Diskursanalyse zum postsowjetischen russischen Rechtsextremismus | Mit einem Vorwort von Dirk Uffelmann | ISBN 978-3-89821-813-9

60 *Олег Рябов* | «Россия-Матушка». Национализм, гендер и война в России XX века | С предисловием Елены Гощило | ISBN 978-3-89821-487-2

61 *Ivan Maistrenko* | Borot'bism. A Chapter in the History of the Ukrainian Revolution | With a new Introduction by Chris Ford | Translated by George S. N. Luckyj with the assistance of Ivan L. Rudnytsky | Second, Revised and Expanded Edition ISBN 978-3-8382-1107-7

62 *Maryna Romanets* | Anamorphosic Texts and Reconfigured Visions. Improvised Traditions in Contemporary Ukrainian and Irish Literature | ISBN 978-3-89821-576-3

63 *Paul D'Anieri and Taras Kuzio (Eds.)* | Aspects of the Orange Revolution I. Democratization and Elections in Post-Communist Ukraine | ISBN 978-3-89821-698-2

64 *Bohdan Harasymiw in collaboration with Oleh S. Ilnytzkyj (Eds.)* | Aspects of the Orange Revolution II. Information and Manipulation Strategies in the 2004 Ukrainian Presidential Elections | ISBN 978-3-89821-699-9

65 *Ingmar Bredies, Andreas Umland and Valentin Yakushik (Eds.)* | Aspects of the Orange Revolution III. The Context and Dynamics of the 2004 Ukrainian Presidential Elections | ISBN 978-3-89821-803-0

66 *Ingmar Bredies, Andreas Umland and Valentin Yakushik (Eds.)* | Aspects of the Orange Revolution IV. Foreign Assistance and Civic Action in the 2004 Ukrainian Presidential Elections | ISBN 978-3-89821-808-5

67 *Ingmar Bredies, Andreas Umland and Valentin Yakushik (Eds.)* | Aspects of the Orange Revolution V. Institutional Observation Reports on the 2004 Ukrainian Presidential Elections | ISBN 978-3-89821-809-2

68 *Taras Kuzio (Ed.)* | Aspects of the Orange Revolution VI. Post-Communist Democratic Revolutions in Comparative Perspective | ISBN 978-3-89821-820-7

69 *Tim Bohse* | Autoritarismus statt Selbstverwaltung. Die Transformation der kommunalen Politik in der Stadt Kaliningrad 1990-2005 | Mit einem Geleitwort von Stefan Troebst | ISBN 978-3-89821-782-8

70 *David Rupp* | Die Rußländische Föderation und die russischsprachige Minderheit in Lettland. Eine Fallstudie zur Anwaltspolitik Moskaus gegenüber den russophonen Minderheiten im „Nahen Ausland" von 1991 bis 2002 | Mit einem Vorwort von Helmut Wagner | ISBN 978-3-89821-778-1

71 *Taras Kuzio* | Theoretical and Comparative Perspectives on Nationalism. New Directions in Cross-Cultural and Post-Communist Studies | With a foreword by Paul Robert Magocsi | ISBN 978-3-89821-815-3

72 *Christine Teichmann* | Die Hochschultransformation im heutigen Osteuropa. Kontinuität und Wandel bei der Entwicklung des postkommunistischen Universitätswesens | Mit einem Vorwort von Oskar Anweiler | ISBN 978-3-89821-842-9

73 *Julia Kusznir* | Der politische Einfluss von Wirtschaftseliten in russischen Regionen. Eine Analyse am Beispiel der Erdöl- und Erdgasindustrie, 1992-2005 | Mit einem Vorwort von Wolfgang Eichwede | ISBN 978-3-89821-821-4

74 *Alena Vysotskaya* | Russland, Belarus und die EU-Osterweiterung. Zur Minderheitenfrage und zum Problem der Freizügigkeit des Personenverkehrs | Mit einem Vorwort von Katlijn Malfliet | ISBN 978-3-89821-822-1

75 *Heiko Pleines (Hrsg.)* | Corporate Governance in post-sozialistischen Volkswirtschaften | ISBN 978-3-89821-766-8

76 *Stefan Ihrig* | Wer sind die Moldawier? Rumänismus versus Moldowanismus in Historiographie und Schulbüchern der Republik Moldova, 1991-2006 | Mit einem Vorwort von Holm Sundhaussen | ISBN 978-3-89821-466-7

77 *Galina Kozhevnikova in collaboration with Alexander Verkhovsky and Eugene Veklerov* | Ultra-Nationalism and Hate Crimes in Contemporary Russia. The 2004-2006 Annual Reports of Moscow's SOVA Center | With a foreword by Stephen D. Shenfield | ISBN 978-3-89821-868-9

78 *Florian Küchler* | The Role of the European Union in Moldova's Transnistria Conflict | With a foreword by Christopher Hill | ISBN 978-3-89821-850-4

79 *Bernd Rechel* | The Long Way Back to Europe. Minority Protection in Bulgaria | With a foreword by Richard Crampton | ISBN 978-3-89821-863-4

80 *Peter W. Rodgers* | Nation, Region and History in Post-Communist Transitions. Identity Politics in Ukraine, 1991-2006 | With a foreword by Vera Tolz | ISBN 978-3-89821-903-7

81 *Stephanie Solywoda* | The Life and Work of Semen L. Frank. A Study of Russian Religious Philosophy | With a foreword by Philip Walters | ISBN 978-3-89821-457-5

82 *Vera Sokolova* | Cultural Politics of Ethnicity. Discourses on Roma in Communist Czechoslovakia | ISBN 978-3-89821-864-1

83 *Natalya Shevchik Ketenci* | Kazakhstani Enterprises in Transition. The Role of Historical Regional Development in Kazakhstan's Post-Soviet Economic Transformation | ISBN 978-3-89821-831-3

84 *Martin Malek, Anna Schor-Tschudnowskaja (Hgg.)* | Europa im Tschetschenienkrieg. Zwischen politischer Ohnmacht und Gleichgültigkeit | Mit einem Vorwort von Lipchan Basajewa | ISBN 978-3-89821-676-0

85 *Stefan Meister* | Das postsowjetische Universitätswesen zwischen nationalem und internationalem Wandel. Die Entwicklung der regionalen Hochschule in Russland als Gradmesser der Systemtransformation | Mit einem Vorwort von Joan DeBardeleben | ISBN 978-3-89821-891-7

86 *Konstantin Sheiko in collaboration with Stephen Brown* | Nationalist Imaginings of the Russian Past. Anatolii Fomenko and the Rise of Alternative History in Post-Communist Russia | With a foreword by Donald Ostrowski | ISBN 978-3-89821-915-0

87 *Sabine Jenni* | Wie stark ist das „Einige Russland"? Zur Parteibindung der Eliten und zum Wahlerfolg der Machtpartei im Dezember 2007 | Mit einem Vorwort von Klaus Armingeon | ISBN 978-3-89821-961-7

88 *Thomas Borén* | Meeting-Places of Transformation. Urban Identity, Spatial Representations and Local Politics in Post-Soviet St Petersburg | ISBN 978-3-89821-739-2

89 *Aygul Ashirova* | Stalinismus und Stalin-Kult in Zentralasien. Turkmenistan 1924-1953 | Mit einem Vorwort von Leonid Luks | ISBN 978-3-89821-987-7

90 *Leonid Luks* | Freiheit oder imperiale Größe? Essays zu einem russischen Dilemma | ISBN 978-3-8382-0011-8

91 *Christopher Gilley* | The 'Change of Signposts' in the Ukrainian Emigration. A Contribution to the History of Sovietophilism in the 1920s | With a foreword by Frank Golczewski | ISBN 978-3-89821-965-5

92 *Philipp Casula, Jeronim Perovic (Eds.)* | Identities and Politics During the Putin Presidency. The Discursive Foundations of Russia's Stability | With a foreword by Heiko Haumann | ISBN 978-3-8382-0015-6

93 *Marcel Viëtor* | Europa und die Frage nach seinen Grenzen im Osten. Zur Konstruktion ‚europäischer Identität' in Geschichte und Gegenwart | Mit einem Vorwort von Albrecht Lehmann | ISBN 978-3-8382-0045-3

94 *Ben Hellman, Andrei Rogachevskii* | Filming the Unfilmable. Casper Wrede's 'One Day in the Life of Ivan Denisovich' | Second, Revised and Expanded Edition | ISBN 978-3-8382-0044-6

95 *Eva Fuchslocher* | Vaterland, Sprache, Glaube. Orthodoxie und Nationenbildung am Beispiel Georgiens | Mit einem Vorwort von Christina von Braun | ISBN 978-3-89821-884-9

96 *Vladimir Kantor* | Das Westlertum und der Weg Russlands. Zur Entwicklung der russischen Literatur und Philosophie | Ediert von Dagmar Herrmann | Mit einem Beitrag von Nikolaus Lobkowicz | ISBN 978-3-8382-0102-3

97 *Kamran Musayev* | Die postsowjetische Transformation im Baltikum und Südkaukasus. Eine vergleichende Untersuchung der politischen Entwicklung Lettlands und Aserbaidschans 1985-2009 | Mit einem Vorwort von Leonid Luks | Ediert von Sandro Henschel | ISBN 978-3-8382-0103-0

98 *Tatiana Zhurzhenko* | Borderlands into Bordered Lands. Geopolitics of Identity in Post-Soviet Ukraine | With a foreword by Dieter Segert | ISBN 978-3-8382-0042-2

99 *Кирилл Галушко, Лидия Смола (ред.)* | Пределы падения – варианты украинского будущего. Аналитико-прогностические исследования | ISBN 978-3-8382-0148-1

100 *Michael Minkenberg (Ed.)* | Historical Legacies and the Radical Right in Post-Cold War Central and Eastern Europe | With an afterword by Sabrina P. Ramet | ISBN 978-3-8382-0124-5

101 *David-Emil Wickström* | Rocking St. Petersburg. Transcultural Flows and Identity Politics in the St. Petersburg Popular Music Scene | With a foreword by Yngvar B. Steinholt | Second, Revised and Expanded Edition | ISBN 978-3-8382-0100-9

102 *Eva Zabka* | Eine neue „Zeit der Wirren"? Der spät- und postsowjetische Systemwandel 1985-2000 im Spiegel russischer gesellschaftspolitischer Diskurse | Mit einem Vorwort von Margareta Mommsen | ISBN 978-3-8382-0161-0

103 *Ulrike Ziemer* | Ethnic Belonging, Gender and Cultural Practices. Youth Identitites in Contemporary Russia | With a foreword by Anoop Nayak | ISBN 978-3-8382-0152-8

104 *Ksenia Chepikova* | ‚Einiges Russland' - eine zweite KPdSU? Aspekte der Identitätskonstruktion einer postsowjetischen „Partei der Macht" | Mit einem Vorwort von Torsten Oppelland | ISBN 978-3-8382-0311-9

105 *Леонид Люкс* | Западничество или евразийство? Демократия или идеократия? Сборник статей об исторических дилеммах России | С предисловием Владимира Кантора | ISBN 978-3-8382-0211-2

106 *Anna Dost* | Das russische Verfassungsrecht auf dem Weg zum Föderalismus und zurück. Zum Konflikt von Rechtsnormen und -wirklichkeit in der Russländischen Föderation von 1991 bis 2009 | Mit einem Vorwort von Alexander Blankenagel | ISBN 978-3-8382-0292-1

107 *Philipp Herzog* | Sozialistische Völkerfreundschaft, nationaler Widerstand oder harmloser Zeitvertreib? Zur politischen Funktion der Volkskunst im sowjetischen Estland | Mit einem Vorwort von Andreas Kappeler | ISBN 978-3-8382-0216-7

108 *Marlène Laruelle (Ed.)* | Russian Nationalism, Foreign Policy, and Identity Debates in Putin's Russia. New Ideological Patterns after the Orange Revolution | ISBN 978-3-8382-0325-6

109 *Michail Logvinov* | Russlands Kampf gegen den internationalen Terrorismus. Eine kritische Bestandsaufnahme des Bekämpfungsansatzes | Mit einem Geleitwort von Hans-Henning Schröder und einem Vorwort von Eckhard Jesse | ISBN 978-3-8382-0329-4

110 *John B. Dunlop* | The Moscow Bombings of September 1999. Examinations of Russian Terrorist Attacks at the Onset of Vladimir Putin's Rule | Second, Revised and Expanded Edition | ISBN 978-3-8382-0388-1

111 *Андрей А. Ковалёв* | Свидетельство из-за кулис российской политики I. Можно ли делать добро из зла? (Воспоминания и размышления о последних советских и первых послесоветских годах) | With a foreword by Peter Reddaway | ISBN 978-3-8382-0302-7

112 *Андрей А. Ковалёв* | Свидетельство из-за кулис российской политики II. Угроза для себя и окружающих (Наблюдения и предостережения относительно происходящего после 2000 г.) | ISBN 978-3-8382-0303-4

113 *Bernd Kappenberg* | Zeichen setzen für Europa. Der Gebrauch europäischer lateinischer Sonderzeichen in der deutschen Öffentlichkeit | Mit einem Vorwort von Peter Schlobinski | ISBN 978-3-89821-749-1

114 *Ivo Mijnssen* | The Quest for an Ideal Youth in Putin's Russia I. Back to Our Future! History, Modernity, and Patriotism according to Nashi, 2005-2013 | With a foreword by Jeronim Perović | Second, Revised and Expanded Edition | ISBN 978-3-8382-0368-3

115 *Jussi Lassila* | The Quest for an Ideal Youth in Putin's Russia II. The Search for Distinctive Conformism in the Political Communication of Nashi, 2005-2009 | With a foreword by Kirill Postoutenko | Second, Revised and Expanded Edition | ISBN 978-3-8382-0415-4

116 *Valerio Trabandt* | Neue Nachbarn, gute Nachbarschaft? Die EU als internationaler Akteur am Beispiel ihrer Demokratieförderung in Belarus und der Ukraine 2004-2009 | Mit einem Vorwort von Jutta Joachim | ISBN 978-3-8382-0437-6

117 *Fabian Pfeiffer* | Estlands Außen- und Sicherheitspolitik I. Der estnische Atlantizismus nach der wiedererlangten Unabhängigkeit 1991-2004 | Mit einem Vorwort von Helmut Hubel | ISBN 978-3-8382-0127-6

118 *Jana Podßuweit* | Estlands Außen- und Sicherheitspolitik II. Handlungsoptionen eines Kleinstaates im Rahmen seiner EU-Mitgliedschaft (2004-2008) | Mit einem Vorwort von Helmut Hubel | ISBN 978-3-8382-0440-6

119 *Karin Pointner* | Estlands Außen- und Sicherheitspolitik III. Eine gedächtnispolitische Analyse estnischer Entwicklungskooperation 2006-2010 | Mit einem Vorwort von Karin Liebhart | ISBN 978-3-8382-0435-2

120 *Ruslana Vovk* | Die Offenheit der ukrainischen Verfassung für das Völkerrecht und die europäische Integration | Mit einem Vorwort von Alexander Blankenagel | ISBN 978-3-8382-0481-9

121 *Mykhaylo Banakh* | Die Relevanz der Zivilgesellschaft bei den postkommunistischen Transformationsprozessen in mittel- und osteuropäischen Ländern. Das Beispiel der spät- und postsowjetischen Ukraine 1986-2009 | Mit einem Vorwort von Gerhard Simon | ISBN 978-3-8382-0499-4

122 *Michael Moser* | Language Policy and the Discourse on Languages in Ukraine under President Viktor Yanukovych (25 February 2010–28 October 2012) | ISBN 978-3-8382-0497-0 (Paperback edition) | ISBN 978-3-8382-0507-6 (Hardcover edition)

123 *Nicole Krome* | Russischer Netzwerkkapitalismus Restrukturierungsprozesse in der Russischen Föderation am Beispiel des Luftfahrtunternehmens „Aviastar" | Mit einem Vorwort von Petra Stykow | ISBN 978-3-8382-0534-2

124 *David R. Marples* | 'Our Glorious Past'. Lukashenka's Belarus and the Great Patriotic War | ISBN 978-3-8382-0574-8 (Paperback edition) | ISBN 978-3-8382-0675-2 (Hardcover edition)

125 *Ulf Walther* | Russlands „neuer Adel". Die Macht des Geheimdienstes von Gorbatschow bis Putin | Mit einem Vorwort von Hans-Georg Wieck | ISBN 978-3-8382-0584-7

126 *Simon Geissbühler (Hrsg.)* | Kiew – Revolution 3.0. Der Euromaidan 2013/14 und die Zukunftsperspektiven der Ukraine | ISBN 978-3-8382-0581-6 (Paperback edition) | ISBN 978-3-8382-0681-3 (Hardcover edition)

127 *Andrey Makarychev* | Russia and the EU in a Multipolar World. Discourses, Identities, Norms | With a foreword by Klaus Segbers | ISBN 978-3-8382-0629-5

128 *Roland Scharff* | Kasachstan als postsowjetischer Wohlfahrtsstaat. Die Transformation des sozialen Schutzsystems | Mit einem Vorwort von Joachim Ahrens | ISBN 978-3-8382-0622-6

129 *Katja Grupp* | Bild Lücke Deutschland. Kaliningrader Studierende sprechen über Deutschland | Mit einem Vorwort von Martin Schulz | ISBN 978-3-8382-0552-6

130 *Konstantin Sheiko, Stephen Brown* | History as Therapy. Alternative History and Nationalist Imaginings in Russia, 1991-2014 | ISBN 978-3-8382-0665-3

131 *Elisa Kriza* | Alexander Solzhenitsyn: Cold War Icon, Gulag Author, Russian Nationalist? A Study of the Western Reception of his Literary Writings, Historical Interpretations, and Political Ideas | With a foreword by Andrei Rogatchevski | ISBN 978-3-8382-0589-2 (Paperback edition) | ISBN 978-3-8382-0690-5 (Hardcover edition)

132 *Serghei Golunov* | The Elephant in the Room. Corruption and Cheating in Russian Universities | ISBN 978-3-8382-0570-0

133 *Manja Hussner, Rainer Arnold (Hgg.)* | Verfassungsgerichtsbarkeit in Zentralasien I. Sammlung von Verfassungstexten | ISBN 978-3-8382-0595-3

134 *Nikolay Mitrokhin* | Die „Russische Partei". Die Bewegung der russischen Nationalisten in der UdSSR 1953-1985 | Aus dem Russischen übertragen von einem Übersetzerteam unter der Leitung von Larisa Schippel | ISBN 978-3-8382-0024-8

135 *Manja Hussner, Rainer Arnold (Hgg.)* | Verfassungsgerichtsbarkeit in Zentralasien II. Sammlung von Verfassungstexten | ISBN 978-3-8382-0597-7

136 *Manfred Zeller* | Das sowjetische Fieber. Fußballfans im poststalinistischen Vielvölkerreich | Mit einem Vorwort von Nikolaus Katzer | ISBN 978-3-8382-0757-5

137 *Kristin Schreiter* | Stellung und Entwicklungspotential zivilgesellschaftlicher Gruppen in Russland. Menschenrechtsorganisationen im Vergleich | ISBN 978-3-8382-0673-8

138 *David R. Marples, Frederick V. Mills (Eds.)* | Ukraine's Euromaidan. Analyses of a Civil Revolution | ISBN 978-3-8382-0660-8

139 *Bernd Kappenberg* | Setting Signs for Europe. Why Diacritics Matter for European Integration | With a foreword by Peter Schlobinski | ISBN 978-3-8382-0663-9

140 *René Lenz* | Internationalisierung, Kooperation und Transfer. Externe bildungspolitische Akteure in der Russischen Föderation | Mit einem Vorwort von Frank Ettrich | ISBN 978-3-8382-0751-3

141 *Juri Plusnin, Yana Zausaeva, Natalia Zhidkevich, Artemy Pozanenko* | Wandering Workers. Mores, Behavior, Way of Life, and Political Status of Domestic Russian Labor Migrants | Translated by Julia Kazantseva | ISBN 978-3-8382-0653-0

142 *David J. Smith (Eds.)* | Latvia – A Work in Progress? 100 Years of State- and Nation-Building | ISBN 978-3-8382-0648-6

143 *Инна Чувычкина (ред.)* | Экспортные нефте- и газопроводы на постсоветском пространстве. Анализ трубопроводной политики в свете теории международных отношений | ISBN 978-3-8382-0822-3

144 *Johann Zajaczkowski* | Russland – eine pragmatische Großmacht? Eine rollentheoretische Untersuchung russischer Außenpolitik am Beispiel der Zusammenarbeit mit den USA nach 9/11 und des Georgienkrieges von 2008 | Mit einem Vorwort von Siegfried Schieder | ISBN 978-3-8382-0837-4

145 *Boris Popivanov* | Changing Images of the Left in Bulgaria. The Challenge of Post-Communism in the Early 21st Century | ISBN 978-3-8382-0667-7

146 *Lenka Krátká* | A History of the Czechoslovak Ocean Shipping Company 1948-1989. How a Small, Landlocked Country Ran Maritime Business During the Cold War | ISBN 978-3-8382-0666-0

147 *Alexander Sergunin* | Explaining Russian Foreign Policy Behavior. Theory and Practice | ISBN 978-3-8382-0752-0

148 *Darya Malyutina* | Migrant Friendships in a Super-Diverse City. Russian-Speakers and their Social Relationships in London in the 21st Century | With a foreword by Claire Dwyer | ISBN 978-3-8382-0652-3

149 *Alexander Sergunin, Valery Konyshev* | Russia in the Arctic. Hard or Soft Power? | ISBN 978-3-8382-0753-7

150 *John J. Maresca* | Helsinki Revisited. A Key U.S. Negotiator's Memoirs on the Development of the CSCE into the OSCE | With a foreword by Hafiz Pashayev | ISBN 978-3-8382-0852-7

151 *Jardar Østbø* | The New Third Rome. Readings of a Russian Nationalist Myth | With a foreword by Pål Kolstø | ISBN 978-3-8382-0870-1

152 *Simon Kordonsky* | Socio-Economic Foundations of the Russian Post-Soviet Regime. The Resource-Based Economy and Estate-Based Social Structure of Contemporary Russia | With a foreword by Svetlana Barsukova | ISBN 978-3-8382-0775-9

153 *Duncan Leitch* | Assisting Reform in Post-Communist Ukraine 2000–2012. The Illusions of Donors and the Disillusion of Beneficiaries | With a foreword by Kataryna Wolczuk | ISBN 978-3-8382-0844-2

154 *Abel Polese* | Limits of a Post-Soviet State. How Informality Replaces, Renegotiates, and Reshapes Governance in Contemporary Ukraine | With a foreword by Colin Williams | ISBN 978-3-8382-0845-9

155 *Mikhail Suslov (Ed.)* | Digital Orthodoxy in the Post-Soviet World. The Russian Orthodox Church and Web 2.0 | With a foreword by Father Cyril Hovorun | ISBN 978-3-8382-0871-8

156 *Leonid Luks* | Zwei „Sonderwege"? Russisch-deutsche Parallelen und Kontraste (1917-2014). Vergleichende Essays | ISBN 978-3-8382-0823-7

157 *Vladimir V. Karacharovskiy, Ovsey I. Shkaratan, Gordey A. Yastrebov* | Towards a New Russian Work Culture. Can Western Companies and Expatriates Change Russian Society? | With a foreword by Elena N. Danilova | Translated by Julia Kazantseva | ISBN 978-3-8382-0902-9

158 *Edmund Griffiths* | Aleksandr Prokhanov and Post-Soviet Esotericism | ISBN 978-3-8382-0903-6

159 *Timm Beichelt, Susann Worschech (Eds.)* | Transnational Ukraine? Networks and Ties that Influence(d) Contemporary Ukraine | ISBN 978-3-8382-0944-9

160 *Mieste Hotopp-Riecke* | Die Tataren der Krim zwischen Assimilation und Selbstbehauptung. Der Aufbau des krimtatarischen Bildungswesens nach Deportation und Heimkehr (1990-2005) | Mit einem Vorwort von Swetlana Czerwonnaja | ISBN 978-3-89821-940-2

161 *Olga Bertelsen (Ed.)* | Revolution and War in Contemporary Ukraine. The Challenge of Change | ISBN 978-3-8382-1016-2

162 *Natalya Ryabinska* | Ukraine's Post-Communist Mass Media. Between Capture and Commercialization | With a foreword by Marta Dyczok | ISBN 978-3-8382-1011-7

163 *Alexandra Cotofana, James M. Nyce (Eds.)* | Religion and Magic in Socialist and Post-Socialist Contexts. Historic and Ethnographic Case Studies of Orthodoxy, Heterodoxy, and Alternative Spirituality | With a foreword by Patrick L. Michelson | ISBN 978-3-8382-0989-0

164 *Nozima Akhrarkhodjaeva* | The Instrumentalisation of Mass Media in Electoral Authoritarian Regimes. Evidence from Russia's Presidential Election Campaigns of 2000 and 2008 | ISBN 978-3-8382-1013-1

165 *Yulia Krasheninnikova* | Informal Healthcare in Contemporary Russia. Sociographic Essays on the Post-Soviet Infrastructure for Alternative Healing Practices | ISBN 978-3-8382-0970-8

166 *Peter Kaiser* | Das Schachbrett der Macht. Die Handlungsspielräume eines sowjetischen Funktionärs unter Stalin am Beispiel des Generalsekretärs des Komsomol Aleksandr Kosarev (1929-1938) | Mit einem Vorwort von Dietmar Neutatz | ISBN 978-3-8382-1052-0

167 *Oksana Kim* | The Effects and Implications of Kazakhstan's Adoption of International Financial Reporting Standards. A Resource Dependence Perspective | With a foreword by Svetlana Vlady | ISBN 978-3-8382-0987-6

168 *Anna Sanina* | Patriotic Education in Contemporary Russia. Sociological Studies in the Making of the Post-Soviet Citizen | With a foreword by Anna Oldfield | ISBN 978-3-8382-0993-7

169 *Rudolf Wolters* | Spezialist in Sibirien Faksimile der 1933 erschienenen ersten Ausgabe | Mit einem Vorwort von Dmitrij Chmelnizki | ISBN 978-3-8382-0515-1

170 *Michal Vít, Magdalena M. Baran (Eds.)* | Transregional versus National Perspectives on Contemporary Central European History. Studies on the Building of Nation-States and Their Cooperation in the 20th and 21st Century | With a foreword by Petr Vágner | ISBN 978-3-8382-1015-5

171 *Philip Gamaghelyan* | Conflict Resolution Beyond the International Relations Paradigm. Evolving Designs as a Transformative Practice in Nagorno-Karabakh and Syria | With a foreword by Susan Allen | ISBN 978-3-8382-1057-5

172 *Maria Shagina* | Joining a Prestigious Club. Cooperation with Europarties and Its Impact on Party Development in Georgia, Moldova, and Ukraine 2004–2015 | With a foreword by Kataryna Wolczuk | ISBN 978-3-8382-1084-1

173 *Alexandra Cotofana, James M. Nyce (Eds.)* | Religion and Magic in Socialist and Post-Socialist Contexts II. Baltic, Eastern European, and Post-USSR Case Studies | With a foreword by Anita Stasulane | ISBN 978-3-8382-0990-6

174 *Barbara Kunz* | Kind Words, Cruise Missiles, and Everything in Between. The Use of Power Resources in U.S. Policies towards Poland, Ukraine, and Belarus 1989–2008 | With a foreword by William Hill | ISBN 978-3-8382-1065-0

175 *Eduard Klein* | Bildungskorruption in Russland und der Ukraine. Eine komparative Analyse der Performanz staatlicher Antikorruptionsmaßnahmen im Hochschulsektor am Beispiel universitärer Aufnahmeprüfungen | Mit einem Vorwort von Heiko Pleines | ISBN 978-3-8382-0995-1

176 *Markus Soldner* | Politischer Kapitalismus im postsowjetischen Russland. Die politische, wirtschaftliche und mediale Transformation in den 1990er Jahren | Mit einem Vorwort von Wolfgang Ismayr | ISBN 978-3-8382-1222-7

177 *Anton Oleinik* | Building Ukraine from Within. A Sociological, Institutional, and Economic Analysis of a Nation-State in the Making | ISBN 978-3-8382-1150-3

178 *Peter Rollberg, Marlene Laruelle (Eds.)* | Mass Media in the Post-Soviet World. Market Forces, State Actors, and Political Manipulation in the Informational Environment after Communism | ISBN 978-3-8382-1116-9

179 *Mikhail Minakov* | Development and Dystopia. Studies in Post-Soviet Ukraine and Eastern Europe | With a foreword by Alexander Etkind | ISBN 978-3-8382-1112-1

180 *Aijan Sharshenova* | The European Union's Democracy Promotion in Central Asia. A Study of Political Interests, Influence, and Development in Kazakhstan and Kyrgyzstan in 2007–2013 | With a foreword by Gordon Crawford | ISBN 978-3-8382-1151-0

181 *Andrey Makarychev, Alexandra Yatsyk (Eds.)* | Boris Nemtsov and Russian Politics. Power and Resistance | With a foreword by Zhanna Nemtsova | ISBN 978-3-8382-1122-0

182 *Sophie Falsini* | The Euromaidan's Effect on Civil Society. Why and How Ukrainian Social Capital Increased after the Revolution of Dignity | With a foreword by Susann Worschech | ISBN 978-3-8382-1131-2

183 *Valentyna Romanova, Andreas Umland (Eds.)* | Ukraine's Decentralization. Challenges and Implications of the Local Governance Reform after the Euromaidan Revolution | ISBN 978-3-8382-1162-6

184 *Leonid Luks* | A Fateful Triangle. Essays on Contemporary Russian, German and Polish History | ISBN 978-3-8382-1143-5

185 *John B. Dunlop* | The February 2015 Assassination of Boris Nemtsov and the Flawed Trial of his Alleged Killers. An Exploration of Russia's "Crime of the 21st Century" | ISBN 978-3-8382-1188-6

186 *Vasile Rotaru* | Russia, the EU, and the Eastern Partnership. Building Bridges or Digging Trenches? | ISBN 978-3-8382-1134-3

187 *Marina Lebedeva* | Russian Studies of International Relations. From the Soviet Past to the Post-Cold-War Present | With a foreword by Andrei P. Tsygankov | ISBN 978-3-8382-0851-0

188 *Tomasz Stępniewski, George Soroka (Eds.)* | Ukraine after Maidan. Revisiting Domestic and Regional Security | ISBN 978-3-8382-1075-9

189 *Petar Cholakov* | Ethnic Entrepreneurs Unmasked. Political Institutions and Ethnic Conflicts in Contemporary Bulgaria | ISBN 978-3-8382-1189-3

190 *A. Salem, G. Hazeldine, D. Morgan (Eds.)* | Higher Education in Post-Communist States. Comparative and Sociological Perspectives | ISBN 978-3-8382-1183-1

191 *Igor Torbakov* | After Empire. Nationalist Imagination and Symbolic Politics in Russia and Eurasia in the Twentieth and Twenty-First Century | With a foreword by Serhii Plokhy | ISBN 978-3-8382-1217-3

192 *Aleksandr Burakovskiy* | Jewish-Ukrainian Relations in Late and Post-Soviet Ukraine. Articles, Lectures and Essays from 1986 to 2016 | ISBN 978-3-8382-1210-4

193 *Natalia Shapovalova, Olga Burlyuk (Eds.)* | Civil Society in Post-Euromaidan Ukraine. From Revolution to Consolidation | With a foreword by Richard Youngs | ISBN 978-3-8382-1216-6

194 *Franz Preissler* | Positionsverteidigung, Imperialismus oder Irredentismus? Russland und die „Russischsprachigen", 1991–2015 | ISBN 978-3-8382-1262-3

195 *Marian Madeła* | Der Reformprozess in der Ukraine 2014-2017. Eine Fallstudie zur Reform der öffentlichen Verwaltung | Mit einem Vorwort von Martin Malek | ISBN 978-3-8382-1266-1

196 *Anke Giesen* | „Wie kann denn der Sieger ein Verbrecher sein?" Eine diskursanalytische Untersuchung der russlandweiten Debatte über Konzept und Verstaatlichungsprozess der Lagergedenkstätte „Perm'-36" im Ural | ISBN 978-3-8382-1284-5

197 *Alla Leukavets* | The Integration Policies of Belarus and Ukraine vis-à-vis the EU and Russia. A Comparative Case Study Through the Prism of a Two-Level Game Approach | ISBN 978-3-8382-1247-0

198 *Oksana Kim* | The Development and Challenges of Russian Corporate Governance I. The Roles and Functions of Boards of Directors | With a foreword by Sheila M. Puffer | ISBN 978-3-8382-1287-6

199 *Thomas D. Grant* | International Law and the Post-Soviet Space I. Essays on Chechnya and the Baltic States | With a foreword by Stephen M. Schwebel | ISBN 978-3-8382-1279-1

200 *Thomas D. Grant* | International Law and the Post-Soviet Space II. Essays on Ukraine, Intervention, and Non-Proliferation | ISBN 978-3-8382-1280-7

201 *Slavomír Michálek, Michal Štefansky* | The Age of Fear. The Cold War and Its Influence on Czechoslovakia 1945–1968 | ISBN 978-3-8382-1285-2

202 *Iulia-Sabina Joja* | Romania's Strategic Culture 1990–2014. Continuity and Change in a Post-Communist Country's Evolution of National Interests and Security Policies | With a foreword by Heiko Biehl | ISBN 978-3-8382-1286-9

203 *Andrei Rogatchevski, Yngvar B. Steinholt, Arve Hansen, David-Emil Wickström* | War of Songs. Popular Music and Recent Russia-Ukraine Relations | With a foreword by Artemy Troitsky | ISBN 978-3-8382-1173-2

204 *Maria Lipman (Ed.)* | Russian Voices on Post-Crimea Russia. An Almanac of Counterpoint Essays from 2015–2018 | ISBN 978-3-8382-1251-7

205 *Ksenia Maksimovtsova* | Language Conflicts in Contemporary Estonia, Latvia, and Ukraine. A Comparative Exploration of Discourses in Post-Soviet Russian-Language Digital Media | With a foreword by Ammon Cheskin | ISBN 978-3-8382-1282-1

206 *Michal Vit* | The EU's Impact on Identity Formation in East-Central Europe between 2004 and 2013. Perceptions of the Nation and Europe in Political Parties of the Czech Republic, Poland, and Slovakia | With a foreword by Andrea Pető | ISBN 978-3-8382-1275-3

207 *Per A. Rudling* | Tarnished Heroes. The Organization of Ukrainian Nationalists in the Memory Politics of Post-Soviet Ukraine | ISBN 978-3-8382-0999-9

208 *Kaja Gadowska, Peter Solomon (Eds.)* | Legal Change in Post-Communist States. Progress, Reversions, Explanations | ISBN 978-3-8382-1312-5

209 *Pawel Kowal, Georges Mink, Iwona Reichardt (Eds.)* | Three Revolutions: Mobilization and Change in Contemporary Ukraine I. Theoretical Aspects and Analyses on Religion, Memory, and Identity | ISBN 978-3-8382-1321-7

210 *Pawel Kowal, Georges Mink, Adam Reichardt, Iwona Reichardt (Eds.)* | Three Revolutions: Mobilization and Change in Contemporary Ukraine II. An Oral History of the Revolution on Granite, Orange Revolution, and Revolution of Dignity | ISBN 978-3-8382-1323-1

211 *Li Bennich-Björkman, Sergiy Kurbatov (Eds.)* | When the Future Came. The Collapse of the USSR and the Emergence of National Memory in Post-Soviet History Textbooks | ISBN 978-3-8382-1335-4

212 *Olga R. Gulina* | Migration as a (Geo-)Political Challenge in the Post-Soviet Space. Border Regimes, Policy Choices, Visa Agendas | With a foreword by Nils Muižnieks | ISBN 978-3-8382-1338-5

213 *Sanna Turoma, Kaarina Aitamurto, Slobodanka Vladiv-Glover (Eds.)* | Religion, Expression, and Patriotism in Russia. Essays on Post-Soviet Society and the State. ISBN 978-3-8382-1346-0

214 *Vasif Huseynov* | Geopolitical Rivalries in the "Common Neighborhood". Russia's Conflict with the West, Soft Power, and Neoclassical Realism | With a foreword by Nicholas Ross Smith | ISBN 978-3-8382-1277-7

215 *Mikhail Suslov* | Geopolitical Imagination. Ideology and Utopia in Post-Soviet Russia | With a foreword by Mark Bassin | ISBN 978-3-8382-1361-3

216 *Alexander Etkind, Mikhail Minakov (Eds.)* | Ideology after Union. Political Doctrines, Discourses, and Debates in Post-Soviet Societies | ISBN 978-3-8382-1388-0

217 *Jakob Mischke, Oleksandr Zabirko (Hgg.)* | Protestbewegungen im langen Schatten des Kreml. Aufbruch und Resignation in Russland und der Ukraine | ISBN 978-3-8382-0926-5

218 *Oksana Huss* | How Corruption and Anti-Corruption Policies Sustain Hybrid Regimes. Strategies of Political Domination under Ukraine's Presidents in 1994-2014. With a foreword by Tobias Debiel and Andrea Gawrich | ISBN 978-3-8382-1430-6

219 *Dmitry Travin, Vladimir Gel'man, Otar Marganiya* | The Russian Path. Ideas, Interests, Institutions, Illusions. With a foreword by Vladimir Ryzhkov | ISBN 978-3-8382-1421-4

220 *Gergana Dimova* | Political Uncertainty. A Comparative Exploration. With a foreword by Todor Yalamov and Rumena Filipova | ISBN 978-3-8382-1385-9

221 *Torben Waschke* | Russland in Transition. Geopolitik zwischen Raum, Identität und Machtinteressen. Mit einem Vorwort von Andreas Dittmann | ISBN 978-3-8382-1480-1

222 *Steven Jobbitt, Zsolt Bottlik, Marton Berki (Eds.)* | Power and Identity in the Post-Soviet Realm. Geographies of Ethnicity and Nationality after 1991 | ISBN 978-3-8382-1399-6

223 *Daria Buteiko* | Erinnerungsort. Ort des Gedenkens, der Erholung oder der Einkehr? Kommunismus-Erinnerung am Beispiel der Gedenkstätte Berliner Mauer sowie des Soloveckij-Klosters und -Museumsparks | ISBN 978-3-8382-1367-5

224 *Olga Bertelsen (Ed.)* | Russian Active Measures. Yesterday, Today, Tomorrow | With a foreword by Jan Goldman | ISBN 978-3-8382-1529-7

225 *David Mandel* | "Optimizing" Higher Education in Russia. University Teachers and their Union "Universitetskaya solidarnost'" | ISBN 978-3-8382-1519-8

226 *Mikhail Minakov, Gwendolyn Sasse, Daria Isachenko (Eds.)* | Post-Soviet Secessionism. Nation-Building and State-Failure after Communism | ISBN 978-3-8382-1538-9

227 *Jakob Hauter (Ed.)* | Civil War? Interstate War? Hybrid War? Dimensions and Interpretations of the Donbas Conflict in 2014–2020 | With a foreword by Andrew Wilson | ISBN 978-3-8382-1383-5

228 *Tima T. Moldogaziev, Gene A. Brewer, J. Edward Kellough (Eds.)* | Public Policy and Politics in Georgia. Lessons from Post-Soviet Transition | With a foreword by Dan Durning | ISBN 978-3-8382-1535-8

229 *Oxana Schmies (Ed.)* | NATO's Enlargement and Russia. A Strategic Challenge in the Past and Future | With a foreword by Vladimir Kara-Murza | ISBN 978-3-8382-1478-8

230 *Christopher Ford* | Ukapisme – Une Gauche perdue. Le marxisme anti-colonial dans la révolution ukrainienne 1917-1925 | Avec une préface de Vincent Présumey | ISBN 978-3-8382-0899-2

231 *Anna Kutkina* | Between Lenin and Bandera. Decommunization and Multivocality in Post-Euromaidan Ukraine | With a foreword by Juri Mykkänen | ISBN 978-3-8382-1506-8

232 *Lincoln E. Flake* | Defending the Faith. The Russian Orthodox Church and the Demise of Religious Pluralism | With a foreword by Peter Martland | ISBN 978-3-8382-1378-1

233 *Nikoloz Samkharadze* | Russia's Recognition of the Independence of Abkhazia and South Ossetia. Analysis of a Deviant Case in Moscow's Foreign Policy Behavior | With a foreword by Neil MacFarlane | ISBN 978-3-8382-1414-6

ibidem.eu